DODGE, PLYMO & CHRYSLER POLICE CARS 1979–1994

Edwin J. Sanow and John L. Bellah
with Galen Govier

Motorbooks International
Publishers & Wholesalers ®

*To our wives, Cindy and Chris, who offered
moral support and understanding, who were patient
during the entire writing process, who have listened
attentively for years to "car talk", and who are our
car show, swap meet, and police event partners.*

First published in 1996 by Motorbooks International Publishers & Wholesalers, 729 Prospect Avenue, PO Box 1, Osceola, WI 54020-0001 USA

© Edwin J. Sanow, 1996

Motorbooks International is a certified trademark, registered with the United States Patent Office

The information in this book is true and complete to the best of our knowledge. All recommendations are made without any guarantee on the part of the author or Publisher, who also disclaim any liability incurred in connection with the use of this data or specific details

We recognize that some words, model names and designations, for example, mentioned herein are the property of the trademark holder. We use them for identification purposes only. This is not an official publication

Motorbooks International books are also available at discounts in bulk quantity for industrial or sales-promotional use. For details write to Special Sales Manager at the Publisher's address

Library of Congress Cataloging-in-Publication Data Available

ISBN 0-7603-0197-2

On the front cover: .This 1989 Diplomat was in service with the Wilmington, Delaware Police. *Courtesy of Dupont Fibers Aramid (Kevlar) Products*

On the back cover: The California Highway Patrol employed this 1980 Dodge St. Regis. The white 1981 Dodge Diplomat belonged to the Indiana State Police.

Printed and bound in the United States of America

Contents

Acknowledgments

Both Volumes I and II of "Dodge, Plymouth & Chrysler Police Cars" were made possible only by the assistance of police officers, historians and car enthusiasts nationwide. This assistance was in the form of photographs, technical bulletins, police car literature, car magazine articles, interviews and encouragement.

Thanks for a good start goes to Sgt. Robert Helmick with the Crime Scene Section, Technical Services Division of the Pinellas County, Florida Sheriff's Office and Deputy Howard Kotarski, Court House Security with the Tarrant County Texas Sheriff's Office.

F/Lt. (ret.) Curtis VanDenBerg of the Michigan State Police (MSP) provided a large volume of vehicle testing data and historical photos. Sgt. Joe Gavula with the Philadelphia, Pennsylvania Police provided technical service bulletins and critical information on the radical "transverse" torsion bar Diplomat/Gran Fury front suspension.

Chrysler Fleet Operations was able to provide some old police car literature for which we are thankful. Hard to find police literature also came from Police Car Owners of America member Bob Kilgore, owner of a beautiful ex-Ohio Highway Patrol Gran Fury M-body.

Thanks to Communications Officer Darryl Lindsay with the Sunnyvale, California Public Safety Department, who provided police literature unable to be found anywhere else. Officer Lindsay also provided select photos, including some of his perfect 1965 ex-California Highway Patrol Dodge Polara.

A very special thanks goes to CHP Commissioner, Maury Hannigan, for writing the Foreward to Volume II. The narrator of "Real Stories of the Highway Patrol" has spent his career in Dodges. Commissioner, thanks again.

Lt. Greg Manuel, Commander of Public Affairs with the California Highway Patrol, and CHP Zenith 12000 Editor, Alice Huffaker were extremely cooperative in supplying historical photos.

Brandt Rosenbusch with the Chrysler Corporation Historical Collection put in hours of searching for police cars from the corporate photo file. Rosenbusch was also a law enforcement student at the time.

Trooper Richard Wilson, with the Kansas Highway Patrol and former magazine coordinator of *The Kansas Trooper*, took an active interest in this project. The KHP used Dodges and Plymouths right up to 1989 and Wilson contributed many photos to these two books.

Special Agent Ned Schwartz, member of the Police Car Owners of America (PCOOA), was instrumental in providing photos from the New York City area. Patrol cars are not a high priority in the NYC-PD's way of life so the photos had to come from private collections. Schwartz came through with New York City photos which gave balance to both books.

Trooper Jim Benjaminson with the North Dakota Highway Patrol is the membership secretary of the Plymouth Owner's Club and a historian and accomplished writer in his own right. He serves as Technical Advisor for the 1940 model year with the Club. Benjaminson supplied a large number of photos for both books.

Patrolman Dave Dotson of the Sparta, Illinois Police was the host of the first annual National Convention held by the Police Car Owners of America. He is also the owner of numerous makes of squad cars and has hands-on police car contacts all over the country. He supplied a wide variety of photos and reference material and remains one of the PCOOA's best assets. Dotson really can find anything.

Sgt. David Morrison is a Public Information Officer with the Indiana State Police. He, too, is an author and departmental historian. While he specializes in 1930s era police work, he is a squad car enthusiast, too. Photos with Indiana State Police (ISP) markings came from his personal file and are now on display at the ISP Museum. Virginia State Police (VSP) trooper Louis Mavredes and special agent Ed McDowell provided photos of various makes, models and years of VSP squad cars.

Officer Greg Reynolds of the Chicago Police Dept. is a Illinois state representative for the PCOOA and a Chevy-man, but don't hold that against him. Reynolds contributed a great deal to Volume II. He opened up his entire color collection of police car photos for our use. Patrolman Mark Wilson of the Greenwich, CT Police Dept. also submitted excellent Mopar photos. We also thank David Gasperetti for his technical contributions on the 318ci, 4-bbl engine.

On the West Coast front, key people stand out from the multiple dozens that assisted John Bellah. The first is Lt. Gary Kamm who is retired from the LAPD. He is former freeway interceptor driver and interceptor supervisor. He also served as watch commander with LAPD and was the acting chief of the California State University, Long Beach Police until his recent retirement.

Second is Officer Charles Casner, also retired from the LAPD. Casner was a freeway interceptor driver, driver training instructor and chief test driver. He is also a former stock car auto racer.

Thanks goes to George Caravas, a 20-year veteran traffic officer with the California Highway Patrol. His career included both vehicle patrol and motorcycle patrol. Caravas is an active west coast member of the PCOOA and owns two meticulously accurate CHP squads, a 1961 Dodge Polara and a 1973 Dodge Polara. Thanks, too, goes to Chuck Swift of Sacramento's Swift Dodge for helping us put the C.H.P. St. Regis controversy in perspective.

A special thanks goes to Lee Kelly, publisher of *Motor Trend* and William Jeanes, publisher of *Car & Driver*. These magazines were supportive enough to allow excerpts to be used from old police car articles, asking only the proper credit in return. Both magazines are to be commended for their cooperation and enthusiasm for the sport of police car collecting.

Another special thanks goes to Roland Osborne, editor of *Chrysler Power*, for giving us each our first automotive break. Thanks, too, goes to Kevin Trickey, Buckeye State Mopar enthusiast, for proofing the final text.

Special thanks, too, goes to Galen Govier, the author of our VIN decoding chapter. Govier is the document expert on pre-1980 Chrysler Corp. decoding. He writes a regular column in *Mopar Muscle* on the subject of VIN, sales code and fender tag decoding.

A very special thanks goes to some of the Old Guard at Chrysler Corp.: Bob Lees, Engine Group; Frank Davis, Product Planning; Don Sierbert, Proving Grounds; and Don Sierra, Product Planning. These were the last of the V-8, rear-drive men at a time when the entire corporation was devoted exclusively to 4 and 6-cylinder, front-drive vehicles. Lees, especially, provided a great deal of info on the 318ci, 2-bbl and 4-bbl engines which powered the 1981 to 1989 Diplomat and Gran Fury.

Finally, a special thanks goes to Cindy Sanow for the encouragement to do both books, for helping with interviews and photography, and for actually typing the finished product. At nearly 140,000 words of text and over 200 pages of complex tables of specs, features, and options, Cindy put in as much old-fashioned hard work on the project as the two authors. It helped that she grew up in a family of Chrysler enthusiasts. Thanks again, Cindy.

In addition to these people mentioned above, a large number of individuals and police departments made contributions of documents and photos. These are listed in the Appendix. We hope we have not overlooked anyone.

Foreword

By Maurice (Maury) J. Hannigan, Commissioner, California Highway Patrol
and Narrator, *Real Stories of the Highway Patrol.*

In February, 1992 John Bellah contacted me about a former California Highway Patrol car that he had located and intended to restore as a CHP unit. The way his 1963 Dodge had been equipped, along with Bellah's meticulous research of the history of the former cruiser, indicated that it had served at either the East Los Angeles or South Los Angeles Area office. Bellah included photographs of the somewhat worse-for-wear cruiser.

Bellah's letter and photographs brought back old memories of my early days with the California Highway Patrol. My first duty assignment with the CHP was our of the South Los Angeles Area office and it is very possible that while stationed at that command, I may have driven his car.

Eight months later, in October, 1992, I had the opportunity to meet Mr. Bellah and to see his car up-close when he placed it on display at the CHP's Retiree's Day. Subsequent CHP events showed the steady progression of Bellah's restoration efforts.

In late 1994, Mr. Bellah presented me with a copy of *Dodge, Plymouth & Chrysler Police Cars 1956-1978*, which he co-authored with Ed Sanow, a publication which holds many fond memories for me and law enforcement officers across the United States.

The automobile is as much a tool to the modern law enforcement officer as a badge, gun, night-stick, pencil or computer terminal. In addition to use in transporting the officer from one location to another, the police car must perform reliably and safely in apprehending lawbreakers and responding to calls for service. A police car also serves various secondary functions such as to provide protection against weather conditions while writing a report, interviewing witnesses or eating a quick lunch in between calls. The hood is often used as a desk to write a citation or to place a cup of coffee in a late night strategy session. The police car must also have the capability to push disabled vehicles out of traffic, serve as a temporary jail, and provide protection to the officers in tactical situations. The patrol car is, in other words, the officer's office during the eight or more hours the officer is on patrol, thus it must be comfortable.

Both Dodge, Plymouth & Chrysler Police Cars 1956-1978 and 1979-1994 bring back fond memories of my 31 year career with the CHP.

Starting as a patrol officer in late 1964, I remember the pushbutton transmissions, the incredibly noisy Jones Motrola police speedometer and drum brakes that were only good for a couple of panic stops before brake fade would develop.

The next year, 1965, the automatic transmission control was mounted on the steering column, making the pushbutton transmission controls a thing of the past along with the extra police speedometer. 1965 also was the first year for disc brakes, as a result of the CHP tests of disc brakes the previous year.

Exhaust emission controls came about in 1966 along with the famed 440ci engine, the engine that would set the standard for highway patrol agencies across the U.S. for many years to come.

The CHP switched to Oldsmobile in 1967, but returned to Dodge in 1968 and again in 1969. The 1969 model Dodge was the fastest. Running the 1969 Dodge at full-throttle near it's top speed would create so much wind pressure that the side windows and their frames would be forced outward about an inch from the outside of the car.

The 1970s started out with Mercury being used by the CHP, but the next year we brought Dodge back. Towards the mid-1970s, environmental concerns and the first Energy Crisis eventually brought about the downsizing of cars, lowered compression ratios, unleaded

Commissioner Maurice J. (Maury) Hannigan was appointed as the chief executive officer of the California Highway Patrol February 23, 1989. He commands 6,300 uniformed and 2.300 non-uniformed personnel. He was appointed to the Highway Patrol November 30, 1964. He was promoted through the ranks of the department, and served as Deputy Commissioner for five years before being appointed Commissioner.

gasoline and the catalytic converter. As a result, the CHP undertook the Special Purpose Vehicle Study in 1979 to research the predicted available vehicles for law enforcement purposes in the future.

The culmination of the 1970s automotive trends resulted in the CHP changing from cruisers being powered form 440ci engines in 1978 to the 318ci Dodge St. Regis just two years later. As the 1980s progressed, Ford and Chevrolet were added to the CHP's fleet, along with Mustang and Camaro as pursuit vehicles.

The last year of the CHP Dodge was 1988. CHP Motor Transport section personnel staged a celebration after the last Diplomat was outfitted, thus ending a traditon spanning a thirty-two year time period. I ended up driving my assigned Dodge Diplomat for three years, which is two years longer than what is considered the norm.

Ed Sanow and John Bellah's book has done a credible job of preserving law enforcement and automotive history, in addition to preserving CHP history. I hope the reader gets as much enjoyment from it as I have.

—*Maury Hannigan*
Commissioner, California Highway Patrol
Sacramento, California
October 1995

Introduction

In the book, *Dodge, Plymouth & Chrysler Police Cars, 1956-1978*, we explain exactly what a police car is and what it is not. It has nothing to do with engine size and everything to do with drivetrain durability. Police cars have different engines, depending on the task at hand. This concept was developed into a science by City of Los Angeles Police Transportation Superintendent, G. Ray Wynne. It was later re-invented by Los Angeles County Sheriff reserve deputy and *Motor Trend* editor, John Christy.

We also made it clear that a police car is only a police car if it has a police package designed by the car maker. The use of any retail car as a police car by a police department does not make it a police car. A police car is determined by the engineered package of components, not by its end use. Many police cars are, in fact, used to transport detectives and other non-uniformed, non-emergency personnel. They are still police cars.

In 1956, Dodge division released the first Mopar police car based on the Coronet. Many of these were powered by the 230hp, 315ci V-8, while a D-500 315ci hemi was available. Dodge immediately gained a reputation among state cops for pure performance.

By 1957, Plymouth entered the police car market, using the drivetrain technology it gained from building taxis. Plymouth became one of the "low price three," which also included Ford and Chevrolet.

Then in 1958, Mopar squads received the 350ci and 361ci Wedge engines. In 1959, the squads were upgraded to the venerable 383ci big block. By 1960, Dodges powered by dual quad 383s totally dominated police car tests conducted by the California Highway Patrol (CHP).

In 1961, Chrysler introduced the Newport-based Enforcer police car. The down-sized squads of 1962 led to the development of the 1963-64 Dodge 880, a big car powered by the 413ci Wedge.

Then in 1965, Dodge extended the wheelbase of the Polara by 1in to meet CHP specifications. By 1966, the mighty 440ci hit the streets, while in 1967, the workhorse 318ci "LA" small block joined the force. By this time, Dodge and Plymouth had wrestled nearly all of the police car business from Ford.

In 1968, 4-door Road Runners and 4-door Super Bees were thinly-disguised as police cars. The 1969 Plymouth Belvedere

This Oklahoma Highway Patrol battle cruiser is a 1980 Plymouth Gran Fury. *Dave Dotson*

The 1980 Plymouth Gran Fury is powered by a 360ci, 4-bbl and was used by the Arizona Highway Patrol. *Greg Reynolds*

383ci and Dodge Polara 440ci were voted among the best Mopar police cars ever made.

Then in 1970, low compression engines hit hard. By 1971, even the big block performance was crippled by emission controls. For 1972, the power loss was so severe, that mid-size cars like the Plymouth Satellite and Dodge Coronet were available with 400 and 440ci big blocks for the first time.

In 1973, the Mopar squads received disc brakes. By 1975, all the squads had catalytic converters. The 1976 model year saw the release of the Dodge Dart and Plymouth Valiant to battle the Chevy Nova in the mid-size class. In 1977, the Dodge Aspen and Plymouth Volare debuted, and came with engines as powerful as the 360ci, 4-bbl.

Then in 1978, all of law enforcement enjoyed their last big block engines. After 1978, the 400 and 440ci were both discontinued. Squad cars like the Plymouth Fury were voted as the second most popular Mopar police cars of all time.

Almost as soon as they were introduced, the big Dodges captured the hearts of cops looking for unbridled performance. In the 1950s, Dodges were the police car of choice for most state troopers and highway patrolmen. Plymouth, on the other hand, became a major force with urban police departments.

Throughout the 1960s and 1970s, Chrysler-made police cars had a lock on the police car market. At one time, eight out of every ten police cars on the road were a Dodge or Plymouth.

This all changed in 1979. With the loss of the big block,

The R-body Mopar like this 1979 Texas DPS Chrysler Newport was the most popular squad car in the post-big-block era. *Greg Reynolds*

The slick-top 1988 Dodge Diplomat was used by the Illinois State Police. *Greg Reynolds*

The Aries K and Reliant K were available with a genuine police package from 1982 through 1987. *Greg Reynolds*

Chrysler Corp. did not have the engine sizes to power the vehicle sizes. Neither did anyone else at the time, which caused some serious investigating into the problem.

While the R-Body St. Regis and Gran Fury were voted the best Mopar police cars ever made, they were only produced for three years. These R-body cars really needed the 360ci power plant. The 318ci was deemed too small for the R-body, while at the same time marginally acceptable in the M-body Diplomat and Gran Fury.

The late 1970s and early 1980s saw increased competition from the Impala/Caprice powered by the 350ci small block. It took half of the 1980s to happen, but the Bowtie squad car slowly replaced the Mopar squad cars. At the same time, Chrysler Corp. made plans to withdraw from the police car market all together.

The Mopar police car era from 1956 to 1978 was one of total dominance. In contrast, the era from 1979 to 1994 was very turbulent, with both extreme highs and extreme lows. Some of the best police cars ever produced by Chrysler Corp. were during this era. So were some of the most frustrating problems.

In spite of the loss of the big block, the 1979 model year started off extremely well. Let's pick up now where we left off with the first book—the 1979 Dodge, Plymouth & Chrysler Police Cars.

The Jeep Cherokee, like this Perry County, Illinois Sheriff's unit, was available as a police package from 1992. *Greg Reynolds*

The M-body Plymouth Caravelle served Canadian law enforcement like this 1987 Calgary Police Service unit. *Rob Elliott*

Chapter 1

1979: Dodge St. Regis and Chrysler Newport

In 1979 Chrysler Corp. released the famous, short-lived, and highly controversial R-body. It was called the St. Regis by Dodge and the Newport by Chrysler. They were new full-size police pursuits from Chrysler Corp.

As for Plymouth, the Fury name had been dropped. The Fury was introduced in mid-1956 as a high performance sport coupe. The first Plymouth police car in 1957 was available with "Fury 301" and "Fury V800" engines. In 1979, the Plymouth division had no full-size, (aka regular-size, aka family-size) vehicles. The largest Plymouth in 1979 was the Volare.

From the Dodge division, the Monaco was also history. And at high-end Chrysler, all of the super-long, 123.9-inch wheelbase Chrysler-marque luxury cars were gone. The largest Chrysler-marque passenger cars were the 118.5-inch, R-body Newport and New Yorker.

St. Regis pursuit...an all-new regular-size Dodge. The all-new Dodge St. Regis has more interior space than 1978 Monaco Pursuit sedans and plenty of stowage space in the big, flat-floored trunk. Also a new powerful V-8 engine option that's the first subject of discussion.

For Peak St. Regis Performance...a new optional 360ci V-8. A 360ci V-8 with 4-barrel carburetor is a new engine available on Dodge Police Pursuits. And it gives its peak performance on the new St. Regis. Because one of its features is a free-breathing full dual exhaust system. When the utmost is demanded from a police car, this is the engine to have.

With a tough automatic transmission to match. The 3-speed TorqueFlite automatic transmission is standard with all engines on St. Regis Police Pursuit Packages. Included is an auxiliary transmission oil cooler. If you know Dodge police cars, you know TorqueFlite. It is famous for its ruggedness and dependability.

Lots of room out back. The St. Regis Police Pursuit has a large uncluttered trunk with a flat floor, which gives you the room you need to carry the equipment police departments often consider essential for law enforcement work. The regular police special spare tire is located under the shelf panel. (Passenger cars got space-saver spare tires.)

Full Instrumentation. When looking at the instrument panel of a St.Regis Pursuit, the driver sees instruments, real instruments. So the driver always gets an accurate reading of what's

This Tennessee State Police 1979 Chrysler Newport is powered by a 360ci, 4-bbl. *Dave Dotson*

Famous for their use of Chrysler-marque squads, here is a Missouri State Highway Patrol 1979 Chrysler Newport. *Ken Kerrick*

going on under the hood with the easy-to-read oil pressure and temperature gauges and ammeter, plus fuel gauge. There's no guesswork. The facts are all right there, all the time.

Lots of room up front. In comparison with the 1978 mid-sized Dodge Monaco Police Pursuit, the 1979 St. Regis comes out ahead in interior room. There are two inches more shoulder-room. And three inches more rear leg room. Overall, the new St. Regis is bigger inside than its 1978 counterpart, according to the sum of eight interior comfort dimensions.

More you should know about St.Regis:
-Pursuit tires are standard. They're fabric-belted, radial-ply blackwalls and certified for high-speed performance. With all St. Regis Pursuit Packages.
-Heavy-duty wheels have 7-inch wide rims and openings for brake cooling.
-Power brakes are heavy-duty discs with semi-metallic pads up front and 11x2-1/2-inch drums with automatic adjuster at the rear.
-The battery is a 500amp (85amp-hour) long-life heavy-duty unit with heat shield.
-Adequate cooling under all conditions is assured by a high-capacity radiator and coolant recovery system.
-The certified speedometer is calibrated with marked 2 mile-an-hour increments to 120mph.
-The catalytic converter is equipped with a grass shield.

This Delaware State Police 1979 Chrysler Newport is powered by the 195hp heavy-duty 360 V-8. *Delaware State Police*

Line by line, the exact same things could be said for the Chrysler Newport Police Pursuit.

The St. Regis and Newport were brand new car designs with a new wheelbase and a special emphasis on weight reduction. At 118.5in, these 1979 squads would have been considered mid-size cars as recently as 1977. They were not called 4-door sedans; they were called 4-door pillared hardtops.

The R-body squads had the same basic front and rear suspensions as the full and mid-size Mopar squads they replaced. The St. Regis and Newport used the classic longitudinal torsion bar front suspension pioneered by Chrysler Corp. in 1957. The Volare and Aspen, of course, retained their transverse torsion front suspension first introduced in 1976.

The St. Regis and Newport police pursuits had specially-engineered, heavy-duty suspension components. However, these were not classified as extra heavy-duty as in the past. Nor did these cars come with 1-3/8in rear shocks as in the past. And a 120mph certified speedometer, in place of a 140mph certified speedo, was simply another reminder that big blocks were no longer available.

The Philadelphia, Pennsylvania Police used these blue and white 1979 Newport Pursuits. *Ned Schwartz*

This former New Jersey State Police 1979 Dodge St. Regis is now used as a daily driver. *Joe Gavula*

11

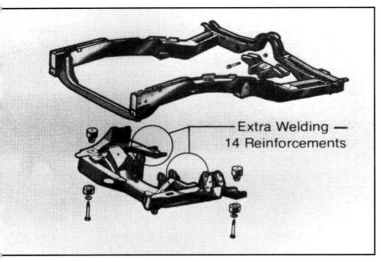

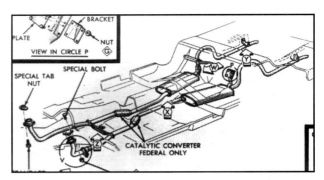

The 1979 Newport and St. Regis with 360ci, 4-bbl engines used a true dual exhaust with dual catalytic converters and dual mufflers. *Chrysler*

The R-body Newport and St.Regis had extra welds around front suspension crossmembers as part of the police package. *Chrysler*

The same exact police suspension used on the St. Regis and Newport was available on R-body passenger cars. It was called the Open Road Handling Package. For $216, the car was outfitted with the police suspension including the firm-feel police power steering with oil cooler.

Both the R-body St. Regis and Newport and the F-body Aspen and Volare police pursuits came standard with the "Special Service Package." On all A38 police package cars, this included extra chassis welds and reinforcements. On the St. Regis and Newport, this included seven areas of extra welding. The police

car literature showed by sketch specifically where these weldments were.

"Strongly Reinforced Body and Suspension. St. Regis front crossmembers and side rails are strengthened with additional welding of the crossmember and front side rail assemblies. This gives additional strength and rigidity to the entire front end. At the rear, the floor pan assembly and crossmember are given extra strength by additional welds."

The 1979 model year was the 'year of fuel efficiency.' And this time, Chrysler Corp. meant it. The R-body St. Regis and Newport were made 700 to 800 pounds lighter than previous full-size cars in an attempt to boost mileage. The full-size Chevrolet and Ford had already been down-sized. In order to meet federal Corporate Average Fuel Economy (CAFE) standards, the 400 and 440ci big blocks were dropped.

The St. Regis and Newport squads came with chrome-plated, stamped aluminum bumpers in the front and rear. This saved

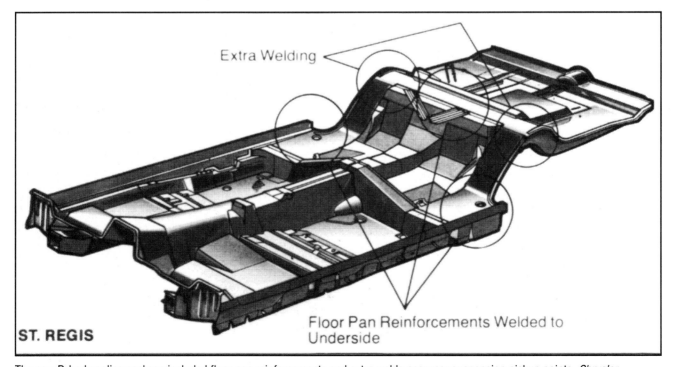

The new R-body police package included floor pan reinforcements and extra welds near rear suspension pickup points. *Chrysler*

Scottsdale, Arizona Police prowled the streets in this 1979 Dodge Aspen. A Slant Six and two V-8s were available. *Chrysler*

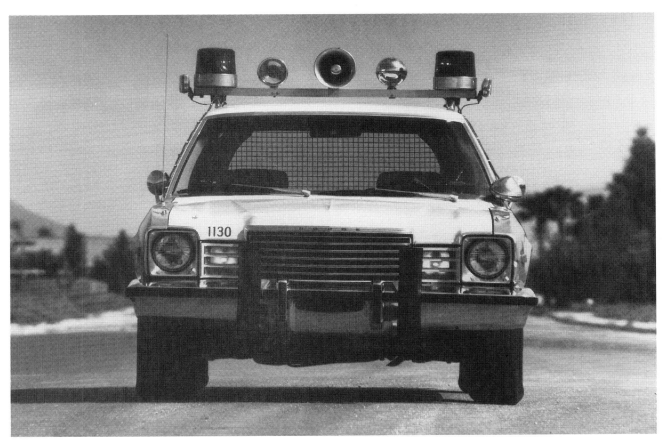

With a massive Federal Vis-A-Bar and four-way takedown and alley lights, this Scottsdale, Arizona Police 1979 Dodge Aspen would be a rearview mirror full. *Chrysler*

The 1979 Dodge Aspen (shown) and Plymouth Volare were available with a 360ci V-8. These could reach 100mph in 22.8 seconds. *Chrysler*

The 1979 Plymouth Volare police car was built specifically to compete with the Chevy Malibu. The Mopar F-bodies were quicker. *Chrysler*

The Tulsa, Oklahoma Police Explorer show off their 1979 Plymouth Volare police cars. *Ron Trekell*

55 pounds over steel. Mopars generally had lightweight radiators and aluminum/plastic master brake cylinders. Passenger cars came with high-pressure, "space-saver" spare tires, but Mopar cop cars through 1989 came standard with regular size pursuit tires.

Lock-up torque converters were available on all "normal-duty" engines. However, none of these lockup units made it into Mopar squads. For the first time since 1974, all engines available on police package cars were "heavy-duty" engines.

Another weight-saving trick, and not a welcomed one, was that in 1979, both the St. Regis/Newport and Aspen/Volare came with smaller tires. In 1978 the E58 Aspen and Volare came standard with the GR70-15. In 1979 the largest tire size was FR70-

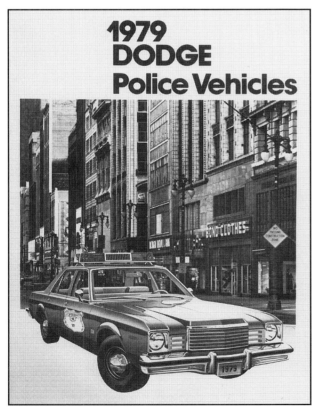

In 1979, Dodge police cars included the Aspen and St. Regis. *Chrysler*

In 1979, Chrysler produced the Newport police car while the only Plymouth squad was the Volare. *Chrysler*

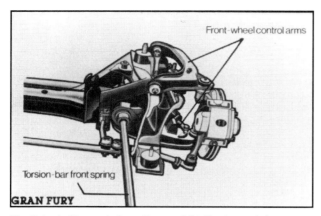

The R-body Newport, Gran Fury and St. Regis used the proven longitudinal torsion bar suspension pioneered by Chrysler Corp. in 1957. *Chrysler*

15. The 117.4in 1978 Monaco and Fury had GR70s standard and HR70s optional. The bigger 118.5in 1979 St. Regis and Newport had FR70s standard and GR70s optional. The worst places to scrimp are on tires, wheels and brakes. Fortunately, the 11in diameter front discs and 2-1/2in wide rear drums were retained for all A38 package squads.

The total variety of Mopar squads was dramatically reduced. In 1977, Chrysler Corp. fielded 34 different police package cars, counting station wagons, but not including vans. By 1979, this number dropped to just six. The six cars available with the A38 police package were:

NL41 Aspen 4-door sedan
HL41 Volare 4-door sedan
EH42 St. Regis 4-door pillared hardtop
TH42 Newport 4-door pillared hardtop
NL45 Aspen 4-door station wagon
HL45 Volare 4-door station wagon

The Aspen and Volare were carry-overs from 1978 in almost all regards. These F-body squads retained the 112.7-inch wheelbase that they shared with the M-body Diplomat and LeBaron passenger cars.

As a minor point, the Aspen and Volare were now available with a 2.4:1 rear gear for improved mileage. This ran contrary to *Motor Trend* and Los Angeles County Sheriff's Department test results, but the low numeric gear ratio was a reality, anyhow. In fact, this rear gear was standard equipment with the Federal E45 318ci, 2-bbl engine and with the California E47 318ci, 4-bbl engine.

Dodge, Plymouth and Chrysler continued the successful practice of offering factory-installed, special-order equipment for radio, siren and lightbar installation. In 1979, they added a battery feed wire into the passenger compartment, special accessory wiring with relays and 10 to 13 grounding straps for radio noise suppression to the list of options.

Good news, of sorts, for the Aspen and Volare came from Chevrolet, of all places. The Nova 9C1 had been Chevrolet's main entry in the police market since 1974. It had been widely used all across the nation, not just in Southern California. The

Pictured is a 1979 Philadelphia, Pennsylvania Police Chrysler Newport Pursuit. This was an extremely popular car among cops driving them. *Greg Reynolds*

facts are, for better or for worse, the Aspen and Volare did not make as good of a police car as the Nova.

For 1979, the Nova was no longer available as a police package. The replacement car was the Chevrolet Malibu. And the Aspen and Volare could outrun the Malibu. *Police Product News* (*PPN*), now called simply *Police*, put these two compact squads through their paces at the International Raceway in Orange County, California.

Squad Car	Engine	0-60mph	0-100mph
Plymouth Volare A38	E58 360ci, 4-bbl	8.7sec	22.8sec
Chevrolet Malibu Police	350ci, 4-bbl	8.9sec	28.5sec

Check that 0 to 100mph time again. Recall that the 1978 Plymouth Fury A38 with the E86 440ci, 4-bbl had a 0 to 100mph time of 24.8 seconds!

PPN also said, "The Volare is a much more solid riding car than the Malibu. We had several large officers, one of them 6 foot 5 inches tall and 250lbs, in both cars. They all preferred the Volare for comfort and for ease in getting in and out of both front and rear."

In spite of good performance and comfort, the problematic transverse torsion bar front suspension design still haunted these Mopar squads.

As for the Volare, several departments who have been using Volares for a year or more were contacted. A few departments stated that the Volare was great for city driving, but didn't seem to hold up well under heavy open road-type patrol done by county sheriffs. When Volares were driven from 120 to 170 miles per shift, there were complaints about front end misalignment and the cars being "squirrelly" at continuous high-speed driving.

The Volare and Aspen were whip-quick for good reason. Their optional E58 360ci, 4-bbl pumped out 20 more net hp in federal trim and an incredible 30 more net hp in California trim over the same 1978 H.D. engine. The Volare and Aspen used a dual exhaust system, with dual cats and a single oversize tailpipe.

The St. Regis and Newport, with this more powerful E58 engine, used a true dual exhaust with dual cats and tailpipes. Of course, the 360ci, 4-bbl was more potent! It had to fill the patrol shoes of a big block, and not come off appearing flat-footed.

The optional 360 4-bbl engine had the following features for longer life and better performance: A double roller timing chain; a Lubrite-treated camshaft; a water pump with larger bearing; heavy-duty valve springs; Nimonic exhaust valves; special Silichrome-1 high-temperature steel intake valves; heads with special valve seat section for better cooling; an anti-turbulence windage tray between the crankshaft and oil sump; a crankshaft of shot-peened cast nodular iron; high-temperature valve seals & shields; high-strength rocker arms; Magnafluxed forged connecting rods; heavy chrome oil rings; and a dual snorkel air cleaner.

As a passing note, the Mopar SWAT vans were available with 225, 318 and 360ci engines in 1979. As a sign of the times, the 1979 Mopar vans from Dodge and Plymouth had a 243ci, 6-cyl diesel engine as an option.

The number of different police car trim models was reduced, and so was the total number of engines available for law enforcement service. As recently as 1977, 17 different engines were available in police package cars. That number was now just six. All the high-altitude emission package engines were gone and all the 2-bbl versions of the 360ci wedge were gone.

This 1979 Plymouth Volare is attached to the U.S. Air Force Security Police. *Greg Reynolds*

1979 Dodge, Plymouth and Chrysler Engines Available for Law Enforcement Service
Engines with Federal Emissions Control Package

Code	Engine & Carb	Net Torque (ft-lb)	Net hp	Aspen Volare	St. Regis Newport
E25	225 Six 1-bbl H.D.	165@1600rpm	100@3600rpm	X	n/a
E45	318 V-8 2-bbl H.D.	250@1600rpm	135@4000rpm	X	X
E58	360 V-8 4-bbl H.D.	280@2400rpm	195@4000rpm	X	X

Engines with California Emissions Control Package

Code	Engine & Carb	Net Torque (ft-lb)	Net hp	Aspen Volare	St. Regis Newport
E25	225 Six 1-bbl H.D.	160@1600rpm	80@3600rpm	X	n/a
E47	318 V-8 4-bbl H.D.	245@1600rpm	155@4000rpm	X	X
E58	360 V-8 4-bbl H.D.	275@2000rpm	190@4000rpm	X	X

1979 Police & Passenger Car Performance

Vehicle	Engine	0-60 mph	0-100 mph	Top Speed	1/4 mile ET	1/4 mile Trap	Brake Power	MIS Road Course	Reference
Dodge St. Regis A38	360ci 4-bbl (E58)	10.1sec	30.2sec	122.9mph	n/a	n/a	21.4fps2	91.6sec	MSP-79
Chrysler Newport A38	360ci 4-bbl (E58)	10.2sec	31.5sec	121.3mph	n/a	n/a	21.8fps2	91.4sec	MSP-79
Chevrolet Impala 9C1	350ci 4-bbl	11.1sec	35.3sec	112.5mph	n/a	n/a	23.8fps2	93.5sec	MSP-79
Ford LTD Police	351Wci 2-bbl	12.3sec	63.3sec	105.4mph	n/a	n/a	18.6fps2	95.1sec	MSP-79
Ford LTD II Police	351Wci 2-bbl	14.8sec	66.7sec	111.1mph	n/a	n/a	20.1fps2	97.9sec	MSP-79
Chevrolet Corvette L82	350ci 4-bbl	6.6sec	n/a	127mph	15.3sec	95mph	n/a	n/a	CD Sept. '79
Pontiac Trans Am	400ci 4-bbl	6.7sec	n/a	124mph	15.3sec	97mph	n/a	n/a	CD Jan. '79
Chrysler 300	360ci 4-bbl	9.5sec	n/a	118mph	17.3sec	79mph	n/a	n/a	MT June '79

The Aspen and Volare came in 225, 318 and 360ci engine sizes in both federal and California trim. The St. Regis and Newport came in 318 and 360ci engine sizes, both federal and California trim. Again, all engines available for police package cars were H.D. engines.

In 1979, Chrysler Corp. released a 4-bbl version of the durable 318ci wedge. This was the first LA-cast 318ci engine to receive a 4-bbl. The 155 net hp E47 was only available with the California emissions package, and it was available on both the Aspen/Volare and Newport/St. Regis.

The optional 318ci, 4-bbl heavy-duty engines have the following features for longer life and better oil economy at high mileage: A double roller timing chain; high-temperature valve seals and shields; and a Lubrite-treated camshaft.

This 318ci, 4-bbl engine would be the focus of intense controversy in 1980. Yet it was the squad car this engine powered, not the engine itself, that caused all the fuss. In fact, this 318ci, 4-bbl engine would become the workhorse of the entire Mopar police pursuit fleet for the next ten years. The agency that cursed it in 1980 would praise it in 1981.

References
Standard Catalog of Chrysler, John Lee, Jim Benjaminson, John Gunnell, Krause Publications.
Chrysler/Plymouth Police Vehicles, Chrysler Corporation, 1979
Dodge Police Vehicles, Chrysler Corporation, 1979
"Police Packs '79," Bob Lay, *Police Product News*, 1979
"Chrysler New Yorker," Chuck Nerpel, *Motor Trend*, May 1979
Patrol Vehicle Specifications, Evaluation and Purchasing Program, Michigan State Police, 1979

Chapter 2

1980: Best Mopar Squad Ever

A survey of 200 city, county, state police and highway patrol departments found the 1980 Dodge St. Regis with the E58 360ci, 4-bbl to be the best Mopar squad ever. The reason being it encompassed everything needed in a squad car.

The E58 St. Regis was not as fast as the big block Mopar squads of old, but it was fast enough. The Michigan State Police got the 360ci, 4-bbl St. Regis to 60mph in 11.5 seconds, to 100mph in 36.7 seconds and to a top speed of 123mph. It ran the quarter mile in 18.4 seconds at 77.5mph.

For the average trained police officer, involved in various traffic and emergency situations, that was enough horsepower. Enough, but not too much. Remember, according to LAPD's G. Ray Wynne, both the extremes of too much power and too little power can cause problems. A plurality of officers answering the survey agreed.

The 1980 model year would be the last year for theE58 360ci, the most durable and powerful of the "smog" smallblocks. Released in 1971 as a 2-bbl engine, and upgraded to 4-bbl status

in 1974, the 360ci had put in an average amount of police service. Even cops get burned out after nine years of service.

In 1981, the 360ci was replaced with the 318ci. The 318ci powered the Mopar police fleet through the 1989 model year.

The 1980 St. Regis and Gran Fury powered by the E58 360ci, 4-bbl featured the classic dual carburetor air intake snorkels. These R-body Pursuits also had a true dual exhaust system, including dual catalytic converters and dual tailpipes. Chrysler Corp. stated the dual snorkel and dual exhausts give this optional V-8 the 'free-breathing' needed for fast-action pursuit jobs. It got the St. Regis and Gran Fury off to a fast start and had the power and stamina required for high-speed police work.

'Free-breathing' may not have been the most realistic way to describe a 1980 police engine to cops who could remember 1969 engines, but for the era, the E58 really was the top of the cop mill.

A considerable amount of confusion exists as to how many kinds of 360ci, 4-bbl engines were available in 1980. For all practical purposes the answer is one—the federal version of the

Indiana State Police used the 1980 Dodge St. Regis powered by the 360ci, 4-bbl. *Dave Morrison*

The 1980 Dodge St. Regis with a 185hp, 360ci V-8 had a 122mph top end and ran the quarter mile in 18 seconds. *Dave Morrison*

During Michigan State Police testing, the 1980 Dodge St. Regis (shown) and Plymouth Gran Fury had the fastest acceleration and quickest road course times. *Michigan State Police*

E58. Effective as of the 1980 model year, the E58 was not available in California.

However, the confusion is understandable since the most technically correct answer is actually four. These other three engines are the EC5 van engine, available in both federal and California trim and the Canadian version of the E58. Of these three, the Canadian E58 was the most powerful at 190 net hp.

The difference between the federal E58 car engine and the federal EC5 van-only engine is simply exhaust. The van engine paid a 5 net hp penalty for a single exhaust system. California emissions stole another 10 net hp from the EC5. The only 360ci, 4-bbl engine for California in 1980 was this EC5.

The differences between the federal E58 and the Canadian E58 were mostly exhaust. The Canadian version produced 5 net hp more than the federal version, because the Canadian squads did not have catalytic converters. The Canadian E58 also had more compression—8.4 versus 8.0.

The Canadian and federal E58 engines used different Carter ThermoQuad 4-bbl carbs. However, the primaries and secondaries were the same. Slight differences existed between the secondary air valve spring tension and the accelerator pump stroke. While both engines used the same camshaft, the distributors were different. The Canadian version had a basic advance of 10 degrees BTDC, compared to 16 degrees for the federal version.

Also making the R-body great in 1980 were its brakes. The St. Regis had a highly developed and proven braking system. The brakes were 11-inch diameter front discs with semi-metallic pads and 11x2-1/2-inch wide rear drums. As in the past, they

Illinois State Police patrolled the interstates in white 1980 Dodge St. Regis squads with yellow stripes. *Dave Link*

were vacuum-assisted, power brakes working through a dual-tandem, dual master cylinder.

These were not anti-lock brakes. No Chrysler Corp. police package car ever had anti-lock brakes. However, they generated far in excess of the 20 feet per second squared deceleration deemed necessary for police use. Dodge and Plymouth squads had braking power that was consistently better than some makes and frequently the overall best brakes period.

The suspension on the memorable 1980 St. Regis had been proven since 1957. This was the last of the fore-to-aft, longitudinal torsion bar front suspension Mopars. The F-bodied Aspen/Volare and the M-bodied Diplomat/Gran Fury to come, used the cross-body, transverse torsion bar front suspension design.

Police and enthusiast drivers alike consistently praised the original torsion bar suspension used on the R-body. And they were anywhere from neutral to highly critical of the transverse torsion bar suspension. The St. Regis suspension was not bone-jarring stiff, nor did it allow the squad to wallow in the curves. Instead, it was balanced like everything else in/on the squad car.

The St. Regis also received much praise for officer comfort and equipment storage space. Sgt. Dave Morrison with the Indiana State Police summed up the enthusiasm of numerous officers in citing, "The St. Regis was the best office I ever had."

The largest Mopar squad next to the St. Regis was the 112.7-inch wheelbase Diplomat, LeBaron and Gran Fury. These M-bodies proved to have just barely enough room and ride comfort.

Favorable comments regarding the St. Regis could also be shared by the R-body Newport from 1979, and the R-body Gran Fury, available in 1980 and 1981. After a two year leave, the Plymouth Gran Fury replaced the Chrysler Newport. Very little difference existed between the 1979 R-body Newport and the 1980 R-body Gran Fury.

The St. Regis was remembered by more police officers because it was available for one year longer than the Gran Fury. But more importantly, the St. Regis was available in two of the three years that the E58 360ci, 4-bbl was available in an R-body. The Gran Fury was available in 1981, but the E58 engine was not, or at least not in 4-door police cars. The St. Regis had the name recognition while the strong 360ci, 4-bbl was available.

A fair number of officers selected the St. Regis with the 318ci, 2-bbl (E45) and 318ci, 4-bbl (E47) engines. These were officers who used the St. Regis as a patrol-class squad, as opposed to a pursuit vehicle. B.L. "Butch" Pritchett, Sheriff of Benton County, Indiana was with the Lafayette, Indiana City Police during this era. "The St. Regis had the best combination of handling, ride and economy. It was comfortable and the 318 had plenty of power for our use."

The beat officer, road deputy and state trooper who used their cars for eight to 12 hours a day, selected the 1980 Dodge St. Regis E58 as the best Chrysler Corp. police car of all time.

The E58 St. Regis is the reference by which all squad cars are judged today. This was the 'perfect police car." Chrysler Corp. dominated the police car market for over thirty years. And the E58 St. Regis was indeed its best police car.

The Dodge Diplomat and Plymouth Gran Fury took over where the R-body squads left off. The M-body cars, in turn dominated the police market until the late 1980s. The squad that surmounted the Diplomat paralled the standard set by the St. Regis.

The squad displacing the Diplomat/Gran Fury was the Chevrolet Impala, aka Caprice. When the St. Regis E58 was ruling the roads, the Impala could not even meet the minimum acceleration requirement set by the Michigan State Police. In the mid-1980s, this made the Diplomat/Gran Fury the best of the

North Dakota State Patrol used the 1980 Plymouth Gran Fury with a 360ci, 4-bbl for traffic enforcement. *Jim Benjaminson*

available squads for the job. Ford was never a threat. Buick and Pontiac didn't even try.

The Diplomat and Gran Fury were not perfect, but they were fast enough. Lighter than the St. Regis, they had almost as good acceleration and top speed from the lighter ELE 318ci, 4-bbl. And the Diplomat/Gran Fury had outstanding brakes. With their stiff suspension, they made acceptable pursuit-class cars.

The downfall came when the Diplomat and Gran Fury were used in patrol-class and taxi-class roles. These cars were plagued by the transverse torsion bar suspension. The pounding from city and county duty on the suspension caused tire wear and brake grabbing problems.

The 1980 vehicle specifications from the Los Angeles County Sheriff's Dept. brought this into sharp focus:

V-8 not to exceed 360ci	no problem
0-60mph in 14sec	no problem
100mph minimum top speed	no problem
106 to 114in wheelbase	no problem
power discs/drums	no problem
FR70 tires on 14x6 (min) wheels	no problem
transverse torsion bars not acceptable	big problem

North Dakota State Highway Department used the 1980 Plymouth Gran Fury with the 318ci, 2-bbl to enforce truck laws. *Jim Benjaminson*

The 1980 Plymouth Gran Fury (shown) and Dodge St. Regis used an aluminum front bumper to save weight. The chrome plating would frequently peel. *D.J. Smith*

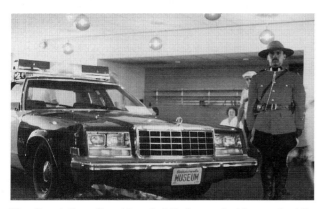

The Royal Canadian Mounted Police rode blue and white Plymouth Gran Furys in 1980. They still got their man. *Larry Knutson*

Car & Driver reviewed the then-new Dodge Mirada CMX powered by the E58 360ci, 4-bbl with dual exhaust and wide ratio TorqueFlite. They praised the powertrain, but "not much can be done for the chassis. The Mirada must make do with the tried-but-not-so-true transverse torsion bar front suspension."

At any rate, due to the transverse front suspension, the Aspen, Volare, Diplomat, LeBaron and Gran Fury (M-body) were essentially banned from the largest, most progressive and one of the most influential Sheriff's Departments in the United States.

More importantly, in this patrol-class setting, the compact 112.7-inch wheelbase really became an issue. In a pursuit-class car, the M-body cars had enough room. However, in patrol and taxi situations, especially with a two-officer unit, the M-body was a little small.

In the mid to late 1980s, Chevrolet finally figured out how to get some horsepower out of the fleet mouse motor. The Caprice had plenty of room and brakes to match the horsepower. And that spelled curtains for the Diplomat. The point is this: The changes in the mid-1980s to the Caprice made it almost identical to the 1980 St. Regis, and the St. Regis was a cop's cop car.

In 1980, Chrysler Corp. submitted the following bids for vehicles meeting the Michigan State Police (MSP) specs. The MSP sets the pace for squad car specifications for most major police departments east of the Rockies.

Year and model	Total cost
1980 Dodge St. Regis A38/E58	$6,572.80
1980 Plymouth Gran Fury A38/E58	$6,536.80
1980 Dodge Aspen A38/E47	$5,969.33
1980 Plymouth Volare A38/E47	$5,802.51

New for 1980: With the glaring exception of the loss of the E58 360ci, 4-bbl for the California cruisers, the 1980 model year was marked by only subtle changes and improvements. Halogen headlights started to become available. The St. Regis and the new Gran Fury came with a steel rear bumper, instead of an aluminum one. This was because an aluminum bumper was prone to flaking and peeling of the chrome plating. For 1980, Dodge and Plymouth pruned the diversity of the police fleet once again. Station wagons were no longer available with the A38 police package. The emergency wagons of the early-1960s gave way to the SWAT vans of the late-1970s. This left just five Chrysler Corp. models eligible to be police cars. Not counting vans, but including station wagons, this was the least diverse fleet since 1959. The five models included:

HL41 Plymouth Volare 4-door sedan
JL42 Plymouth Gran Fury 4-door pillared hardtop
JH42 Plymouth Gran Fury Salon 4-door pillared hardtop
NL41 Dodge Aspen 4-door sedan
EH42 Dodge St. Regis 4-door pillared hardtop

To make up for the lack of a medium trim level Plymouth and a medium and high trim level Dodge, Chrysler Corp. released vented, full-diameter wheel covers. These dress hub caps were available for both the 14in Volare/Aspen wheels and the 15in St. Regis/Gran Fury wheels.

The lack of fleet diversity made keeping track of the available engines very easy. For 1980, Dodge and Plymouth shared a total of five police engines—the fewest in the history of Chrysler Corp. police cars. The Aspen/Volare were available with:

E25 225ci, 1-bbl Slant Six, Federal and California
E45 318ci, 2-bbl V-8, Federal only
E47 318ci, 4-bbl V-8, Federal and California
E58 360ci, 4-bbl V-8, Federal only

The St. Regis and Gran Fury were available in all three federal V-8 engines, with only the E47 318ci, 4-bbl available in California, causing great controversy. The E47 in Federal and California trim were the same engine according to MSP spec sheets. The California version was simply made available intact for the other 49 states.

This was not the case for the E25 Slant Six, even though the Federal and California horsepower and torque figures were the same. For one thing, the distributors on these two E25 engines were different.

A Canadian version of the E47 318ci 4-bbl was also produced in 1980. With the same 8.5:1 compression and single exhaust, the Canadian engine had a 5 net hp and 5lb-ft advantage over the California version. The reason again was that the Canadian 318ci, 4-bbl did not have the restriction of the catalytic converter.

In 1980, Chrysler Corp. began describing the engine displacement in terms of metric liters. The 318ci engine was now called a "5.2 liter" engine. The practice of listing both "ci" and "liters" continued through 1989.

In 1979, the Mopar squads were available with either 2.71 or 3.21 rear gear ratios, depending on the squad, emissions, and the engine. For1980, Chrysler Corp. split the difference between these ratios and released a 2.94 rear gear, period. The 8-

This is the door shield on the 1980 Gran Fury used by the Royal Canadian Mounted Police, Gendarmerie Royale du Canada. *Larry Knutson*

1/4in Aspen/Volare and the 9-1/4in St. Regis/ Gran Fury all got the 2.94:1 gear. A limited-slip "Sure-Grip" differential was again available.

A most subtle change took place with tires in 1980. The police tire specifications had the new P-metric designation. The P215/70R15, for example, had a 215mm sidewall cross-section width, when mounted on a specified rim.

Block heaters became available as an option for the first time in 1980. They were not available in California, which didn't matter. But it sure made cold winter starts more reliable for most cops in the other 49 states.

Certified speedometers, the mark of a cop car, were available again in 1980. This time they were calibrated to 125mph, and they came standard with an oil pressure gauge in lieu of an oil pressure light. What made this certified speedometer available on both the F-body and R-body worthy of note, is the harsh warning found in the police literature:

Warning: certified speedometer with scale over 85mph may legally be purchased only by law enforcement agencies for the purpose of law enforcement.

In 1980, the Michigan State Police expanded their vehicle test program to include:

1. Full-size sedans (114.4 to 119.9in wheelbase) with 350 to 360ci V-8 engines.

2. Mid-Size sedans (105.5 to 112.7in wheelbase) with 225ci 6-cyl to 318ci V-8 engines.

3. Mid-size sedans with 350 to 360ci V-8 engines.

No clear trends in the results exist. A great deal of overlap between these three different kinds of squads was evident. One fact was however, very obvious. The E58 360ci, 4-bbl powered

Mopar squads, full-size or mid-size, were faster than the competition. In most cases, they were a lot faster. The E58 powered cruisers were not America's fastest sedans, in terms of top speed, but only the Corvette L82 was faster.

The Los Angeles County Sheriff's Department used this rollbar-equipped 1980 Gran Fury for EVOC training at the Pomona Fairgrounds. *John Bellah*

Troopers with the Kansas Highway Patrol thrash this 1980 Gran Fury A38 on their EVOC course. *Rick Wilson*

The police in New York City are not really interested in cars. Count this as one of the dozens of differences between the cops in Los Angeles and the cops in New York City. In the Big Apple, the enforcement scenario obviously calls for patrol-class and taxi-class squads. These cops, for the most part, were perfectly happy with 225ci, 1-bbl and 318ci, 2-bbl powered cruisers. In fact, in the 1980s, only the NYC-PD highway units got the V-8 and 4-bbl squads.

However, in 1980, the NYC-PD fleet folks did something foolish. New York cops take most everything in stride, but this went too far—or should we say "too small."

The First Precinct seriously deployed a fleet of Plymouth Horizon squad cars. No, these were not police package vehicles! The headlines of the October 28, 1980 *New York Post* read:

Detectives with the Los Angeles Police Department used this 1980 Gran Fury. This "plain wrapper" had a spotlight but was still a pure cop car. *John Bellah*

No prisoners please, the car's too small.

Question: How do you fit a big police officer into a small car? Answer: Snugly! Officers big and small are fast learning to cope with smaller new police cars."

The Plymouth Horizon, Ford Fairmont and Chevy Citation are among the new smaller—and more fuel efficient—cars replacing previous roomier models.

All of them have been test-driven by the Motor Transport Division and found to be "safe and serviceable," according to a police spokesman.

Six-foot-two 265lb Police Officer Matthew Johnson of Manhattan's Ericsson Place stationhouse is one of many officers filling out a two page questionnaire to evaluate the cars' performance.

And how do the officers like the smaller models?

Well, the Plymouth Horizon has been catching most of the complaints, with the others ranking just a drop better, we're told.

The most frequent complaint is of officers having trouble getting a prisoner into the back seat unless he's cooperative.

For the record, the Dodge Omni and Plymouth Horizon had a 99.2-inch wheelbase. That is 13-1/2in shorter than a Volare/Aspen or later Diplomat/Gran Fury squads. These micro-squads were also 39in shorter overall than the Volare/Aspen. For the performance curious reader, the Omni/Horizon squads were powered by a 105ci, 4-cylinder engine producing 65 net bhp. Yes, they got 30mpg. No, they could not exceed 85mph, even downhill.

Fortunately, the NYC-PD Horizon never went beyond the field testing stage. Within just two months, all of these matchbox cars were taken out of service.

In 1978, Chrysler Corp. transmissions received lockup torque converters except for H.D. police engines and those engines with California or high altitude emissions packages. In 1980, Chrysler Corp. passenger cars received another improvement in the transmission—a wide ratio gear set.

First gear on the TorqueFlite was dropped from 2.45 down to 2.74. Second gear was geared down from 1.45 to 1.54. Third gear, or drive, remained at 1.00 to one. This new gearing added quite a bit more low-end and mid-range responsiveness. The wide ratio came with the 225, 318 and 360ci engines in all levels of carburetion and with all emissions packages. However, neither lockup torque converters nor wide ratio transmissions were available on police packages, yet. These changes would take place in 1981, with the exception of one engine.

As a production side-note, in early 1980, the Hamtramck, Michigan assembly plant closed. Hamtramck assembled many of the great muscle cars of the 1960s and 1970s. As of 1980, "Dodge Main" was gone. At the end of 1980, the Lynch Road assembly plant in Detroit also shut down. Chrysler's financial woes were the result of extremely sluggish car sales which all car makers experienced. Chrysler was undergoing a painful transition from larger, rear wheel drive to smaller, front wheel drive cars. And, according to the market, Chrysler was a little behind the other manufacturers.

In 1980, the Diplomat and LeBaron M-body passenger cars were significantly restyled. They now had the square-jawed and sharp-creased look that a legendary cop car would have beginning in 1981. As of 1980, the Diplomat and LeBaron shared the same 112.7-inch wheelbase as the Aspen and Volare. As a result, these became natural replacements for the Aspen and Volare which were dropped after the 1980 model year.

The fabulous St. Regis and Gran Fury were available in 1981 for the last time. Chrysler Corp. only made the R-body St. Regis, Newport and Gran Fury for three years. While the R-body

Indiana State Police used the 1980 Dodge Aspen with 360ci engines. These cars were faster than the Mopar R-bodies. *Dave Morrison*

By 1980, the New Albany, Indiana Police were among many departments who gave the mid-size squads a try. *Darryl Lindsay and Ned Schwartz*

Nevada Highway Patrol could catch anything with these 1980 Plymouth Volare cruisers equipped with 360ci, 4-bbl engines. *Darryl Lindsay and Ned Schwartz*

was available in 1981, support for it was not. As California highway cops clearly expressed in 1980, a 318ci engine—even with a 4-bbl carb—is not big enough to make a pursuit-class car. The 1981 R-bodies were vastly upstaged by the 1981 M-bodies powered by the same engines.

1980 Dodge St. Regis
Standard Equipment with (A38) Pursuit Package
Air Cleaner-dry-type, replaceable element
Alternator-heavy-duty 65 ampere Chrysler with electronic regulator
Ammeter
Antifreeze-for minus 35 degrees F
Armrests-front and rear (rear includes ash receivers on St. Regis)
Ash Receiver-front
Ash Receiver-rear
Automatic Air Conditioning Hi-Pressure Clutch Cutoff Switch-for compressor, with optional air conditioning only
Axle Ratios - 2.94:1
Axle Size - 9.25in
Battery-500 ampere (85 ampere-hours) with Thermo-Guard heat shield
Brakes-heavy duty power brakes with dual master cylinder; disc front brakes with semi-metallic front pads; 11x2.5in rear drum brakes
Brakes, Power Booster-dual tandem
Catalytic Converter
Coolant Recovery System
Coolant System-maximum capacity radiator with 20in diameter seven-blade fan with thermal torque drive
Easy-Fill Oil Filler Tube
Electronic Ignition
Engine Mounts-spool-type
Front Fender-wheelhouse panel high-temperature aluminized shields

Gauge-engine temperature, ammeter, fuel
Grass Shield for Catalytic Converter
Heater with Defroster
Heavy-Duty Service Package-extra welds and reinforcements
Hood Release-instrument panel mounted
Horns-dual
Interior Trim, St. Regis-heavy-duty cloth and vinyl straight bench (K1) available in dark blue or cashmere
Mirror-inside day/night; outside flag-type, left and right, manual
Oil Filter-full flow, throwaway
Oil Pressure Warning Light (n/a with certified speedometer)
Parking Brake Warning Light
Police Accessory Feed Wire
Power Steering Oil Pump Cooler

New York City Police crushed crime in this blue and white 1980 Plymouth Volare. These were powered by the Slant Six. *Ned Schwartz*

Seat Belts-three front, three rear
Seat, Front-heavy duty seat construction
Splash Shield, Rubber-special heat-reflective, right side
Speedometer-non-certified, 85mph
Steering, Power-Pursuit Firm-Feel type
Stoplight Switch-heavy duty
Suspension-Specially designed & engineered suspension for pursuit-type work, with the following heavy-duty components matched for high speed handling: front anti-sway bar, torsion bars, rear anti-sway bar, extended-life upper & lower control arm bushings & heavy duty rear leaf springs with special bushings & heavy duty 1-3/16in front & rear shock absorbers
Tinted Glass-all windows (including shaded windshield)
Tire, Spare, Conventional
Transmission Auxiliary Oil Cooler
Transmission Low-Gear Blockout
Transmission, TorqueFlite Automatic
Wheels-extra heavy duty (15x7in)
Windshield Wipers-two-speed with electric washers
Tires: P215/70R15 police-type
1980 Dodge St. Regis
Optional Equipment with (A38) Pursuit Packages
Air Conditioning
Alternator-100 ampere, dual belt drive
Clear Windshield-with tinted side and back window glass
Deactivate Door Switch
Deck-Lid Release, Remote
Defroster, Rear Window (2)-electrically heated
Engine Block Heater-not available in California
Engine Oil Cooler-Optional E58 engine only
Fast-Idle Throttle Control-manual locking type

New York City Police actually tested the Plymouth Horizon to see how it would work as a precinct car. They had a tough time getting prisoners in the back seat. *Sandra James*

Hose Clamps-stainless steel, worm type
Keys, Single/Keys, Universal Single System
Lamp, Glove Box
Lamp, Luggage Compartment
Lamp, Under hood
Light, Additional Dome
Locking Gas Cap
Mats, Floor-heavy duty black, front and rear

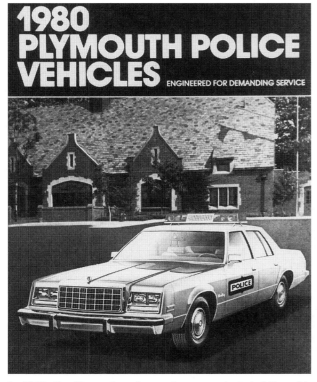

In 1980, the Plymouth police package cars included the mid-size Volare and full-size Gran Fury. *Chrysler*

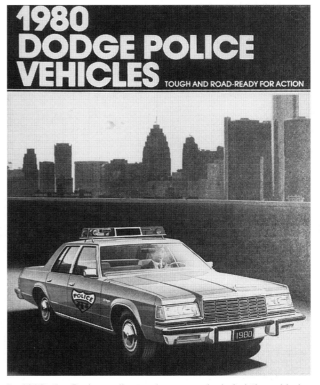

In 1980, the Dodge police package cars included the mid-size Aspen and full-size St. Regis. *Chrysler*

Mirror, Right, Outside-remote control
Police Bonding Strap Package
Radiator, Silicone Heater and Bypass Hose
Radio Cable Conduit
Radio Suppression Package
Relay Control System
Roof Reinforcement Plate
Roof Wire

Seat, Rear-heavy duty construction with full foam cushion
Speedometer (3)-certified to 125mph: includes oil pressure gauge in lieu of warning light
Spotlight, Left, 6in windshield-pillar mounted
Spotlight, Right, 6in windshield-pillar mounted
Sure-Grip Rear Axle - 2.94 ratio
Wheel covers-vented 15in
Tires: P225/70R15 police-type

1980 360ci, 4-bbl Engines

Vehicle	car	car	van	van
Emission Pkg.	Federal	Canada	Federal	California
Engine Code	E58	E58	EC5	EC5
SAE Net HP	185@4000	190@4000	180@4000	170@4000
Net Torque	275@2000	280@2000	270@4000	270@2000
Carburetor	Carter TQ	Carter TQ	Carter TQ	Carter TQ
Carb Number	9244S	9236S	n/a	n/a
Exhaust	dual	dual	single	single
Catalysts	dual	NONE	single	single
Compression	8.0:1	8.4:1	8.0:1	8.0:1
Timing	16BTDC	10BTDC	16BTDC	16BTDC
Fuel	Unleaded	Regular or unleaded	Unleaded	Unleaded

1980 St. Regis Versus 1989 Diplomat & Caprice

(Michigan State Police Vehicle Tests)

Category	1980 Dodge St. Regis	1989 Dodge Diplomat	1989 Chevrolet Caprice
Police Package	A38	AHB	9C1
Engine Size	360ci (E58)	318ci (ELE)	350ci
Induction	ThermoQuad 4-bbl	QuadraJet 4-bbl	Throttle Body Inj.
Exhaust	dual	single	single
SAE Net HP	185@4000	175@4000	190@4400
Torque, Net	275@2000	250@3200	285@2400
Compression Ratio	8.0:1	8.0:1	9.3:1
Axle Ratio	2.94:1	2.94:1	3.42:1
Transmission	A727, 3-sp auto	A999, 3-sp auto	700R4, 4-sp auto
Lock-up	no	yes	yes
Tires	GR70-15(Flexten)	P21570R-15(GT+4)	P22570R-15(GT+4)
Steering	15.7:1 firm-feel	15.7:1 firm-feel	n/a ratio, power
Front Suspension	torsion, sway bar	torsion, sway bar	coil spr, sway bar
Rear Suspension	leaf, sway bar	leaf, sway bar	coil, sway bar
Brakes, f/r	power disc/drum	power disc/drum	power disc/drum
Swept Area, f/r	224 in2/166 in2	205 in2/166 in2	273in2/138in2
Wheelbase	118.5in	112.7in	116.0in
Overall Length	220.2in	204.6in	212.2in
MSP Test Weight	4173lb	3894lb	3965lb
Head Room, Front	38.2in	39.3in	39.5in
Leg Room, Front	42.3in	42.5in	42.2in
Shoulder Rm, Front	61.0in	56.0in	60.5in
Hip Room, Front	57.4 in	53.5in	55.0in
MIS Road Course	91.8sec	88.7sec	86.2sec
0 to 60mph	11.5sec	11.8sec	9.8sec
0 to 100mph	36.7sec	38.9sec	29.4sec
Top Speed	122.7mph	119.1mph	122.0mph
Distance to 110mph	.90mi	1.10mi	.95mi
Quarter Mile ET	18.40sec	18.79sec	17.62sec
Quarter Mile Trap	77.5mph	75.5mph	79.8mph
Brake Power	23.5fps2*	26.3 fps2*	26.0fps2*
Ergonomics	180.1pts	190.2pts	189.6pts
Fuel Economy, city	11mpg	12.7mpg	14.3mpg

Note: In 1980, the Chevrolet Impala 350ci was eliminated from the MSP bid process due to its inability to meet the established minimum acceleration requirements!!!
*fps2 stands for 'feet per second squared.'

1980 Dodge and Plymouth Heavy Duty Police Engines
Engines with Federal Emissions Control Package

Code	Engine & Carburetor	Net Torque (ft-lb)	Net Horsepower	Aspen Volare	St. Regis Gran Fury
E25	3.7 liter (225ci) 1-bbl Slant Six	160@1600rpm	90@3600rpm	X	n/a
E45	5.2 liter (318ci) 2-bbl V-8	245@1600rpm	120@3600rpm	X	X
E47	5.2 liter (318ci) 4-bbl V-8	240@2000rpm	155@4000rpm	X	X
E58	5.9 liter (360ci) 4-bbl V-8	275@2000rpm	185@4000rpm	X	X

Engines with California Emissions Control Package

Code	Engine & Carburetor	Net Torque (ft-lb)	Net Horsepower	Aspen Volare	St. Regis Gran Fury
E25	3.7 liter (225ci) 1-bbl Slant Six	160@1600rpm	90@3600rpm	X	n/a
E47	5.2 liter (318ci) 4-bbl V-8	240@2000rpm	155@4000rpm	X	X

1980 Police and Passenger Car Performance

Vehicle	Engine&Carb	MIS Road Course	0-60 mph	0-100 mph	Top Speed	1/4 Mile ET	Trap	Brake Power	Reference
Plymouth Gran Fury A38	360ci 4-bbl E58	90.8sec	11.3sec	35.4sec	125mph	18.15sec	76.6mph	22.5fps2	MSP-80
Dodge St. Regis A38	360ci 4-bbl E58	91.8sec	11.5sec	36.7sec	123mph	18.40sec	77.5mph	23.5fps2	MSP-80
Ford LTD-S Police	351ci 2VV	92.2sec	11.5sec	37.3sec	121mph	18.50sec	77.8mph	22.0fps2	MSP-80
Chevrolet Impala 9C1	350ci 4-bbl	92.8sec	12.9sec	46.2sec	110mph	19.08sec	73.3mph	23.7fps2	MSP-80
Buick LeSabre Police	350ci 4-bbl	96.2sec	13.4sec	49.4sec	113mph	19.50sec	74.3mph	22.7fps2	MSP-80
Dodge St. Regis A38	318ci 4-bbl E48	93.9sec	13.1sec	45.7sec	115mph	19.60sec	74.5mph	23.5fps2	MSP-80*
Dodge Aspen A38	360ci 4-bbl E58	92.7sec	10.9sec	n/a	122mph	17.95sec	77.5mph	23.3fps2	MSP-80
Chevrolet Malibu 9C1	350ci 4-bbl	92.2sec	12.3sec	n/a	111mph	19.00sec	74.3mph	24.7fps2	MSP-80
Chevrolet Malibu 9C1	305ci 4-bbl	93.3sec	12.8sec	n/a	113mph	19.20sec	73.5mph	24.1fps2	MSP-80
Plymouth Volare A38	318ci 4-bbl E45	96.2sec	12.6sec	n/a	120mph	19.33sec	74.8mph	23.9fps2	MSP-80
Dodge Aspen A38	318ci 4-bbl E45	96.2sec	13.2sec	n/a	117mph	19.55sec	73.3mph	22.3fps2	MSP-80
Ford Fairmont Police	255ci 2-bbl	95.7sec	15.9sec	n/a	112mph	20.65sec	68.5mph	24.2 fps2	MSP-80
Chevrolet Corvette L82	350ci 4-bbl	n/a	7.4sec	n/a	130mph	15.5sec	92.0mph	n/a	MT Dec.'79
Pontiac Trans Am Turbo	301ci 4-bbl	n/a	8.2sec	n/a	116mph	16.7sec	86.0mph	n/a	CD Oct.'79
Chevrolet Camaro Z28	350ci 4-bbl	n/a	8.5sec	n/a	120mph	16.4sec	86.0mph	n/a	CD Apr.'80
Dodge Mirada CMX	360ci 4-bbl E58	n/a	10.5sec	n/a	118mph	17.8sec	79.4mph	n/a	MTOct.'79
Dodge Diplomat	225ci 1-bbl E25	n/a	15.0sec	n/a	95mph	20.1sec	68.4mph	n/a	MT Apr.'80

*Reference only

References

Plymouth Police Vehicles, Chrysler Corporation, 1980
Dodge Police Vehicles, Chrysler Corporation, 1980
Plymouth Gran Fury (Canada), Chrysler Corporation 1980
Patrol Vehicle Specifications, Evaluation and Purchasing Program, Michigan State Police, 1980
"Dodge Diplomat," Chuck Nerpel, *Motor Trend*, April 1980
"Dodge Mirada," Ron McGonegal, *Motor Trend*, October 1979
Vehicle Testing and Evaluation Program, Los Angeles County Sheriff's Dept., 1980
"Dodge Mirada," Rich Ceppos, *Car & Driver*, October 1979
"No Prisoners Please," staff reporter, *New York Post*, October 28, 1980
Illustrated Text Section, Passenger Car Parts Catalog, Chrysler Corp., 1980

This 1980 Pinellas County, Florida Sheriff's St. Regis uses propane fuel to improve performance and prevent vapor lock. *Robert Helmick*

Chapter 3

Year of the Dog in California

1978: *THE PREDICTION*. With their highly refined satire, the August 1978 issue of *Car & Driver* featured an article entitled "The Incredible Shrinking Cop Car." The subtitle was even more prophetic, "And while its shrinking, it's also getting (heh, heh), slower." Superimposed over the awesome CHP Dodge Monaco, powered by the 440 Magnum, was a Dodge Omni, complete with oversized lightbar.

C&D made some chillingly accurate predictions about the 'Great New Car Down-sizing Revolution of 1982.'

"For by 1982, four years from the moment you read these words, the fearsome California Highway Patrol could well be reduced to impotent pursuit cars."

Evidence for their view was the loss at year's end of the Chrysler Corp. big blocks, which were victims of CAFE laws. Actually, it took only two years, instead of the four predicted by *C&D*. For Californians, 1980 became the Year of the Dog.

C&D mused about "Dirty Harry" and "Smokey and the Bandit" sequels being filmed using black and white Ford Fiestas. Recall the New York City Police Dept. with the Plymouth Horizon. That was 1980.

Another uncanny prediction was the assumption that police would be exempt from smog and fuel standards and that they would appeal to Congress to allow them to keep their high performance engines. Evidence in 1978 to support this theory was that the CHP had already joined with the International Association of Chiefs of Police (IACP) in their effort to get emergency vehicles excluded from CAFE standards.

This prediction became true when the California legislature relaxed air pollution standards for emergency vehicles in mid-1981. For the 1982 model year, cop cars needed only to comply with federal emissions standards, not the stricter California standards.

In 1978, Chrysler Corp. was seeking congressional exemption from CAFE penalties for certain cars. Dave Hubbs, Chrysler's Fleet Sales Manager, is quoted by *C&D* saying:

"Unless we get some kind of exception, performance engines will go away. Even with an exemption, we won't be building any more King Kong motors. Without an exemption, there is no solution. It is a very bleak future and I have nothing to offer in the way of encouragement."

The 1979 CHP Special Purpose Vehicle Study introduced the Camaro Z28 as a pursuit vehicle. *Darryl Lindsay*

In 1980, the largest engine to power the St. Regis in California was the 155hp, 318ci V-8. The CHP was not amused but all of the West Coast speeders sure were. *California Highway Patrol*

Chevrolet's Harry Hammond put a different and much more accurate spin on the whole problem. Remember, this is a 1978 quote.

"The need for a pursuit vehicle is emotional. There is other technology that will do as well. Remember also that in the final analysis, it is safer not to pursue."

Hammond insightfully identified pursuit vehicles as emotional. The lack of pursuit vehicles would indeed become an emotional issue and not one of true substance. The CHP repeatedly pointed to "image" and "morale" problems with the slower 1980 cars, and not necessarily tangible enforcement drawbacks. It was clearly a case of symbolism over substance. This is especially evident when the actual timed performance of the "problem" car and the "solution" car are analyzed.

The CHP fleet personnel knew that vehicle specifications would have to be modified to what the car makers could build. In the severely depressed car market of the late 1970s and early 1980s, nobody was going to build a special police car, not even for the CHP. Engine emission certifications costs and CAFE penalties were just too high.

The CHP knew by 1981 they were going to have to "bite the bullet." The CHP got small displacement V-8 mid-size cars by 1981, but the bullet biting took place one year earlier than hoped.

Led by SCCA A/Production Corvette road racer and CHP Fleet Manager John Grow, the CHP began to re-evaluate its overall vehicle needs. This led to an 18-month study on four very different kinds of 1979 model year squad cars.

1979: THE EXPERIMENT. Late in 1978, the CHP began their now-famous Special Purpose Vehicle Study. This involved short wheelbase patrol-cars with small V-8s, pursuit-class pony cars with bigger V-8s, and utility-class down-sized station wagons with small V-8s. The CHP was currently cruising around in the 1979 Dodge St. Regis, powered by the E58 360ci, 4-bbl. They were happy with the squad's performance but knew it would not carryover to 1980.

The researchers studied the following:

1. 1979 Chevrolet Malibu: 305ci, 4-bbl V-8 engine with a 108in wheelbase and a 2.73 rear gear
2. 1979 Ford Fairmont: 302ci, 4-bbl V-8 engine with a 105.5in wheelbase and a 2.73 rear gear
3. 1979 Plymouth Volare station wagon: 318ci, 4-bbl V-8 engine with a 112.7in wheelbase and a 2.41 rear gear
4. 1979 Chevrolet Camaro Z28: 350ci, 4-bbl V-8 engine with a 108in wheelbase and a 3.08 rear gear

The Z28 was complete with front air dam and rear spoiler. It was also equipped with "Nova Police" brakes. The Nova cop car was legendary in California. The CHP received an exemption from the California Air Resources Board (CARB) to use a 3.08 axle in the Z28 to increase its top speed. These were otherwise stock Z28s that rolled off the Van Nuys assembly plant, complete with every last bit of smog gear.

The Volare wagon was a bit ahead of its time. Wagons have never been well-accepted by cops. However, the Volare wagon had three times the cargo space as the current 4-door, long wheelbase St. Regis.

The CHP purchased twelve of each of these four test squads. They sent three of each to carefully selected parts of the state. The locations were: West Los Angeles, which was heavily urbanized, densely populated, congested with traffic; El Centro, near the Mexican border with an extremely hot climate; Redding with long mountain grades, cold weather and snow; and Bakersfield, the high speed link between northern and southern California

The CHP kept detailed maintenance, downtime and fuel mileage records of all 48 test vehicles. They put an average of 57,000 miles on each car.

The Malibus had a few engine and transmission problems. The heat from El Centro affected them. The Malibu averaged 34 hours of downtime per month and had a total cost of 32 cents per mile.

The Fairmont performed equally well state-wide with only a few head gasket and transmission problems. It had the

31

least downtime at 20 hours per month and a total cost of 25 cents per mile.

The Volare had transmission troubles and 32 hours of downtime per month. However, the Mopar wagon had the lowest operating cost of any vehicle at just 21 cents per mile.

The Camaro Z28 was an entirely different story. The heat of El Centro, the continuous high speeds around Bakersfield, and the mountain grades around Redding, took a heavy toll. Of the twelve Z28 test cars, nine had to have the engine replaced altogether. Five of the engines were overhauled, due to piston or main bearing failure at least once before being replaced by a different engine. Only the three Z28s driven in the urban Los Angeles traffic did not need new engines.

The Camaros logged the most downtime at 52 hours per month and of course the highest operating costs at 48 cents per mile.

CHP mechanics were not fond of the Z28. Cited in *Police Produce News* they said:

"GM has a long way to go before they can market a high speed machine that can match the endurance of the old Dodge gunboat."

The average CHP car spends most of its time at cruise speeds, and in 1979 got in an average of one high-speed pursuit a day. Speeds over 100mph for 50 miles or more are common.

The Z28s came with 2-bolt main 350ci small blocks. Nine of the twelve Z28 test cars had to have the engine replaced. Chevy replaced them with the bullet-proof 4-bolt main 350ci mill. That solved the problem.

The CHP declared the experiment a success. A great deal was learned about small block, patrol-class mid-size cars and pony car-based pursuit-class cars.

1980: *THE PROBLEM.* In 1980, California cops got ambushed by California emissions standards. In the protracted firefight that followed, the good name of the Dodge St. Regis got caught in the crossfire.

In 1980, the E58 360ci, 4-bbl was no longer available in California police cars. The biggest available engine for the 118.5in wheelbase St. Regis was the E47 318ci, 4-bbl with 155 net hp.

The CHP fleet folks were aware the CAFE and emissions laws would slow down emergency vehicles. In fact, the CHP had omitted any performance specification for acceleration or top speed on the 1980 bid. This was not an oversight. Instead, the CHP fleet personnel were simply facing reality.

Chuck Swift of Swift Dodge in Sacramento, California had won the CHP "class E" squad car contract for years, supplying all the CHP Dodges. According to Swift, no 1980 CARB-approved car could meet the old CHP requirements for acceleration and top speed. The three squads that were CARB-certified to bid on the 1980 CHP contract were:

1. Dodge St. Regis, 318ci, 4-bbl
2. Chevrolet Impala, 350ci, 4-bbl
3. Ford LTD, 351ci, 2VV

The St. Regis was awarded the contract.

Halfway into the 1980 model year, CHP officers began to complain about the 318ci powered Dodge. The CHiPs were used to the power of the 440ci. They accepted the still powerful 360ci St. Regis "like a trooper." However, the 318ci powered squad just didn't make the cut.

Fleet personnel may have known what was going on, but the rest of the state, including many CHP patrolmen, were caught off guard by how slow the 1980 squads were. Friendly competition between the old 1978 440ci Monacos ready for retirement and the brand new 1980 318ci St. Regis' made the huge acceleration differences even more obvious. The 318ci powered St. Regis made a great patrol-class car, but a horrible pursuit-class car.

Wild reports started to surface: CHP cruisers were being outrun by Volkswagen Beetles. The St. Regis only had a top speed of 65mph on a mountain grade. Being laughed at by speeders, squads were too slow to merge into traffic. They were too slow to pace and then overtake speeders. They had no power at all, not even to push stalled vehicles out of the traffic lane. Speeders intentionally flaunted their speed because they knew they could outrun the CHiPs.

CHP patrol officers felt they had to thank drivers of high-performance cars who honored the "continuously glowing red light" and pulled over, knowing they could outrun the squad. Officers were unable to overtake drivers on the freeway, even when drivers were not trying to elude the CHP. Speeders often got lost in traffic before the patrolman could accelerate to overtake speeders.

The list of gripes seemed endless. The St. Regis was called a dog, a stone, the patrolman's bad dream and a car that "couldn't catch its own shadow, let alone a speeder on a mountain grade."

California magazine and *Car & Driver* ran hypothetical stories of Corvettes and Camaros simply running away from the CHP Dodges at will. The top speed of the St. Regis was "unofficially" claimed to be 85mph on level ground and 65mph up a mountain grade.

Chuck Swift properly identified these claims for exactly what they were—exaggerations. The facts were that these officers were simply suffering from "big block withdrawal," the same malady car enthusiasts suffered in the mid-1970s.

The facts were also that while the 1980 St. Regis was slow, it was not that slow. According to Swift and some CHP patrol officers, the St. Regis would run between 105 and 107mph on level ground with a full lightbar and twin spotlights.

This seems to be confirmed by the Michigan State Police test of a 318ci, 4-bbl powered 1981 Dodge St. Regis. Without either lightbar or spotlights, the MSP recorded a top speed of 114.7mph. The O to 60mph time for the St. Regis with the 318ci was just 1.6 seconds slower than the same car powered by the 360ci, and just 3 seconds slower than the 440ci powered Monaco.

According to Swift, there was no problem with the 1980 CHP St. Regis, except it had a small V-8 engine. He maintains the California emissions requirements caused the lack-luster performance. Again, all CARB-approved squads were slow.

This 1981 CHP Dodge Diplomat saved the Dodge performance reputation which was more than tarnished by the 318ci powered St. Regis. *California Highway Patrol*

And of course, the 318ci powered squad was slower than the same squad with a larger engine.

That was not the point. The point was, the St. Regis was faster than any other make of police car certified by CARB. Specifically, the St. Regis outran the Chevrolet Impala and the Ford LTD. It was the best full-size squad car available in the State of California in 1980, period.

Not good enough. The CHP had a performance problem, real or perceived, and that caused a "wimpy squad" image and low patrol officer morale. Quite honestly, the CHP called this an "embarrassing problem."

All of this was quite a handful for perhaps the most respected and influential police department anywhere. The CHP had a positive enforcement reputation, rivalled only by the Royal Canadian Mounted Police on this continent. And a problem in California was a big problem. The CHP alone logged between 90 and 110 million miles a year on patrol. Yep. The distance from the earth to the sun.

Not surprisingly, the CHP's embarrassing problem became a political football at the urging of the California Association of Highway Patrolmen. And who could blame them? Members of a California watchdog group even threatened to sue Chrysler Corp.

The only problem with the law suit was Chrysler made no breech of contract regarding acceleration rates or top speed. No specs were written. No performance promise was made. No performance promise was broken. Dodge Division was not liable for the cost to modify the CHP cars, or to replace them with faster cars. Even still, it was widely agreed, something had to be done.

1980 1/2: *THE SOLUTION*. The California Highway Patrol, the California Air Resources Board, the California Association of Highway Patrolmen, and Chrysler Corp. and Swift Dodge all came together in October, 1980 to reach an agreement. Like a bunch of gearheads standing in the pit area of a drag strip, these officials brainstormed a way to improve acceleration or top speed—or both. That had to have been the Car Clinic of the Decade. We wonder if Ronnie Sox or Dick Landy was invited.

The suggestions ranged from mild to wild, just like all bench-racing sessions:
1. Remove the air-intake emissions control flap
2. Remove the entire air-intake snorkel system
3. Install a catalytic converter exhaust cutout
4. Install a turbocharger (really!)
5. Install a B&M shift kit
6. Change the rear gear from 2.94 to 3.21 or 3.55
7. Replace the muffler with a straight pipe
8. Modify California emissions to federal emissions level

The CARB flatly blamed Chrysler for failing to engineer their cars for performance. We know, how could anyone accuse Chrysler Corp., of all car companies, for failing to design performance cars? At any rate, the CARB absolutely refused to budge on anything related to smog gear. The California legislature favorably handled this issue in less than a year.

At $800, the turbocharger was too expensive. Chuck Swift advised against the change from a 2.94 rear ratio to a 3.55 gear. He cited warranty problems from cars that would rev much higher at cruising speeds. The 3.21 ratio was never acted upon, perhaps due to cost. This used to be the standard police gear ratio, and would have improved both acceleration and top speed.

This group decided on a three-step plan of attack.

First, sell off some squads to local jurisdictions. These would be agencies who needed a patrol-class car. The St. Regis with the 318ci, 4-bbl was certainly an excellent patrol-class car. The CHP sold off 86 of these squads for the same $7,091 price they paid.

In 1982, the CHP selected the Mustang 5.0 LX to restore morale among highway patrolmen and to strike fear in the hearts of speeders. For the first time ever, Chrysler had to "no bid." *Ford*

The number of new cars sold to local agencies was limited because the CHP urgently needed squad cars as replacements. After all, the decision to sell was approved after the 1981 passenger cars had already been released. Rather than devoting effort to coordinating further sales, the CHP focused on the best possible specs for the 1981 squad cars. At any rate, this action resulted in the Los Angeles Times headline, "CHP Unloading Its 'Dog Cars,'" with the subtitle "900 New Vehicles Too Slow to Catch Speeders."

The second part of the plan was to modify all of the existing squads. CARB authorized the removal of the muffler (not catalyst) and the installation of a straight pipe in its place. They did this only after tests were run to see how much noisier the cars would be and how much it improved top speed.

CARB tests found the catalysts quieted the engines so much that a muffler was not needed to pass CARB noise ordinances. Again, the catalytic converters remained on the CHP squads untouched. Only the mufflers were straight-piped. The result was a 5 to 10 net hp increase which was good for 2 to 4mph on the top end.

The only other authorized modification was a shift kit and recalibrated valve body for the highest possible shift points. The shifts were much firmer and well past the peak power of the 318ci, 4-bbl wedge.

Few people would be naive enough to think that the modifications all stopped there. Yes, some unauthorized changes were made. By far, the most common was plugging the exhaust gas recirculation valve. Every bit of exhaust gas that gets routed back into the intake manifold lowers the horsepower. Other popular changes were enriching the air to fuel mixture on the Thermo-Quad carb, loosening the air cleaner, and advancing the basic timing. Squads that came in for transmission service came out with non-lock-up torque converters. All these changes produced cars that would run 117mph on a level road.

The third plan of attack was to simply use these squads up as fast as possible. They were assigned to high mileage patrols and heavy shift work in an attempt to hit 70,000 miles in the shortest possible time.

Some of the motorists stopped by these heavily modified St. Regis squads were surprised at how quick the Dodges were. Word of sluggish CHP cars travelled fast. Some highway patrolmen, proud of the improved performance from the tricked-up

Dodges, let it be known that they were running experimental 440ci engines. Just a little bit of police humor.

1981: *THE TEST.* This image and morale problem was not going to happen again to the CHP. Long known as having the hottest Dodges in the country, and after taking heat from the press, politicians and their own patrolmen, the 1981 cars were going to be faster.

By the time the December 1980 bid process got underway, the CHP already had an excellent idea of how the 1981 squads were performing. The Michigan State Police tests on 1981 mid-size and full-size cars were performed in September 1980. However, few of the cars that MSP tested could pass the tough CARB standards.

The MSP tests, however, gave the CHP a realistic look at where police cars were in 1981. This allowed the CHP to set minimum and realistic acceleration and top speed standards. The standards were:

0 to 60mph	13sec max.
0 to 100mph	43sec max.
top speed	110mph min. in 2 miles

The CHP kept this standard for the rest of the 1980s.

In the meantime, CARB had approved three police cars for use in California. Eligible to quote were:

Chevrolet Malibu	350ci, 4-bbl, 165 net hp
Dodge Diplomat	318ci, 4-bbl, 165 net hp (E48)
Ford LTD	351ci, 2VV, 165 net hp

Dodge was the low bid among the contracts at $8,162. However, the CHP was not going to spend a penny until they could confirm the winning car could meet the specifications. In February 1981, all of the interested parties gathered at Mather Air Force Base for some high stakes drag racing:

	0-60	0-100	top speed
Malibu 350	11.42sec	40.27sec	111.9mph
Diplomat 318	12.84sec	42.71sec	116.3mph
Ford LTD 351	12.76sec	42.16sec	116.4mph

The good name of Dodge had been vindicated by the Dodge Diplomat in its very first year as a police package car. With all the pressure put on this test, and the storming controversy leading up to the test, the Dodge Diplomat A38 was an instant legend.

In time for the 1982 model year cars, the California legislature passed into law a bill which exempted emergency vehicles from state smog control standards. This became California Vehicle Code Section 27156.2. The 1982 emergency vehicles still had to meet federal emissions standards.

1982: *THE PURSUIT.* The Dodge Diplomat, and for 1982, the Plymouth Gran Fury, powered by the 318ci, 4-bbl made reasonable patrol-class cars. However, not since the big blocks of pre-1979 did law enforcement have a true pursuit-class car. The 1978 Monaco 440 was great, the 1979 St. Regis 360 was acceptable, the 1980 St. Regis 318 was not acceptable, and the 1981 Diplomat was the fastest 4-door police sedan available.

Not fast enough. The 18-month 1979 Specialty Vehicle study was just being completed as the St. Regis problems got statewide attention. Stung by low top speed cars for too long, the CHP wanted a good old fashioned pursuit car. What was the fastest domestic-made car in America in 1982? The Ford Mustang. It outran the 125mph Chevrolet Corvette by 1 to 3mph.

Armed with the 18-month study involving the Camaro Z28 and tired of slow cars, the CHP set up some pursuit car specs:

0 to 60	10sec maximum
top speed	120mph minimum

Chrysler Corp. had supplied the CHP with police cars since the first Dodge police car in 1956, with one Mercury and one Oldsmobile as the only exceptions. However, in 1982, Chrysler did not have a single high-performance car in any of the three divisions that could meet those specifications. For the first time in 25 years, Chrysler Corp. had to "no bid" the CHP.

The Camaro Z28 bid $11,445 against the Mustang GL bid of $6,868.67. The car that chases Porsches for a living was born.

The Mustang had been powered by a wimpy 255ci V-8 in 1980 and 1981. In 1982, it received the 157 net hp H.O. 302ci V-8. The CHP Mustang came with the GT suspension, GT steering, Fairmont brakes and wheel and this H.O. engine. The H.O. engine had a special marine cam, double roller timing chain, heav-

This slick-top 1981 CHP Diplomat hit top speeds of 116mph. *Greg Reynolds*

1979 CHP Experiment

Vehicle (1979)	Wheelbase	Engine	SAE Net HP	Top Speed	Mileage
Chevrolet Malibu	108.1in	305ci, 4-bbl	125	110mph	12.2mpg
Chevrolet Camaro Z28	108.0in	350ci, 4-bbl	160	120mph	11.7mpg
Ford Fairmont	105.5in	302ci, 4-bbl	133	108mph	14mpg
Plymouth Volare Wagon	122.7in	318ci, 4-bbl	155	110mph	12.8mpg

CHP Power to Weight Ratios

Year	Squad	Engine	SAE Net HP	Test Wt.	lb:hp Ratio	0-60mph	Top Speed
1978	Monaco	440ci, 4-bbl	255hp	4369lb	17.1:1	9.3sec	133mph
1979	St. Regis	360ci, 4-bbl	195hp	4530lb	23.2:1	10.1sec	123mph
1980	St. Regis	318ci, 4-bbl	155hp	4173lb	26.9:1	13.1sec	115mph
1981	Diplomat	318ci, 4-bbl	165hp	3851lb	23.3:1	12.8sec	116mph
1982	Mustang	302ci, 2-bbl	157hp	3319lb	21.1:1	6.9sec	128mph

SQUAD CAR PERFORMANCE IN THE DOG YEARS**

Vehicle	Engine	SAE HP	0-60 mph	0-100 mph	Top Speed	1/4mi ET	1/4mi Trap	MIS Course	Brake Power
1979 Dodge St. Regis (CHP)	E58 360ci, 4-bbl	195 net hp	10.1sec	30.2sec	122.9mph	n/a	n/a	91.6sec	21.4fps2
1980 Dodge St. Regis	E58 360ci, 4-bbl	185 net hp	11.5sec	36.7sec	122.7mph	18.4sec	77.5mph	91.8sec	23.5fps2
1980 Dodge St. Regis * (CHP)	E47 318ci, 4-bbl	155 net hp	13.1sec	45.7sec	114.7mph	19.6sec	74.5mph	93.9sec	23.7fps2
1980 Dodge Aspen	E48 360ci, 4-bbl	185 net hp	10.9sec	25.7sec	122.2mph	17.9sec	77.5mph	92.7sec	23.3fps2
1980 Dodge Aspen	E47 318ci, 4-bbl	155 net hp	13.2sec	32.3sec	117.3mph	19.6sec	73.2sec	96.2sec	22.3fps2
1981 Dodge St. Regis	E48 318ci, 4-bbl	165 net hp	13.2sec	45.7sec	114.7mph	19.6sec	74.5mph	93.9sec	23.7fps2
1981 Dodge Diplomat (CHP)	E48 318ci, 4-bbl	165 net hp	12.8sec	42.7sec	116.3mph	19.4sec	75.5mph	92.0sec	24.6fps2
1981 Ford LTD	H.O. 351Wci, VV	165 net hp	12.8sec	42.2sec	116.4mph	19.4sec	74.7mph	92.4sec	23.4fps2
1982 Dodge Diplomat	E48 318ci, 4-bbl	165 net hp	12.2sec	40.0sec	115.4mph	19.2sec	75.3mph	93.6sec	23.7fps2
1982 Chevy Impala (CHP)	350ci, 4-bbl	150 net hp	12.7sec	45.8sec	107.8mph	19.4sec	73.0mph	92.0sec	24.0fps2
1982 Ford Mustang (CHP)	H.O. 302ci, 2-bbl	157 net hp	6.9sec	21.1sec	128mph	16.1sec	87.2mph	n/a	n/a
1983 Dodge Diplomat (CHP)	E48 318ci, 4-bbl	165 net hp	12.4sec	39.7sec	120mph	18.2sec	74.6mph	92.6sec	24.9fps2
1983 Ford Mustang (CHP)	H.O. 302ci, 4-bbl	175 net hp	7.7sec	21.2sec	129mph	16.1sec	87.5mph	n/a	n/a
1984 Ford Mustang (CHP)	H.O. 302ci, 4-bbl	205 net hp	7.4sec	20.8sec	130mph	15.3sec	91.8mph	n/a	n/a

*1981 figures are used
**Conducted by the Michigan State Police. Mustang results from Motor Trend magazine.

ier valve springs, an oversize H.O. 351 air cleaner and a larger 356cfm 2-bbl carb.

The CHP ordered a trial shipment of 406 Mustangs. It rapidly became the "darling of the CHP." As early as September of 1982, the CHP was claiming that the Mustang enhanced the image of the CHP with the public. The real problem after all, was one of image. And that is indeed a genuine police concern.

The CHP Mustangs consistently hit 60mph in 7 seconds, 100mph in 21 seconds and had a top speed of nearly 130mph. By 1983, eleven states had adopted the Mustang as a special pursuit car. The Mustang grew to have the same reputation as the old Dodge pursuit cars. The Mustang was the unchallenged squad until the 1991 Camaro B4C blistered it.

However, both the California Highway Patrol and the Michigan State Police looked forward to the day when 4-door cruisers would be fast enough not to need a specialty car. This happened in 1994 with the LT1-powered Caprice under the guidance of Harry Hammond, of Nova 9C1 fame. Neither of these two influential departments are buying any more pursuit Camaros. The pursuit Mustang was discontinued after 1993.

The last full-size, 4-door sedan powerful enough to be both a patrol-class squad and a pursuit-class squad, was the Dodge St. Regis powered by a 360ci, 4-bbl wedge. And that is why cops today have voted it the best Mopar squad of all time.

References

Special Purpose Vehicle Study, California Highway Patrol, September 1980

"CHP 1980 Goes Racy With The Camaro Z28," Bob Hagin, *Police Product News*

"Copstang," Don Fuller, *Motor Trend*, August 1984

"The Fleetest Fleet", Hal Rubin, *Highway Patrolman*, April 1984

"The Incredible Shrinking Cop Car," Leon Mandel, *Car & Driver*, August 1978

"The CHP Ford Mustang," Bob Metallo, *Highway Patrolman*, February 1983

Personal Communication: Chuck Swift, President, Swift Dodge, Sacramento, CA

"Blazing Squad Cars," David Barry, *California*, June 1982

"No CHiPs Off the Old Block", Michael Jordan, *Car & Driver* 1981

"302 GT Mustang," Jim McCraw, *Motor Trend*, September 1981

CHP Class E Special Service Vehicle Specification, Office of Procurement, State of California, November 1983

Patrol Vehicle Specifications, Evaluation and Purchasing Program, Michigan State Police, 1979 thru 1984

Personal Communication, George Caravas, CHP patrolman (retired)

Chapter 4

Reliability Crisis: Maine State Police Problems

This chapter is included in the book as a reality check. It documents some routine and not-so-routine problems faced by all police fleet managers. Police cars are not all about power and speed. They are instead about durability and reliability.

It is a problem when police cars are not powerful enough for the job at hand. Witness the CHP 1980 Dodge St. Regis. But it is a worse problem when police cars are not reliable or suffer extended periods of downtime. Such was the experience of the Maine State Police with 1978 Plymouths and 1980 Dodges.

Reliability is one of the reasons the LAPD/LASD vehicle evaluation includes input from the motor pool personnel on maintenance history, if it is available. Obviously, the maintenance history must be analyzed to be sure it applies. History from a big-block, C-body may not be meaningful, when considering a small-block, M-body. At any rate, the maintenance/motor pool personnel have a formal part in the overall review. At the very least, it gives them a later opportunity to say, 'I warned you!'

Anyone who owns a car knows that cars have problems. They are always aggravating and occasionally expensive. Fleet cars such as cop cars, taxis and rentals have even more problems. They are constantly driven by people with an "it's not my car" attitude. This is why cop cars and taxis have extreme duty parts and why rentals are sold after 1 year or 20,000 miles.

Problems with a taxi or a rental might mean a missed plane departure. Problems with police cars might mean loss of life. As such, maintenance woes with cop cars always seem to take on a sense of urgency and crisis, as they should.

All police cars made by every car maker, even Volvo, have breakdowns. This chapter will discuss the experience one state police department had with one year of Plymouth and one year of Dodge. Were this book written about Chevrolets, Fords, or Pontiacs, exactly the same kinds of problems would be reported. Overall and in spite of this chapter, Chrysler products have a better police in-service record than any other auto maker.

In December 1977, the Maine State Police took delivery of 100 1978 Plymouth Furys. Of these, 30 were powered by the E45 318ci, 2-bbl and 70 were powered by the E68 400ci, 4-bbl. The small block cars were issued to detectives, supervisors, crime lab personnel and other non-emergency officers. These were not police package cars, so any discussion of or complaints concerning these cars is pointless.

The big block cars, however, were equipped with the A38 police package. These were issued to the ground troops. At this time, the Maine State Police was using 1977 model Furys with the E68 400ci, 4-bbl. After logging some times on both the 1977 and 1978 Furys, the Maine troopers experienced some nagging problems.

The most serious was replacement of Lean-Burn computers. Lean-Burn was brand new on the 1976 E64 400ci, 4-bbl. By 1977, all the big blocks and the 360ci engines had Lean-Burn. For all practical purposes, 1977 was the first year for Lean-Burn and the Maine State Police fell victim to this new fangled emissions technology.

The Lean-Burn computer went defective on a number of 1977 Furys. The problem was lessened for 1978, but still existed. Maine fleet management ran an 18-month study on maintenance for these Lean-Burn powered squads. On a fleet of just 108 1977 and 1978 A38 squads, they spent $3150 on replacement electronic computers. That was for parts alone. Installation labor more than doubled that figure.

The other problem was exhaust systems. This was a decade before stainless steel exhausts which first appeared on 1987 model Dodges and Plymouths. On just exhaust and computers alone, Main spent $120 per car in the first 18 months. They could have purchased 1-1/2 more squad cars for the same money spent on just these two areas.

The following complaints against the Maine State Police 1978 Fury E68 will give you an insight into the job of a police fleet manager.

After 5,000 miles of driving, the vehicle used in excess of 30 quarts of oil and it was found that all the ring slots on every piston were lined up.

The vehicle could not go over 2,000 mile periods without having one of the exhaust gaskets replaced.

Exhaust: three times for a manifold gasket repair and four times for catalytic converter.

Several days after receiving the vehicle, I had to take it to a Dealer for a new speedometer. On several different occasions, I had to return the vehicle to have doors and windows adjusted. After approximately one month, I had to have a new transmission installed.

The engine stalls, and backfires through exhaust system, along with the exhaust system requiring a lot of repair work particularly around the engine block.

The trunk hinges broke off and trunk fell off.

This officer has twice had the exhaust manifold gasket go. Once it was fixed under warranty. On one occasion the carburetor backfired and melted inside.

The following problems existed over a five-month period: The right torsion bar was found to be banging and nearly un-

hooked; the front sway bar broke loose twice; a continuing problem with the engine running poorly at low speeds and stalling at idle or when trying to turn in the road and exhaust manifold gaskets.

It was found that the brakes on the rear had never been adjusted at the factory, having no brakes at all on rear. The vehicle now has an exhaust leak, which has been fixed many times, but will leak again within less than a hundred miles. Overall, this has been the poorest cruiser that this officer has ever had. Service at the dealership was even worse.

I found that if the accelerator was depressed in order to accelerate, the vehicle would start to backfire repeatedly through the carburetor, the vehicle would hesitate and skip, miss, buck and at times stall completely.

This officer had and still is having problems with an exhaust leak. The cruiser now has 13,500 miles on it and the exhaust leak had been repaired two (2) times by Plymouth Dealerships and four (4) times by the state police mechanic. Through no fault of the mechanics, the leak kept reoccurring where the small pipe bolts on at the rear of the manifold on the right side of the vehicle.

The vehicle had a new transmission installed within the first 10,000 miles. The exhaust system had to be fixed. The left front sway bar had to be replaced and shocks tightened. Four thermostats had been installed, and even now the vehicle still overheated at high speed.

The vehicle had carburetor problems since it was delivered. Much of the interior trim in the vehicle seemed to be improperly installed or carelessly installed. The gear shift indicator did not line up properly. There were many other minor problems that I found irritating.

There was mis-alignment of power steering pump. It would keep throwing the power steering belt off. This happened about 4 times at approximately 5000 miles on the vehicle. This vehicle had to have the exhaust manifold gasket replaced because of a bad exhaust leak. This officer had to keep the windows cracked to keep from being asphyxiated. This officer, found in pursuit of speeders that the vehicle was terribly unbalanced. The vehicle was extremely light on back and heavy on front. You could lose traction at high speeds traveling on a straight stretch of road.

The vehicle was having problems when it would rain; the rear tail lights would keep going out; this problem was finally corrected by drilling holes in the base of the rear light assembly to allow the water to drain.

In 1979, and strictly on the basis of low bid, Chevrolet was awarded the Maine State Police contract. For better or for worse, Maine spent less money on repairs for the Chevrolets than for the previous year's Plymouths. Several engines and transmissions in the Plymouths failed, while only one engine and no transmissions in the Chevrolets. (Recall, however, that nine out of twelve Camaro engines failed this same model year during the CHP Special Vehicle Study.)

Armed with the 1978 and 1979 maintenance records, Maine fleet personnel attempted to exclude Dodge and Plymouth from bidding on the 1980 contract. That request was denied. Government agencies find it more effective to penalize the vehicle in a monetary way [like the Michigan State Police] than to disqualify a particular car maker from bidding.

A considerable number of discussions were held to exclude the Dodges and Plymouths from bidding. As luck would have it, the 1980 Maine state contract was captured by Dodge. Discussions were then held in an attempt to not base the acceptance of a bid on the lowest bid price alone. Of course, accepting something other than the lowest bid needs to be built in to the purchase specification prior to bid, not after the bids are open.

During all these discussions, Maine was assured by Chrysler Corp. fleet officials that the 1980 Dodge (R-body) was far superior to the 1978 Plymouth.

The quality control was tighter and, in fact, the R-body was an entirely different vehicle. The truth was, the 1980 cars did have a different body and a different variety of police engines. The R-body was well received in 1979 by other police departments.

The Maine State Police purchased the Dodge St. Regis in 1980. And the fleet personnel dutifully recorded every penny of maintenance. Rightly or wrongly, they felt these squads were forced upon them. That alone can be a source of friction as well as cause an intolerant attitude toward any defects.

In preparation for the 1981 contract, Maine fleet officers again sent inquiries to the troopers. They asked for a list of problems experienced with the 1980 Dodge St. Regis. The response this time was much more varied than the problems they experienced with the 1978 Plymouths.

Reports of problems from the field included a bit of everything, including brakes, rear main seal, rear axle seals, fan clutch, window regulators, fuel pumps, wiring problems. In police fleet management, this was to be expected.

The Maine State Police offer a reality check on the 1978 Plymouth Fury and 1980 Dodge St. Regis.

I had taken vehicle in three times for the front brakes and on the fourth time, they had to rebuild the front brake assembly, 20,000 miles. The rear main seal on the engine had to be replaced at 20,000 miles and is leaking now at 27,000 miles.

Presently, I have 31,000 miles on my Dodge cruiser. Problems so far have been the driver's door window wouldn't go up or down. The brakes had to be replaced on the front end with low mileage (disc, pads and calibers). The carburetor has been rebuilt twice and a new one is on order. The rear main seals have been replaced twice. There have been two new computers put in. The fuel pump had to be replaced.

The carburetor was repaired at 700, 1000, 1200 and 1500 miles. Two fuel pumps were installed, one at 6,000 miles and the other at 14,000 miles. The computer was replaced at 8,800 miles.

At approximately 11,000 miles, the electronic computer had to be changed. At approximately 13,000 miles, the rings in the engine had to be replaced. At that time and the present time, the engine leaks oil both from the manifold and the main seal.

At approximately 10,000 miles, a new carburetor had to be installed. At 30,000 miles, the wiring under the hood burned up and had to be replaced.

Carburetor-secondaries do not work. They did not work when the car was new. I had it into dealership on either three or four occasions, and it still does not work.

With less than 200 miles on it, the complete wiring harness burned up.

The biggest problem that I have encountered with the Dodge is the very cheap seat. Prior to driving the Dodge, I never experienced any back trouble. Since that time, I have had constant trouble with it. Recently it was necessary for me to drive a spare car while mine was broken down. During that time, while driving a Chevy with a good seat, I have had no back trouble.

This officer feels that this vehicle is comfortable to work from and has plenty of leg and head room.

This time, even though they were not asked to comment on it, many officers listed minor little problems and went on to say the St. Regis was "entirely satisfactory" as a pursuit-class vehicle. Chrysler fleet officials were right. The 1980 St. Regis was indeed superior to the 1978 Fury. Some Maine troopers took this opportunity to go one step further. They stated the 1980 Dodge St. Regis was far superior to the 1979 Chevrolet Impala they used to be issued.

The damage, traced back to 1977 and 1978, was done. Maine State Police used Plymouths for all of the 1970s, except 1979 when Chevrolet snuck in. In 1980, Maine went with Dodge. In spite of the fact that the 1980 St. Regis was indeed an improvement over the 1978 Fury, and in fact an excellent squad in its own right, this was the last year the Maine State Police patrolled in a Chrysler product. In Maine's opinion, Chrysler had failed to deliver in the one area that a police car must deliver. Durability.

Chapter 5

1981: Dodge Diplomat and Chrysler LeBaron

The 1981 model year saw the release of a brand new A38 police package car, the M-body Dodge Diplomat and Chrysler LeBaron. This also was the year of intense interest in the E48 318ci, 4-bbl engine. All Mopar squads received lockup torque converters, and some got the improved, wide gear ratio TorqueFlite transmission.

The 318ci, 4-bbl was first offered in 1979, but to California cops only. In 1980, this E47 engine became available nationwide. It gained infamy as not having enough power to turn a 4173 pound St. Regis into a pursuit-class squad. The 1980 318ci, 4-bbl was far overshadowed by the federal version of the 360ci, 4-bbl. For 1981, the 360ci was no longer available in 4-door sedans anywhere. The E48 318ci, 4-bbl took center stage.

In 1981, the 318 V-8 became Chrysler Corp.'s largest engine. Ironically, it was one of the smallest displacement engines ever produced by a Corporation famous for "King Kong" big blocks. Only the 301ci V-8 of the 1950s and the 273ci V-8 of the 1960s were smaller V-8 engines.

The 318ci engine was available in two heavy duty versions—the "lively" federal-only E45 2-bbl and the pursuit-oriented E48 4-bbl. These produced 130 net hp and 165 net hp respectively.

The new optional 5.2 liter (318ci) four-barrel V-8 engine is designed for pursuit power! Chrysler, Dodge and Plymouth's new 5.2 liter V-8 is designed for both power and efficiency. It gives LeBaron, St. Regis, Diplomat and Gran Fury the power and stamina required for high-speed police work.

In one year, this E48 4-bbl engine changed from being the black sheep to being the top dog. The simple change from the 118.5 inch R-body to the 112.7-inch M-body gave cops 115mph (plus) speeds again. The 1980 E47 4-bbl engine gained 10 net hp to become the 1981 E48 4-bbl engine.

The optional 5.2 liter (318ci) four-barrel V-8 police engine has the following special features for longer life and better performance:

Anti-turbulence windage tray between crankshaft and oil sump
Chrome plated top piston rings
Crankshaft made of select hardness cast nodular iron
Detonation sensor

The 1981 Dodge Diplomat used by the Indiana State Police was powered by the 318ci V-8. This is one of the smallest V-8s ever made by Chrysler Corp. *Dave Morrison*

In 1981, the Chrysler LeBaron came with the A38 police package. These are the red and white squads used by the Putnam County, New York Sheriff. *Ned Schwartz*

Double roller timing chain
Easy access oil filler
Forged steel connecting rods
Heavy duty chrome plated oil rings
Heavy duty exhaust manifolds
Heavy duty valve springs
High strength rocker arms
High temperature cylinder head cover gaskets
High temperature valve seals and shields
Lubrite treated camshaft
Nimonic exhaust valves
Special Kolene cleaned cylinder heads
Special piston-to-block clearances
Special silichrome-l high temperature steel intake valves
Water pump with oversize bearing

The Chrysler LeBaron was used as an official police car for just the 1981 model year. This fleet of rare Lebarons was used by the Des Moines, Iowa Police. *Darryl Lindsay and Ned Schwartz*

The great E58 360ci was discontinued in 4-door sedans for 1981, but parts of it lived on in the E48, and later ELE, high performance 318ci. The police 318ci, 4-bbl used 360ci heads with their larger valves and passages, according to Chrysler historian Dale Burkhardt. The 4-bbl carb, the 360ci heads and a larger diameter single exhaust system were responsible for the 35 net hp difference between the 4-bbl and 2-bbl 318ci engines.

It is common knowledge the 318ci, 4-bbl police engine used the heads, intake manifold and carburetor from the 360ci, 4-bbl engine. Less commonly known is the camshaft used in the E48/ELE 318ci, 4-bbl police engines. This is a frequent question among enthusiasts who are rebuilding their police engines and others who want to build a police-spec, small-block V-8.

Both the pre-85 E48 4-bbl engine and the post-85 ELE 4-bbl engine used the same cam, Chrysler part number 4227879. This bumpstick had an intake lift of .373in with a duration of 240 degrees and an exhaust lift of .400in with a 248 degree duration. This is quite mild. Enthusiasts can easily perk-up their police mills by selecting a cam with more lift and duration.

As a comparison, the 1974-1976 E58 360ci, 4-bbl HP cam has a lift and duration of .429in(I)/444in(E) and 268deg(I)/276deg(E). This is Mopar cam number 4214671. The 1977-1980 360ci, 4-bbl cam was a bit milder due to the emissions crunch. This had the same specs for both intake and exhaust at a .410in lift and 252 degree duration. The camshaft from the 360ci V-8 is interchangeable with the 318ci V-8.

To put all this in perspective, Crane Cams (for example) makes three performance street cams for the 318ci V-8. These are legal for street-use and also geared for both off-road racing and towing. The local speed shop first recommended a .454in lift, 272 degree duration cam for enthusiasts. One step milder is a cam that almost exactly equals the old Mopar 360hp cam. It has specs of .427in(I)/. 454in(E) and 260deg(I)/272deg(E). One step hotter is the Crane Cam with .454in(I)/.480in(E) and 272deg(I)/284deg(E).

The Virginia State Police used the 1981 Plymouth Gran Fury powered by the 318ci, 4-bbl. These cars had a 115mph top speed. *Louis Mavredes and G.L. Mavredes*

The 318ci 4-bbl was not restricted to "police-only" use. While it was not available in any Dodge or Plymouth passenger car, for the first time, the 318ci, 4-bbl was available in a Chrysler-marque passenger car. Turnaround is only fair, but here's the difference: In the 1950s and 1960s, police cars used the "New Yorker engine". In 1981, the Chrysler New Yorker passenger car used the "police engine".

No Chrysler Corp. V-8 police engine ever came with fuel injection. Engines came in all makes and models of 2-bbl, 4-bbl and dual 4-bbl, but never fuel injection. However, in 1981 Chrysler Corp. made a fuel injected 318ci engine. This electronic fuel injection (e.f.i.) motor was restricted to the Chrysler Imperial passenger car. E.F.I. lasted for three years. The police 4-bbl engine produced more power:

318ci, 2-bbl	130 net hp
318ci, e.f.i.	140 net hp
318ci, 4-bbl	165 net hp

Chrysler Corp. used electronic feedback carburetors for California engines in 1980. In 1981, this carburetion system was standard on nearly all engines. The pressure was still on to reduce exhaust emissions.

Electronic Feedback Carburetor System. All Chrysler-Plymouth police V-8 and California Slant Six engines have an electronic feedback carburetor system that maintains ideal fuel-air mixture in the carburetor for best engine performance and driveability.

It does this by monitoring oxygen content in exhaust gases to determine if the carburetor intake fuel-air mixture is ideal. The instant the mixture varies from ideal, the oxygen monitor signals an electronic computer and the fuel-air mixture is automatically adjusted back to ideal. The result is better engine operation, which improves fuel economy and reduces exhaust emissions.

Catalytic Converters. Various catalytic converter arrangements are used with all Chrysler-Plymouth police engines to reduce exhaust emissions.

Eight-Cylinder Engines. Two three-way catalytic converters adjacent to the engine reduce nitrogen oxides and oxidize combustible emissions as soon as they leave the exhaust manifold. The second catalytic converter, downstream from the first, further oxidizes hydrocarbons and carbon monoxide emissions to acceptable levels.

An air pump in the emissions control system is also used.

Six cylinder engine (except California) employs two full-oxidation catalytic converters.

Six cylinder engine (California) employs a three-way front catalytic converter and a pure oxidation main converter.

(Plymouth Police literature)

In 1981, after all these years, and with only two more years left in its production, the 225ci Slant Six engine received hy-

The full-size Plymouth Gran Fury made a fine squad car for urban patrol. This one was in-service with the Clinton County, New York Sheriff. *Ned Schwartz*

1981 CHRYSLER-PLYMOUTH POLICE VEHICLES

A TRADITION OF ENGINEERING LEADERSHIP!

In 1981, the Chrysler LeBaron was the mid-size squad while the Plymouth Gran Fury was the full-size car. *Chrysler*

draulic lifters. Chrysler Corp. boasted this gave a quieter operation and reduced maintenance over solid lifters. No kidding. Almost as an apology, the police literature stated "V-8 engines also have hydraulic lifters." That statement was correct, and had been correct for twenty years!

In 1978, passenger cars with both the big block 727 and small block 904 Torque Flite trans received lockup torque converters. The 'big block" and "small block" designations are somewhat misleading, since the police-spec, small block 318ci and 360ci used the larger 727 trans through 1983. At any rate, in 1981 all Mopar squads in both emissions packages and both engine sizes received lockup torque converters.

In 1981, the full-size police car from Dodge was the St. Regis. The mid-size cruiser was the Diplomat. *Chrysler*

And a fuel-saving lockup clutch in the torque converter provides a direct mechanical connection between engine and transmission at cruising speeds. This transmission has a reputation for performance, durability and low maintenance requirements.

As a fuel-saving measure, a separate clutch was added to the torque converter. This engaged after the transmission was in 3rd gear and between 27 and 31mph. When engaged, the engine was linked to the transmission as positively as a clutch on a manual transmission. When disengaged, the torque-multiplying converter acted as a normal fluid or turbine drive unit. *Motor Trend* reviewed this lockup device when it first appeared in 1978.

The driving and driven halves of the torque converter lock together with a clutch above a predetermined speed to eliminate slippage and save fuel. (Because this deceases the amount of heat generated within the transmission, durability should be improved, too.) The lockup feature is not noticeable when driving the car. The part-throttle kickdown from 3rd to 2nd gear can't be missed, however, and comes as a surprise until you get used to it. At low to moderate speeds, the slightest pressure on the accelerator pedal causes the transmission to downshift, eliminating fuel-wasting tramps on the throttle.

The lockup disengaged when the transmission was downshifted, either manually or automatically. A fail-safe valve allowed a fast lockup release for responsive forced-downshift performance. The lockup also disengaged below speeds of 30mph.

When the lockup engaged, the engine speed would drop a couple of hundred rpm. The engine did not have to work as hard for the same vehicle speeds, because the losses going through the fluid-drive torque converter were eliminated. Very neat.

The Chrysler lockup converter was strictly fluid pressure controlled. The driver had no control over the lockup whatsoever. The lockup unit increased fuel economy by 4 percent in urban city driving, and 6 percent in rural and interstate driving.

The other transmission improvement for 1981 was the "wide-ratio" gearing. This was released on passenger cars in 1978. For 1981, the 225ci Slant Six and the E45 318ci 2-bbl V-8 came with wide ratio Torque Flites. The then-ELE 318ci, 4-bbl got the wide ratio trans in 1984.

The wide ratio trans was a big help in improving both low end responsiveness and through-gear acceleration.

	pre-81 close ratio	81 & up wide ratio
first gear	2.45:1	2.74:1
second gear	1.45:1	1.54:1
third gear	1.00:1	1.00:1

One of the biggest changes for 1981 was the new M-body Dodge Diplomat and Chrysler LeBaron. The Diplomat started out as an ultra-plush option on a New Yorker, then became an upscale Dodge personal luxury car. For 1981, it was a cop car.

The last time a Chrysler-marque squad hit the streets was 1979 with the R-body Newport. Previous to that there was the A38 police package option on the 1976 Newport 124-inch wheelbase. The 1981 Chrysler LeBaron was the last Chrysler-marque squad car of any kind. The first one was the 1961 Chrysler Newport Enforcer.

The 1981 A38 police package was available on:
FH41 Chrysler LeBaron 4-door sedan (M-body)
EH42 Dodge St. Regis 4-door pillared hardtop (R-body)
GH41 Dodge Diplomat 4-door sedan (M-body)
JL42 Plymouth Gran Fury 4-door pillared hardtop (R-body)

The 1981 M-body LeBaron/Diplomat replaced the 1980 F-body Aspen/Volare. While the R-body St. Regis/Gran Fury was still available, the E58 360ci, 4-bbl was not. All cops in 1981

The 1981 LeBaron was the last Chrysler-marque police car. *Chrysler*

were in the same situation as the California cops were in 1980. As a result, many police departments switched to one of the 112.7-inch M-bodies in 1981.

Fleet managers who did not pay attention to what happened in California in 1980, fell into that same real or imagined performance trap. The alert fleet managers ordered the Diplomat and LeBaron in 1981 if they wanted a pursuit-class car. The ones asleep at the wheel, or still hung up on long wheelbase cars for pursuit, ordered the Gran Fury and St. Regis.

The Gran Fury and St. Regis with the 318ci, 2-bbl and 4-bbl still made excellent patrol-class squads.

By 1981, down-sized Mopar squads had been around for five years for cops to think about. The highly-publicized, and admittedly successful Nova 9C1 had been around even longer. The loss of the 360ci engine just sped up the acceptance and changeover to down-sized cars. By 1982, a long wheelbase Mopar squad would not be an option anyhow.

Much like 1977, the choice was simple. Cops could either have a big car with an engine that was perhaps too small for frequent high speed work, or a midsize car with an engine that was adequate for all but Porsche-chasing. Some fleet managers ordered the small block-powered, fullsize squad. After all, that

The 1981 Plymouth Gran Fury was the last of the long wheelbase police cars. *Chrysler*

The Dodge St. Regis was produced for only three years. This was Chrysler Corp's best police car. *Chrysler*

The 1981 Dodge Diplomat replaced the 1980 Dodge Aspen as mid-size squad car. *Chrysler*

This Arizona Highway Patrol 1981 Gran Fury was powered by a 318ci small block. *Greg Reynolds*

combination had served thousands of police departments well for literally decades.

Most cops, however, went for the enhanced performance of the M-body. R-body St. Regis and Gran Fury production shut down for good before mid-year 1981.

The 1981 M-body Diplomat and LeBaron and the 1982 M-body Gran Fury shared mechanical features with the F-body Volare and Aspen. The brakes, suspension and wheelbase were all identical. The controversial transverse torsion bar front suspension carried over from the F-body to the M-body unchanged.

Diplomat and LeBaron Police Pursuit cars have a transverse torsion bar twin A-arm front suspension system and an iso-clamp multileaf rear spring suspension-all rubber isolated from the car body for ride quietness. Heavy duty bushings and retainers at the front struts, front anti-sway bar cushion brackets and

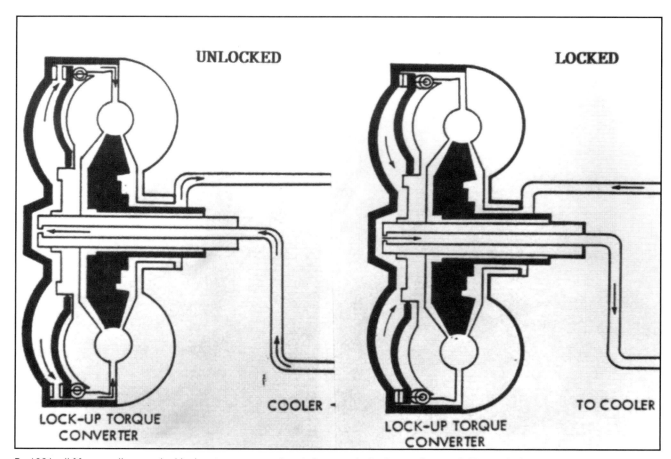

By 1981, all Mopar police cars had lockup torque converters to improve fuel mileage. *Automatic Transmissions*

rear spring front hangers are used for improved handling and durability. Heavy duty shock absorbers and front and rear anti-sway bars are standard on these Police Pursuit models. These tough features provide a stable, smooth ride with excellent handling responsiveness.

This front suspension issue will be discussed in detail in a future chapter. The LeBaron was the first and only Chrysler-marque squad with transverse torsion bars.

On the topic of suspensions, from 1974 through 1980, Chrysler police literature read something like this when dealing with suspensions and tires.

A rear anti-sway bar to provide optimum handling with radial tires is standard on all Pursuit Packages. If bias or bias-belted tires are installed, it is recommended that the rear anti-sway bar be removed because of adverse handling effects with these types of tires.

For 1981, Chrysler Corp. made a major change:

The suspension systems on Chrysler, Dodge and Plymouth A38 Police Pursuit Packages are designed to provide optimum handling with radial tires. The use of bias or bias-belted tires is NOT recommended.

In terms of tires, the P215/70R15 pursuit-spec radials that were optional on the Aspen/Volare became standard equipment on the LeBaron/Diplomat. The M-body squads used this tire size through the 1989 model year. The R-body cars had P225/70R15 pursuit radials as an option.

In 1981, for just the second time, the Michigan State Police ran a field of both full-size and mid-size squad cars. In heads-up competition, the M-body LeBaron did extremely well. Further, both M-body cars beat both R-body cars in all significant areas of performance.

In 1981, both the full-size and mid-size Chevrolets, also ran very well. How could that be? The coy Harry Hammond

told *Car & Driver* in mid-1978, "We aren't working on anything in police cars after model year 1979." Chevrolet, in fact, turned out to be Dodge and Plymouth's toughest competitor for the rest of the Eighties. Buick dropped out. Ford was a distant competitor.

In 1981, Chrysler Corp. released the platform that literally saved the company from bankruptcy. This of course, was the K-car. Chrysler-marque, Dodge and Plymouth based most of their production on this platform, or variations of it, through 1989.

The Aries K and Reliant K were by far the most famous cars of the decade. They were the key to the 1.5 billion dollar loan guarantee the U.S. Congress made to Lee Iacocca and the new Chrysler Corp. The K-car flag-waving was intense. "American way to beat the pump...America's not going to be pushed around any more."

With the K-car, Chrysler Corp. made a 'no-looking-back' shift to front wheel drive cars. In 1981, 74 percent of all Plymouths and 81 percent of all Dodges were front wheel drive. The K-cars alone represented from 33 to 40 percent of passenger car sales. *Motor Trend* awarded the Aries K and Reliant K the "1981 Car of the Year." And in 1982, the K-cars joined the police force.

1981 Chrysler LeBaron & Dodge Diplomat Significant Standard & Optional Equipment
Standard

Automatic Air Conditioning Compressor High-Pressure Clutch Cutoff Switch

Axle Ratio - 2.94

Axle Size - 8.25in

Brakes-Heavy duty power brakes with dual master cylinder; disc front brakes with semi-metallic front pads; 11x2.5in rear drum brakes, Power Booster-single diaphragm

Engine Cooling Package-maximum capacity radiator with 20in diameter seven-blade with thermal drive on 6 cylinder engines

Heavy-Duty Service Package-extra welds and reinforcements

1981 Police H.D. Engines Chrysler, Dodge, Plymouth
Engines with Federal Emissions Control Package

Code	Engine & Carburetor	Net Torque (lb-ft)	Net Horsepower	Chrysler LeBaron/ Dodge Diplomat	Plymouth Gran Fury/ Dodge St. Regis
E25	3.7 liter 225ci, 1-bbl Slant Six	165@1600rpm	85@3600rpm	X	X
E45	5.2 liter 318ci, 2-bbl V-8	230@2000rpm	130@4000rpm	X	X
E48	5.2 liter 318ci, 4-bbl V-8	240@2000rpm	165@4000rpm	X	X

Engines with California Emissions Control Package (Code N95)

Code	Engine & Carburetor	Net Torque (lb-ft)	Net Horsepower	Chrysler LeBaron/ Dodge Diplomat	Plymouth Gran Fury/ Dodge St. Regis
E25	3.7 liter 225ci, 1-bbl Slant Six	165@1200rpm	90@3600rpm	X	X
E48	5.2 liter 318ci, 4-bbl V-8	240@2000rpm	165@4000rpm	X	X

1981 VAN ENGINES
Dodge & Plymouth Police Vans
Engines with Federal Emissions Control Package

Code	Engine & Carb	Net Torque (lb-ft)	Net Horsepower
EA3	3.7 liter 225ci, 1-bbl Slant Six	170@1600rpm	95@3600rpm
EC1	5.2 liter 318ci, 2-bbl V-8	140@2000rpm	140@3600rpm
EC2	5.2 liter 318ci, 4-bbl V-8	245@2000rpm	170@4000rpm
EC5	5.9 liter 360ci, 4-bbl V-8	260@2000rpm	175@4000rpm

Engines with California Emissions Control Package (Code HC5)

Code	Engine & Carb	Net Torque (lb-ft)	Net Horsepower
EA3	3.7 liter 225ci, 1-bbl Slant Six	165@1200rpm	90@3600rpm
EC2	5.2 liter 318ci, 4-bbl V-8	250@2000rpm	160@3600rpm
EC5	5.9 liter 360ci, 4-bbl V-8	260@2000rpm	180@4000rpm

1981 Police Michigan State Police Car Performance

Vehicle	Engine	0-60 mph	0-100 mph	1/4mi ET	Trap	Top Speed	MIS Road Course	Brake Power
Chevrolet Malibu	350ci, 4-bbl	11.42sec	40.27sec	18.15sec	74.75mph	111.9mph	90.37sec	25.71fps2
Chrysler LeBaron	318ci, 4-bbl(E48)	12.86sec	45.24sec	18.90sec	73.50mph	114.7mph	92.54sec	26.02fps2
Chevrolet Impala	350ci, 4-bbl	11.93sec	39.98sec	18.95sec	75.00mph	113.8mph	90.72sec	26.62fps2
Ford LTD	351ci, H.O., 2VV	12.76sec	42.16sec	19.35sec	74.75mph	116.4mph	92.40sec	23.35fps2
Dodge Diplomat	318ci, 4-bbl(E48)	12.84sec	42.71sec	19.38sec	75.50mph	116.3mph	91.98sec	24.63fps2
Plymouth Gran Fury(R)	318ci, 4-bbl(E48)	12.76sec	42.22sec	19.40sec	75.25mph	115.1mph	93.60sec	25.15fps2
Dodge St. Regis(R)	318ci, 4-bbl(E48)	13.14sec	45.72sec	19.63sec	74.50mph	114.7mph	93.93sec	23.67fps2
Ford Fairmont	255ci, V-8, 2-bbl	13.63sec	65.79sec	19.68sec	71.00mph	106.4mph	93.50sec	25.02fps2
Ford Fairmont	200ci, L16, 1-bbl	18.77sec	not*	21.78sec	63.50mph	92.3mph	n/a	25.02fps2
Buick LeSabre	252ci, 4-bbl	17.51sec	not*	21.88sec	66.25mph	97.1mph	98.48sec	23.87fps2
Chrysler LeBaron	225ci, 1-bbl(E25)	21.06sec	not*	22.80sec	61.75mph	92.5mph	n/a	26.02fps2

* "not" means it did not reach 100mph

Police Accessory Feed Wire
Power Steering Oil Pump Cooler
Steering, Power-pursuit Firm-Feel type
Suspension-specially designed and engineered suspension for pursuit-type work; includes front and rear anti-sway bars, heavy-duty rear leaf springs with special bushings, heavy-duty strut bushings and 1-3/16-inch front and rear shock absorbers
Transmission Auxiliary Oil Cooler
Transmission Low-gear Blockout
Wheels-extra heavy duty (15x7.0in)

Optional
Air Conditioning
Deck-Lid Release, Remote
Defroster, Rear Window
Door Switch Deactivator
Engine Block Heater
Engine Oil Cooler
Lamp, Under-Hood
Light, Additional Dome
Police Bonding Strap Package
Radiator, Heater and Bypass Hose, Silicone
Radio Cable Conduit

Radio Suppression Package
Rear Axle, Sure-Grip
Relay Control System
Roof Reinforcement Plate-for light or siren
Speedometer-calibrated 125mph; includes oil pressure gauge
Spotlight, left, 6in windshield-pillar mounted
Spotlight, right, 6in windshield-pillar mounted
Throttle Control, Fast Idle-manual locking type
Wheel Covers-vented 15in

The 318ci-powered 1981 St. Regis was a good urban patrol car with the Camden, NJ Police. *Greg Reynolds*

References
Standard Catalog of Chrysler, John Lee, Jim Benjaminson, John Gunnell, Krause Publications
Dodge Police Vehicles, Chrysler Corporation, 1981
Chrysler-Plymouth Police Vehicles, Chrysler Corporation 1981
"Dodge Magnum XE," John Ethridge, *Motor Trend*, May 1978
Patrol Vehicle Specifications, Evaluation and Purchasing Program, Michigan State Police, 1981
"Aspen R/T," staff report, *Motor Trend*, February 1976
"Burkhardt on Pursuits," Dale Burkhardt, *Chrysler Power*, January 1993
"Hydrodynamic Units." Prof. Mathias F. Brejcha, *Automatic Transmissions,* 2nd edition, Prentiss-Hall, Inc.

This 1981 St. Regis was put to good use by the Minnesota State Patrol. *Greg Reynolds*

Chapter 6

1982: Chrysler's Kwaint Kop Kar

In 1980, the passenger car world was preoccupied with Chrysler's financial problems and the anticipation of the coming "K-car." In 1981, the K-car literally took the buying public by storm in the form of the Dodge Aries K and Plymouth Reliant K. In 1982, after the customary one year release as a passenger car, the K-car was available with an A38 police package.

The Aries K and Reliant K were released as light-duty, urban-oriented, "scout cars." To this day, car makers still call attention to the difference between a full-blown, heavy-duty police package and a "special service" package.

As a rule, "special service" packages, or in this case "scout car" packages, are intended for urban-duty or light traffic enforcement. They are not rugged or durable enough to be a heavy-duty, unlimited-use police car. This is in spite of the fact that many of the components are heavy-duty and the chassis has been beefed-up with extra welds.

For the record, the current Mustang and Camaro pursuit-class cars are, and have always been, "special service package" cars, complete with a durability disclaimer. The Lumina is available in both police package and in light-duty special service package. Ford made a big deal, and rightly so, about the fact that their Taurus was a full-blown police package car. This term has always meant a certain minimum level of ruggedness and reliability.

All this is to indicate the Aries K and Reliant K were not meant to be bullet-proof, 24-hour-a-day, police cars. Dodge and Plymouth made this clear from the first press release.

The new Dodge Aries and Plymouth Reliant: Front-Wheel Drive Police Scout Car. Economical, Roomy, Comfortable, Easy to Service!

The new Scout Car is the ideal police car for in-town and around-town police duties that don't require pursuit work. It's the kind of police work that occupies the most time in many police departments. A few strategically placed pursuit cars can handle the occasional high-speed runs. The Scout Car can handle all the other jobs, and do them more economically!

Front-Wheel Drive, Four-Cylinder Economy. Excellent traction and directional stability are two big benefits of front-wheel drive. The traction benefit result from engine and transaxle weight bearing on the front driving wheels, which gives the tires a better directional stability, especially in cross-winds.

Plymouth and Dodge's proven 2.2 liter (135ci) transverse-mounted four-cylinder, two-barrel engine reflects high technology throughout. An electronic computer, electronic feedback carburetor, electronic spark advance and electronic ignition help provide maximum engine efficiency and performance while reducing recommended maintenance. Aluminum cylinder head and intake manifold, overhead camshaft and hydraulic valve ad-

justers (no periodic adjustments required) are other advance features of this Chrysler-built engine.

Roomy, Comfortable Interior Seats Six Passengers. The Police Scout Car gives you more stretch-out room and comfort than you might expect in a fuel-efficient car. Front head room and leg room-the most important comfort dimensions in police-duty are actually bigger than in the 1981 Ford LTD and Fairmont, Mercury Marquis and Zephyr; and there's more front leg room than in the 1981 Cadillac DeVille and Brougham sedans, according to official MVMA dimensions.

From the beginning, the two overriding design goals for the K-car were an EPA "intermediate" interior volume and a wheelbase of less than 100 inches. Dodge and Plymouth both insisted, with a straight face, that their K-cars were six passenger vehicles. Decide for yourself.

	Aries K	Diplomat
wheelbase	99.9in	112.7in
headroom, front	38.6in	39.3in
headroom, rear	37.8in	37.7in
leg room, front	42.2in	42.5in
leg room, rear	35.4in	36.6in
shoulder room, front	55.4in	56.0in
hip room, front	55.6in	53.5in
hip room, rear	56.2in	53.2in
interior volume	95.5cu-ft.	98.0cu-ft.
trunk volume	15.0cu-ft.	15.6cu-ft.

The Virginia State Police were among many to field the 1982 Plymouth Gran Fury. This squad car had a 116mph top end. *Louis Mavredes and G.L. Mavredes*

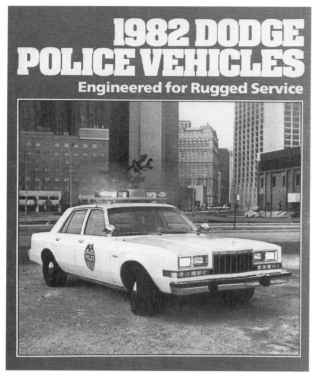

1982 DODGE POLICE VEHICLES
Engineered for Rugged Service

In 1982, Dodge Division built Diplomat police cars and Aries K scout cars. *Chrysler*

These roominess figures from the objective Michigan State Police vehicle evaluation make a strong case the K-car had as much room as the M-body Diplomat and Gran Fury. In fact, gunbelts on cops make the hip room a most critical measurement. In this regard, the K-car has (gasp) more room than the Diplomat.

The A38 police "scout car" package was available only on the DL41 Dodge Aries 4-door sedan and the PL41 Plymouth Reliant 4-door sedan

The A38 scout car package did indeed feature all the normal cop features like a reinforced chassis and additional welding, maximum capacity radiators, heavy duty interior, heavy duty wheels with police-spec tires and even the availability of a 125mph certified speedometer and left and right pillar mounted spotlights.

The K-car used a heavy-duty Iso-Strut front suspension developed for the 1978 Omni/Horizon. This was basically a MacPherson strut setup with a coil spring front suspension and front sway bar. The rear suspension also used coil springs with a rear sway bar, flex-arm beam axle, and trailing arms or trailing links. The K-car came with power-assisted, rack and pinion steering. Front discs, 9.3 inches in diameter, and 7.9-inch rear drum brakes completed the suspension.

The 1982 K-car front suspension was actually an improvement over the original design released in 1981. The 1982 suspension had a new geometry and a new "linkless" front sway bar. This change provided better steering control on rough roads such as Chicago city streets. The K-car was certainly a car of "firsts." This was the first police car since 1956 to use a coil spring suspension. This was the shortest wheelbase squad in the history of Chrysler Corp. police cars. The powertrain also held a number of "firsts" for cops:

The Nassau County, New York Police used this A38-package 1982 Dodge Aries K. The car was used by Emergency Services, not as routine patrol. *Ned Schwartz*

The Peel Regional Police, Ontario used this bright yellow 1982 Reliant K with scout package to deliver warrants and serve summons. *Neil Painchaud and Ned Schwartz*

1. First Chrysler Corp. police car powered by a 4-cylinder engine.

2. First Chrysler Corp. police car powered by an overhead cam engine.

3. First Chrysler Corp. police car powered by a non-Mopar engine. (Mitsubishi 2.6 L, 156ci 2-bbl optional)

4. First front-wheel drive Chrysler Corp. police car.

5. First 4-cylinder engine produced by Chrysler Corp. since the 1930s.

The standard power plant for the K-car was the 2.2L, 135ci, 2-bbl engine built in Trenton, Michigan. This used a cast iron block, an aluminum "hemi" combustion chamber head, and an aluminum, long-runner intake manifold. An electronic feedback Holley 2-bbl carb. mixed the fuel. A cog-belt driven overhead cam worked the valvetrain. The result was 84 SAE net horsepower.

Called the "Trans4", this 4-cylinder engine was transversely mounted in the engine compartment. It was bolted to a Torque-Flite 3-speed transaxle made in Kokomo, Indiana.

The optional engine was a 2.6L, 156ci Mitsubishi-made 4-cylinder. It was also an overhead cam "hemi-head" engine with a cast aluminum head and intake manifold. This Inline 4-cylinder, fed from a Mikuni 2-bbl carb, produced 92 SAE net hp. It used a special three valves per cylinder valvetrain.

The optional Mitsubishi-built 2.6 liter engine is also a high technology engine and its larger displacement provides additional power for your Scout Car. This engine features an MC-JET design combustion system which utilizes a third "jet" valve that feeds a high speed jet of air into the combustion mixture at low engine speeds for rapid and more complete burning of the fuel-air mixture and improved fuel economy. A Silent Shaft design in the 2.6 liter engine utilizes two counterbalancing shafts to dampen vibrations normally associated with four-cylinder engines. Result: engine runs smoothly even when idling.

Motor Trend found the larger 4-cylinder engine was a full second quicker in the quarter mile:

Plymouth Reliant K 2-door	Chrysler 2.2L	Mitsubishi 2.6L
SAE net horsepower	84hp	92hp
0 to 60mph	14.04sec	12.38sec
quarter mile ET	19.63sec	18.64sec
quarter mile trap	69.40mph	73.40mph

The Aries K and Reliant K were perfect examples of a taxi-class squad. When used in that capacity, they worked extremely well. The Fort Worth, Texas Police Dept., for example, used the K-cars after 1983 when the Slant Six engine was discontinued. When restricted to detectives and investigators and other non-emergency officers, the K-car was "cost effective and ergonomically sound."

Some police departments started out using the Aries K and Reliant K as Dodge and Plymouth designed them. However, as policies changed and police departments received pressure to dispatch more uniformed officers on the road as frequently happens, the K-cars were pushed from taxi-class to patrol-class duties. It did not take long to find out this was a bad idea.

The biggest problem early on with the K-cars used as patrol cars was that they bottomed out on streets and either knocked holes in the transaxle oil pan, or knocked the oil pan drain plug completely off. One agency lost a couple of K-car engines when detectives bottomed out, lost all the oil and locked up the engines before they knew what happened. Chrysler Corp. corrected this problem by adding a transaxle shield as standard equipment in 1985.

As for sheer performance, the Dodge Aries K distinguished itself from the 1982 taxi-class squads tested by the Michigan State Police. The Aries K, powered by the E62 135ci, 2-bbl 4-cylinder, turned in the quickest quarter mile ET of any of the 6-cylinder and 4-cylinder "people movers". In fact, it outright smoked the M-body Gran Fury powered by the 225ci Slant Six. The Aries K outran both the Malibu and Fairmont to make quite a name for itself in its rookie year.

As a rule, cops continued to show a very strong preference for the 6-cylinder M-body Diplomat/Gran Fury over the 4-cylinder K-car Aries and Reliant as long as the Slant Six was available. In 1982, cops could still remember the 118.5-inch St. Regis

The Reliant K scout car was introduced in 1982 as America's first front wheel drive cop car. *Chrysler*

of 1980 and the 440ci powered Fury of 1978. The change to a 99.9-inch 4-cylinder cop car met with extreme resistance, even if it made sense for some situations.

The K-car, however, met with overwhelming acceptance by one group of fleet managers for a very good reason. Remember who guaranteed the loans to make the K-car and the new Chrysler Corp. possible? Uncle Sam. So, the government had a vested interest in seeing the K-car succeed. The highest concentration of K-car police cars anywhere was on U.S. military bases and the motorpools of the U.S. Government.

The group of cops with the least sense of humor, the Military Police, received the K-car by the dozens. Now you know why the MPs are always in such a foul mood. As for the ability of the 4-cylinder K-car with two burly MPs on-board to catch a fleeing Corvette, do you know anyone who tried to flee from an MP? It just does not happen.

The M-body Gran Fury prevailed. After 1981, the R-body St. Regis and Gran Fury were discontinued. With the 118.5in R-bodies gone, the 112.7in M-body was the largest platform offered by Chrysler, Dodge or Plymouth. The Dodge division only had two rear-wheel drive cars left—the Diplomat and Mirada. The Plymouth division just had the Gran Fury. In 1982, a mere 10 percent of Dodge and Plymouth passenger car sales were rear-wheel drive.

In 1982, the Gran Fury nameplate was attached to an M-body cruiser, replacing the Chrysler LeBaron. At the end of 1980, production of the LeBaron stopped when the Lynch Road, Detroit plant closed. For 1981, LeBaron was an M-body police car. For 1982, LeBaron became the first Chrysler-marque front-wheel drive luxury car.

In 1982, the A38 police package was available only on these two M-bodies: GL41 Dodge Diplomat 4-door sedan and BL41 Plymouth Gran Fury 4-door sedan.

For VIN buffs, the 1981 Diplomat was GH41. The second digit represents the price level or trim level. In this case "H" means high. The Diplomat was originally the most plush of all

options on the New Yorker Brougham. In 1977, the Diplomat became its own car and the most luxurious of all Dodges. It was aimed at the Cadillac Seville and Lincoln Versailles clientele. By 1982, its real destiny came true. The 1982 GL41 VIN indicates low price level or entry-level trim features. As a general rule, and there are numerous exceptions, cop cars are based on the low trim level models.

Dodge and Plymouth fleet personnel were taking the loss of the big R-body like, well, troopers.

The Tough Midsize Gran Fury and Diplomat Police Car... Responsive, Roomy, Maneuverable!

The 1981 Diplomat and Gran Fury Police Pursuits are tough, maneuverable, mid-size cars, that are over a foot shorter than last year's St. Regis and Gran Fury Police Pursuits. And yet they have over an inch more front seat head room and slightly more front seat leg room. These are the two roominess dimensions that mean the most for driver comfort.

In 1982, like it or not, all police departments across the nation were forced to reconsider their minimum wheelbase requirements. This does not mean that they had to change the minimums, but they had to reevaluate them. This also does not mean that no other options were available. Dodge and Plymouth have always been competitors in the police market.

Squad Car	Wheelbase
Chevrolet Impala	116.0in
Ford LTD	114.3in
Diplomat/Gran Fury	112.7in
Chevrolet Malibu	108.1in
Ford Fairmont	105.5in

Remember the fuss in 1962 when the Dodges dropped to 116in? In 1982, 116in was the largest wheelbase available from any car maker for any police car.

Simply put, most police agencies could not justify the higher price for the LTD or the Impala, especially since neither gave

This 1982 Plymouth Gran Fury served the marshal in Basset, Colorado as a K-9 unit. *Mike Keller*

better overall performance than the Diplomat or Gran Fury. As a result, the rigid wheelbase minumums and rigid vehicle weight minimum requirements which were once disputed, were now quietly changed or ignored.

The California Highway Patrol, once the bastion of such standards, broke the ice for all other departments nationwide by selecting the Dodge Diplomat in 1981. This allowed everyone else a face-saving way around the wheelbase requirements. The California Highway Patrol is influential.

The Michigan State Police (MSP) are the police vehicle specialists east of the Rockies. In 1982, they also adopted shorter wheelbase standards. The MSP serves as a credible check and balance for cops in the other 49 states who do not trust anything that comes from California. In 1982, the MSP lowered their wheelbase minimum to 105.5in for the heavy-duty, 4-door police patrol car. That was the final blow. High speed performance would now be measured with a stopwatch and not the distance in inches between the front and rear wheels.

The MSP also dropped a minimum top speed requirement for 1982 model year cars and relaxed the acceleration times. This really had no effect. The top performing Dodge, Ford and Plymouth squads still ran 115 to 116mph and got to 100mph in well under the tighter CHP standard of 43 seconds.

This action from Michigan's finest did draw attention to one fact: Even the best police cars were still slow. In 1982, larger differences than in the previous years existed between the cop cars and the coupes they chased. Three Porsche models were available. They all ran between 130 and 135mph. The Trans Ams and Camaro Z28s ran 116mph, but got to that speed in half the time it took the battle cruisers. The Corvette was back up to 125mph speeds. And the CHP weren't the only ones tooling around in 128mph 5.0L Mustangs. Traffic violators had them before the CHP did. The CHP was just fighting fire with fire.

In all honesty, through the rest of the 1980s, the difference between the capability of cop cars and typical violator cars became worse. It would take fuel-injection and sleeker body styles for the 4-door cop cars to get back into the 130mph range. That would happen after the Diplomat and Gran Fury tours of duty.

Motor Trend reviewed a 1982 Plymouth Gran Fury Pursuit powered by the E48 318ci, 4-bbl.

Take heart, America; the old police interceptor ain't what she used to be. All in all, this cop car appears to be just a pale shadow of its former self.

Okay. That was the bad news. *Car & Driver* predicted it. Cops in California and the rest of the nation struggled to adapt to it. Now *Motor Trend* tells the whole world. Was there any good news? Actually, yes.

The New Jersey State Police used this 1982 Dodge Diplomat. The 318ci V-8 was available in 2-bbl and 4-bbl versions. *Joe Gavula*

This 1982 Plymouth Gran Fury was the last Mopar squad car used by the Los Angeles County Sheriff's Dept.

The Los Angeles County Sheriff's Dept. made good used of this 1982 Gran Fury. The powerplant was a 318ci, 4-bbl producing 165hp.

In a way, the weakest part of those Mopar missile squad cars of days gone by was the monster 440 Commando Interceptor engine. Sure, that kind of powerplant would move almost any car off the line quickly. But all that weight up front also made the car want to keep traveling in a straight line at the first bend in the road. Handling is therefore one area where the Gran Fury Cop Car is much improved over its legendary predecessors, finding its way around turns on a par with cars like the Volvo sedan.

In case it was unclear, handling "like a Volvo" was considered the highest form of praise from *Motor Trend*. These are the guys whose ideal police car was the Volvo 164, remember? If it weren't for Harry Hammond and his Nova 9C1, every cop in Southern California would still be patrolling in Volvos—and loving it.

At any rate, the Gran Fury and Diplomat did handle very well. Each had a pony car stiff suspension, a tolerable firm-feel steering and about the best police brakes in the business. Heavy sway bars front and rear, the Diplomat and Gran Fury were tightly sprung and really did make up for some of the heavy loss in power with a better overall suspension.

The powerplants for the 1982 M-body police cars were unchanged from 1981 squads. The Chrysler Imperial passenger car still had the electronic fuel injected 318ci engine in 1982, and some cops were wondering if that would be handed down to the cop cars. With fuel-injection and 360ci intake and heads, the 318ci cop motor could push out 15 to 20 net hp more and have a much flatter power curve. That would be just the "ticket."

Instead, the talk around Detroit was about doing away with the rear-wheel drive Diplomat and Gran Fury altogether. And by 1984! A stretched version of the K-car called the E-car would be released in 1983. That was supposed to spell the end of the Windsor, Ontario-made M-body cop cars.

The last Diplomat and Gran Fury were to be 1983 model year cars. At the very latest, after giving the E-car a one-year prove-in, the 1984 model year would be "curtains." These were widely acknowledged plans, as was the fact that Chrysler Corp. would be out of the police car business when this happened.

Chrysler Corp. was indeed out of the police market as soon as they dropped the rear-wheel drive platform. However, the timing of this event was not at all like the 1982 planning.

By 1982 and 1983, the energy crisis was news a decade old. Sick of matchbox cars with squirrel cage engines, the public wanted big cars with powerful V-8 engines again. Demand for the V-8 powered Diplomat and Gran Fury actually increased. Maybe cops would get the fuel-injected 318ci after all. Or hey, how about a fuel-injected 360ci!

In 1982, Dodge cop cars outsold Plymouth squads by a slight margin. This would be the trend for the rest of the 1980s. The 1982 production totals were the Diplomat A38 with 11,787 police cars and the Gran Fury A38 with 9,467 police cars

1982 Dodge Aries and Plymouth Reliant Police Scout Car
(With A38 Scout Car Package)
Standard Equipment
Alternator-SAE 78-ampere Chrysler
Automatic Air Conditioning Compressor High-Pressure Clutch Cutoff Switch
Axle Ratio-2.78 to 1
Battery-500 ampere Long-Life
Body-Reinforced forestructure and additional welding
Body-Reinforced rear structure and additional welding
Brakes-Power brakes with dual master cylinder for separate diagonal (left front with right rear wheel and right front with left rear) braking disc: 9.3in diameter, rear drums: 7.9in diameter

Brakes, Power Booster-single diaphragm
Engine Cooling Package-maximum capacity radiators: 22.5in width radiator with engine; cooling fans: 15in diameter four-blade fan with 2.2 liter engine; five-blade "silent-fan" with optional 2.6 liter engine
Front-Wheel Drive
Seat, Front-heavy duty cushion
Steering, Power-rack and pinion
Suspension-includes front and rear antisway bars, heavy duty front and rear coil springs and heavy duty 1-1/4in front and 1in rear shock absorbers
Tires-P185/70R14
Transaxle, Automatic TorqueFlite-three speed, column-mounted range selector, with auxiliary transmission oil cooler
Transaxle Low-Gear Blockout
Wheels-heavy duty: 14x6.0in JJ

Optional Equipment
Air Conditioning
Dome Light Door Switch Control Deactivation
Engine Block Heater
Gauge Package-includes engine temperature, oil pressure and voltmeter gauges
Hose Clamps-stainless steel, screw type
Lamp, Glove Box
Lamp, Luggage Compartment
Lamp, Underhood
Mats, Floor-heavy duty: black only
Radio Delete Option
Radio Suppression Package
Speedometer, Certified-calibrated to 125mph; includes oil pressure warning light
Spotlight, Left 6in windshield-pillar-mounted
Spotlight, Right 6in windshield-pillar-mounted

1982 Dodge Aries and Plymouth Reliant A38 Police Scout Car Engine
Chrysler-built 2.2L 135ci, 2-bbl, 4-cyl
Hemispherical combustion chambers
Electronic fuel control computer
Electronic feedback carburetor
Electronic spark advance
Electronic ignition

This 1982 Wisconsin State Patrol Dodge Diplomat is fitted with full dress wheel covers and mud flaps. *Dave Dotson*

Overhead camshaft-cog belt driven
Camshaft lobes are Lubrited for long life
Five main crankshaft bearings for strength & durability
Cast iron cylinder block
Cast nodular iron crankshaft
Aluminum cylinder head & intake manifold
Chrome-plated intake & exhaust valve stems
Chrome-vanadium valve springs
Hydraulic valve adjusters-no periodic adjustments required
High quality rubber valve stem seals
Carburetor fresh air induction system with heated air door to aid
    cold weather warmup
Electric motor-driven engine cooling fan

Mitsubishi-built 2.6L 156ci, 2-bbl, 4-cyl
Third-valve combustion chambers
Hemispherical combustion chambers
Transverse mounting
Overhead camshaft
Electronic ignition
Cast iron cylinder block
Forged steel crankshaft
Five main bearings for strength and smoothness
Aluminum cylinder head and intake manifold
Electric motor-driven engine cooling fan with after-run feature
    (continues to cool after engine is shut off)
SAE 75amp alternator with built-in electronic voltage regulator

1982 Dodge and Plymouth Police Car Engines

Code	Engine Displacement & Carb	Net Torque(lb-ft)	Net HP	Aries & Reliant	Diplomat & Gran Fury
E62	2.2L (135ci) 2-bbl Trans-4	111@2400rpm	84@4800rpm	STD	n/a
E72	2.6L (156ci) 2-bbl 4-cyl	131@2500rpm	92@4500rpm	OPT	n/a
E25	3.7L (225ci) 1-bbl Slant Six	160@1600rpm	90@3600rpm	n/a	STD
E45	5.2L (318ci) 2-bbl V-8	230@2000rpm	130@4000rpm	n/a	OPT
E48	5.2L (318ci) 4-bbl V-8	240@2000rpm	165@4000rpm	n/a	OPT

1982 Police and Passenger Car Performance Michigan State Police

Vehicle	Engine	0-60 mph	0-100 mph	Top Speed	1/4 mile ET	1/4 mile Trap	Brake Power	MIS Course
Plymouth Gran Fury A38	E48 318ci, 4-bbl	12.24sec	39.36sec	116.3mph	19.08sec	76.50mph	24.29fps2	92.63sec
Ford LTD Police	H.O. 351ci, 2VV	12.59sec	42.54sec	115.8mph	19.15sec	72.50mph	22.63fps2	91.99sec
Dodge Diplomat A38	E48 318ci, 4-bbl	12.19sec	39.95sec	115.4mph	19.20sec	75.25mph	23.71fps2	92.57sec
Chevrolet Impala 9C1	350ci, 4-bbl	12.74sec	45.79sec	107.8mph	19.40sec	73.00mph	23.99fps2	92.04sec
Chevrolet Malibu Police	350ci, 4-bbl	13.29sec	49.73sec	110.1mph	19.53sec	72.50mph	24.62fps2	92.61sec
Ford Fairmont Police	255ci V-8, 2-bbl	13.80sec	57.04sec	107.0mph	19.88sec	72.00mph	23.17fps2	94.16sec
Dodge K-Aries A38	E62 135ci I4, 2-bbl	17.58sec	not	97.5mph	21.55sec	66.25mph	n/a	n/a
Ford Fairmont Police	140ci, L4, 2-bbl	17.26sec	n/a	103.4mph	21.85sec	67.50mph	n/a	n/a
Chevrolet Malibu Police	229ci, Y6, 2-bbl	17.99sec	n/a	100.6mph	21.85sec	65.25mph	n/a	n/a
Ford Fairmont Police	200ci, L6, 1-bbl	18.72sec	not	97.3mph	22.00sec	64.75mph	n/a	n/a
Plymouth Gran Fury A38	E25, 225ci, 1-bbl	20.36sec	not	96.2mph	22.53sec	62.25mph	n/a	n/a
							References	
Datsun 280 ZX Turbo	2.8L, e.f.i.	7.7sec	n/a	135mph	15.9sec	88mph	MT Feb. 1982	
Porsche 944	2.5L, e.f.i.	7.7sec	n/a	130mph	15.9sec	86mph	MT May 1982	
Ford Mustang CHP	H.O. 302ci, 2-bbl	6.9sec	21.10sec	128mph	16.1sec	87mph	MT Sept. 1981	
Buick Regal Turbo	3.8L, turbo	9.0sec	n/a	113mph	16.7sec	83mph	CD Feb. 1982	
Chevrolet Camaro Z28	305ci, 4-bbl	8.6sec	n/a	116mph	16.7sec	81mph	MT May 1982	

This San Francisco Police 1982 Dodge Diplomat has 16-inch pusher bumpers. *Greg Reynolds*

References

Dodge Police Vehicles, Chrysler Corporation, 1982
Plymouth Police Vehicles, Chrysler Corporation, 1982
Patrol Vehicle Specifications, Evaluation and Purchasing Program, Michigan State Police, 1982
"Plymouth Gran Fury Police Special," Jim Hall, *Motor Trend*, September 1982
Standard Catalog of Chrysler, John Lee, Jim Benjaminson, John Gunnell, Krause Publicatons
"Chrysler: First Family of Front-Drive," Jim McCraw, *Motor Trend*, February 1982
"The New Chrysler," Ron McGonegal, *Motor Trend*, September 1980.

Chapter 7

1983: Totally Improved K-cars

In 1983, Dodge and Plymouth dropped the term "Scout Car" to describe the A38 police package Aries K and Reliant K. These K-cars were now called Police cars or Patrol cars. This was in contrast to the M-body Diplomat and Gran Fury. These were called Pursuits.

How things change. As recently as 1977, the Police Pursuit was a 121.4-inch wheelbase, 440ci Dodge Royal Monaco. In 1983, the Police Pursuit was a 112.7-inch wheelbase, 318ci Dodge Diplomat.

The same thing goes for the most economical of all the patrol or taxi class squads. In 1977 again, a Police Patrol (or Patroller) was a 112.7-inch wheelbase, 225ci Slant Six Plymouth Volare. In 1983, the Police Patrol was a 100.3-inch wheelbase 135ci, Inline four Plymouth Reliant K.

Many police and sheriff's departments have a need for two types of police vehicles-one for pursuit, such as the Gran Fury and Diplomat Police Pursuit. The other for in-town and about-town duties, such as the Reliant and Aries Police car.

For 1983, Chrysler Corp. offered four vehicles with the A38 Pursuit Package or A38 Patrol Package:

GL41	4-door sedan	Dodge Diplomat Pursuit
BL41	4-door sedan	Plymouth Gran Fury Pursuit
DL41	4-door sedan	Dodge Aries Patrol
PL41	4-door sedan	Plymouth Reliant Patrol

Of these squads, the M-body Diplomat and Gran Fury were almost straight carryovers from 1982. On the other hand, the Aries K and Reliant K received the following added features:

1. new suspension
2. new brakes
3. new steering
4. more horsepower

In terms of suspension, the front and rear sway bars were upgraded from "standard" duty in 1982 to "heavy duty" in 1983. The design changed in a subtle way, increasing the effectiveness. Most importantly, the rear heavy duty shock absorbers jumped from a 1-inch diameter to 1-3/16-inch diameter. Cops took Chrysler Corp. seriously when they called the K-car a six passenger car. The huge rear shocks helped.

Of all the K-car changes, the upgrade to the brakes was the most critical. The front disc diameter was increased from a swept area of 157sq-in to 198sq-in. The rear drum width was increased from a swept area of 58sq-in to 85sq-in. All together that represented a 32 percent increase in binder surface area. This was one of the largest improvements in braking in Chrysler Corp. police car history! Enthusiasts with the older K-cars should be aware that these cars are under-braked.

The 1983 change to the rack and pinion steering was also a significant one. The steering ratio was quickened from 18:1 to 14:1. As a point of reference, the Diplomat and Gran Fury used a

15.7:1 ratio. The GM Camaro and Firebird used a 14.4:1 ratio. When Dodge and Plymouth called the K-car steering "quick-ratio," they were not kidding. It was still power-assisted and still had a firm feel.

Horsepower and torque from the 2.2L, 135ci base inline 4-cylinder increased a lot—nearly 12 percent. The intake manifold was reworked, and the fuel/spark controls were recalibrated. In an unthinkable move, compression was increased from 8.5 to 9.0:1. These steps added 10 net hp and 6lb-ft. That kind of increase was hard to come by in the days of CAFE, EPA and CARB.

On the topic of fuel economy, Chrysler Corp. made it clear they were the American leader.

"Chrysler's projected CAFE for the 1983 models is 28.7mpg—better than Ford or GM. And that rating equals the government's requirement for 1985, putting us three years ahead of schedule."

In fact, Aries K and Reliant K were advertised as the highest mileage, six passenger, front wheel drive cars in America. They carried EPA estimates of 29mpg city, and 41mpg highway. That was for the 2.2L, 135ci engine with a 4-speed stick. The A38 package cars came with the 3-speed auto transaxles. They got 28mpg/35mpg. Those were very impressive numbers in 1983.

The other drivetrain change in the K-car lineup was the final drive ratio in the 2.6L, 156ci powered squads. The final ratio increased from 2.78 to 3.02 to 1. This made the 4-cylinder K-cars powered by the optional E72 just that much quicker and more responsive.

This 1983 Dodge Diplomat is equipped with the A38 police package but powered by the 225ci Slant Six. This was the last year for this engine. *Avery Henry*

The Baton Rouge, Louisiana Police equipped their 1983 Dodge Diplomats with pusher bars. *Baton Rouge Police*

In 1983, the K-cars boasted again an exceptional amount of six passenger interior space, bashing the full-size Mercury and Cadillac:

The Dodge Aries and Plymouth Reliant Police Patrol Cars give you more stretch-out room and comfort than you might expect in a fuel-efficient car.

Front headroom and legroom—the most important comfort dimensions in police duty—are actually bigger than the 1982 Ford LTD and Fairmont, Mercury Marquis and Zephyr. And there's more front legroom than in the 1982 Cadillac DeVille and Brougham sedans, according to official MVMA (Motor Vehicle Manufacturers Association) dimensions. Furthermore, the driver's seat adjusts 6.5 inches front to rear in Aries and Reliant for a big range of driver sizes.

This 1983 Plymouth Gran Fury was in-service with the Missouri State Highway Patrol. It is now a daily driver owned by an emergency medical technician.

The K-car was America's newest taxi. Fleet sales of the K-car were up. It was grudgingly accepted as a police car and wildly heralded as America's newest taxi. Chrysler Corp. was producing front wheel drive cars at redline speeds. In fact, in 1983 they purchased the old Volkswagen assembly plant in Sterling Heights, Michigan to make even more compact, front wheel drive cars.

Diplomat and Gran Fury. While the K-cars received all the attention, the Diplomat and Gran Fury were still the backbone of the police fleet.

The Dodge Diplomat Pursuit and Plymouth Gran Fury Pursuit were heavy-muscled cars, built for maximum performance for anything from high-speed pursuits to routine assignments. Evidence was in the continued popularity of these vehicles. It was used in great numbers throughout the country. There was a choice of three heavy-duty engines, with heavy-duty suspension, brakes, steering and electrical equipment necessary for tough pursuit work.

These cars were available with either the E25 225ci Slant Six, the E45 318ci, 2-bbl or the E48 318ci, 4-bbl. The Slant Six and 2-bbl V-8 had the wide ratio A904 TorqueFlite. The 4-bbl V-8 still used the old, close-ratio, big-block A727 TorqueFlite. The V-8 squads all had lockup torque converters for the best fuel economy.

On the topic of economy, the 1983 police and fleet vehicle literature specifically states the 225ci, 1-bbl and the 318ci, 4-bbl must come with the proven 2.94:1 rear gear. No mention is made of the gear for the 318ci, 2-bbl combination, and for good reason. The 2-bbl V-8 squads came with a 2.24:1 final drive. That was the lowest rear gear ratio ever.

Maybe that explains why the car lacked a certain neck-snapping response? Maybe that also explains the 1983 CAFE ratings for Chrysler Corp.?

These 2-bbl V-8 cars were slow, and they used a lot of gas getting up to speed. *Motor Trend* proved nearly 10 years previ-

In 1983, production of the M-body Dodge Diplomat (shown) and Plymouth Gran Fury moved from Windsor, Ontario to outside St. Louis, Missouri.

ous this was the wrong fuel economy approach for realistic police driving. However, it gave the right numbers for the federal fuel test against which Chrysler Corp. was measured. And that was what counted. Imagine that: A 2.24:1 rear gear, installed in near total secrecy. Cops would have had a fit had they known.

Of course, complaints about loss of power in order to economize were closely followed by complaints of the cars being too small. The Diplomat and Gran Fury had no room to brag about, but Chrysler Corp. did anyhow.

"Front seat roominess Provides extra comfort for driver and front passenger. Diplomat and Gran Fury Police Pursuits have over an inch more front seat headroom than the Ford LTD and more front seat legroom than either Impala or Ford LTD. These two dimensions mean the most for driver comfort."

The reality, however, was that all cop cars were shrinking. The one option that cured more problems with lack of front seat space appeared most frequently on Mopar squads. The cure was a tilt steering column. Once a luxury, this was now a real necessity. It was available on both the K-cars and the M-body squads.

The Chrysler Imperial still came with the fuel-injected 318ci V-8. However, 1983 was the last year. The 318ci, 4-bbl had already disappeared from the passenger car lineup. This was also the last year for the Slant Six in police cars. Like the 360ci V-8, the Slant Six continued to serve cops in the police vans. This was also the last year for the Dodge Mirada. In 1984, the only rear-wheel drive cars in the entire Dodge and Plymouth line up would be the M-body 4-door sedans.

Here's an 1983 slick-top Oklahoma Highway Patrol Gran Fury. *Darryl Lindsay*

This 1983 Ripon, Wisconsin Police Gran Fury has classic black and white trim. *Greg Reynolds*

This 1983 Texas DPS Dodge Diplomat has twin spotlights and twin grille lamps. *Dave Dotson*

In the early 1980s, the M-body police cars were assembled in Windsor, Ontario, Canada. During 1983, the production of the rear-wheel drive Diplomat and Gran Fury moved to Fenton, Missouri, near St. Louis, to join the K-cars. The M-body squads were assembled in Fenton, Missouri until mid-year 1987 when the production shifted to Kenosha, Wisconsin.

At the Michigan State Police 'runoffs' for 1983 model year squads, the Mopars felt the heat from the Ford and Chevy squads. The Mopars achieved the highest top speeds, the best brakes and the best zero to 100mph times. The Fords and Chevys did well on the influential road course stage. However, when total performance and total dollars were combined, the Plymouth Gran Fury A38 was still the best cop car for the money.

Meanwhile, in the mini-car runoffs, the Reliant K A38 showed off its new 1983 abilities by humiliating the econo-boxes from Ford and Chevy.

The 1983 production count for America's police cars were the Dodge Diplomat A38 with 13,106 police cars and the Plymouth Gran Fury A38 with 8,400 police cars.

The Mascoutah, Illinois Police used clear but simple markings on their 1983 Diplomat. *Dave Dotson*

1983 Torque and Horsepower Ratings-Police Car Engines
Engines with Federal Emissions Control Package
(California Police and Emergency Vehicles Use Federal Engines)

Code	Engine Displacement & Carb.	Availability	Net Torque (lb-ft)	Net Horsepower
E62	2.2 liter (135ci) 2-bbl, 4cyl	Aries/Reliant	117@3200rpm	94@5200rpm
E72	2.6 liter (156ci) 2-bbl, 4cyl	Aries/Reliant	132@2500rpm	93@4500rpm
E25	3.7 liter (225ci) 1-bbl, Slant Six	Diplomat/Gran Fury	165@1600rpm	90@3500rpm
E45	5.2 liter (318ci) 2-bbl, V-8	Diplomat/Gran Fury	230@2000rpm	130@4000rpm
E48	5.2 liter (318ci) 4-bbl, V-8	Diplomat/Gran Fury	240@2000rpm	165@4000rpm

This New York-New Jersey Port Authority 1983 Dodge Diplomat has some street scars. *Dave Dotson*

This NYPD 1983 Gran Fury is a 4-bbl Highway Patrol unit. *Ned Schwartz*

1983 Passenger Car Performance

Vehicle	Engine	0-60	1/4 mile ET	1/4 mile Trap	Top Speed	Laguna Seca Road Course	Reference
Chevrolet Camaro Z28	305ci, 4-bbl	7.4sec	15.6sec	90.5mph	134mph	85.4sec	MT July 1983
Ford Mustang GT	302ci, 4-bbl	7.7sec	16.0sec	87.5mph	125mph	89.9sec	MT July 1983
Dodge Daytona Z	2.2L (135ci) efi turbo	8.2sec	16.5sec	81.6 mph	119 mph	88.8 sec	MT July 1983
Chevrolet Corvette	350ci, efi	7.3sec	15.8sec	84.0mph	138mph	n/a	MT May 1983
Chevrolet Monte Carlo SS	305ci, 4-bbl	8.0sec	16.1sec	85mph	120mph	n/a	MT April 1983
Olds Hurst/Cutlass	307ci, 4-bbl	8.8sec	16.7sec	83mph	109mph	n/a	CD April 1983

1983 Police Car Performance
Michigan State Police

Vehicle	Engine	0-60mph	0-100mph	1/4 mile ET	1/4 mile Trap	Top Speed	MIS Road Course	Brake Power
Chevy Impala 9C1	350ci, 4-bbl	11.67sec	42.51sec	18.55sec	73.5mph	115.0mph	92.21sec	23.23fps2
Chevy Malibu Police	305ci, 4-bbl	11.71sec	40.73sec	18.78sec	75.0mph	116.3mph	92.13sec	24.51fps2
Ford LTD Police	351ci, 2VV	12.22sec	39.81sec	18.83sec	72.3mph	117.9mph	90.59sec	23.99fps2
Plymouth Gran Fury A38	E48 318ci, 4-bbl	12.38sec	39.68sec	19.10sec	76.5mph	120.0mph	92.64sec	24.92fps2
Dodge Diplomat A38	E48 318ci, 4-bbl	12.81sec	40.46sec	19.30sec	75.5mph	118.8mph	93.54sec	24.26fps2
Ford LTD Police	302ci, p.f.i.	13.94sec	69.01sec	19.93sec	71.3mph	104.4mph	n/a	23.99fps2
Ford Mustang SSP	302ci, 4-bbl	8.32sec	22.71sec	16.68sec	86.3mph	132.0mph	88.31sec	24.97fps2
Plymouth Reliant A38	E72 156ci, 2-bbl	15.49sec	n/a	19.70sec	68.0mph	102.8mph	94.58sec	23.96fps2
Chevy Impala 9C1	229ci, 2-bbl	17.40sec	n/a	21.50sec	67.0mph	104.3mph	n/a	23.23fps2
Ford Fairmont Police	140ci, 1-bbl	18.40sec	not	21.83sec	65.0mph	95.8mph	97.68sec	24.22fps2
Ford Fairmont Police	200ci, 1-bbl	17.68sec	not	21.93sec	66.3mph	97.7mph	n/a	24.22fps2
Dodge Diplomat A38	E25 225ci, 1-bbl	18.75sec	not	22.03sec	63.5mph	96.5mph	n/a	24.26fps2

This Perry County, Illinois Sheriff's 1983 Diplomat is also a D.A.R.E. unit. *Dave Dotson*

References

Standard Catalog of Chrysler, John Lee, Jim Benjaminson, John Gunnell, Krause Publications

Chrysler Corporation Police and Fleet Vehicles, Chrysler Corporation, 1983

"All American GTs," Ron Grable, *Motor Trend*, July 1983

Patrol Vehicle Specifications, Evaluation and Purchasing Program, Michigan State Police, 1983

Chapter 8

Transverse Torsion Bar Blues

In 1957, Chrysler Corp. shocked the motoring world by releasing an entirely new front suspension system on all of its cars. This was the famous torsion bar suspension. In terms of the springs used in front and rear suspension, there were only three designs:

1. coil springs
2. leaf springs
3. torsion bars

Technically, a torsion bar and a coil spring work exactly the same way. A torsion bar is just a straightened out coil spring. The physics of extension and compression are the same for both.

In practical terms, the torsion bar is a much more compact system and really does give better high speed handling. Cops who drive 100mph plus numerous times each patrol shift confirmed this. So did sports car enthusiasts who would not be caught dead in a "4-door sedan." The torsion bar front suspension gained fame as the high speed setup.

In 1976, Chrysler Corp. made what most analysts considered a very subtle change to the torsion bar system. It was called an Isolated Transverse Torsion Bar system. This system was released on the new 1976 F-body Dodge Aspen and Plymouth Volare. In 1977, the M-body cars, which included over time the Dodge Diplomat, the Plymouth Gran Fury and (Canadian) Caravelle and the Chrysler LeBaron, were designed with transverse torsion bars.

While everyone in the auto industry caught the change, it was simply considered a different use of the time-proven torsion bar design. Instead of longitudinal bars running front to back and anchored in the transmission mount cross member, the transverse bars ran left and right and were anchored in structures under the radiator. Some, in fact, have confused the transverse torsion bars for front anti-sway bars. Actually, that was a very easy mistake since the anchor points in the frame and on the lower A-arms were so similar.

In 1976, *Motor Trend* described the transverse suspension and gave it approval.

Perhaps the outstanding feature of these cars is the new transverse torsion bar front suspension. Chrysler pioneered the use of torsion bars in American production cars in 1957 and has used them ever since on all lines. But those bars run longitudinally with the chassis and are springing media only. The new bars run across the front of the car and do double duty as locators for the lower control arms. It is a neat, compact setup and retains the adjustability of the longitudinal bars as before, so that any spring sag that might occur in the life of the car can be compensated for. They are augmented by a sturdy anti-roll bar that allows compliance and controls body roll without changing the ride.

The whole front suspension assembly is hung on a K-member that is isolated from the unitized body by four massive rubber

This is the Tennessee Law Enforcement Academy EVOC fleet. Transverse torsion bars were sensitive to abusive driving. *Dave Dotson*

mounts, so there is no metal-to-metal path through which noise or road vibration can be transmitted to the body.

The handling in the case of the Aspen is not, repeat NOT achieved at the expense of ride comfort. Even the so-called heavy-duty suspension in the R/T and Road Runner packages is free from any harshness—a tribute to the new transverse torsion bar design.

Again, so we keep these two very different suspension designs straight, the transverse bars are mounted cross-wise in the front of the car. The transverse bars react on the outboard ends of the lower control arms. Each torsion bar is anchored in the front crossmember opposite the wheel that it supports. The right wheel's torsion bar is anchored on the left side of the car and vice versa. From the anchor, the bar extends across the front of the car to a "pivot cushion bushing" and then bends and extends rearward to the lower control arm.

By 1980, the automotive press became less enchanted with the transverse bars. *Car & Driver* called it "tried-but-not-so-true." That wasn't the response when the enthusiasts magazine reviewed the old B-body and C-body squads with longitudinal torsion bars. Recall that in 1980 the Los Angeles County Sheriff's Dept. declared "torsion bars designed in a transverse configuration are not acceptable."

Two problems developed from the transverse bars. It is critical to look at the two problems individually since the corrections are separate, even though the two problems were frequently mistaken as being related.

First, the front suspension "sagged" over time. All torsion bar cars did this, but the transverse sprung cars did this rapidly, sometimes within a week. As the front ride height dropped down, the tires would develop negative camber and a toe-out alignment.

The sagging suspension resulted in extreme inside tread wear from the negative camber and, in poor high speed, stability from the toe-out. Toe-out also caused severe brake pull, sometimes from one side to the other, as each front tire traded being in control.

On any Mopar, the proper ride height is absolutely critical to straight-line braking and high speed control. When adjusted properly, these F-body and M-body squads handled just fine.

Chrysler Corp. fleet personnel recommended the ride height be checked with every oil change. If the ride height was okay, the front end tire alignment would be okay, too. The check was simple. The distance from the head of the front K-frame bolt to the ground should be 12in.

The problem was the transverse torsion bars would sag and cause an out-of-alignment situation in exact proportion to how hard the car was driven. If the squad was abused by cutting rough

medians at high speed, driven extensively over pot-holed streets or otherwise thrashed by the officer, the transverse torsion bars would sag rapidly, sometimes within a week!

In this regard, the transverse torsion bar suspension was not like the original longitudinal torsion bar suspension. The original torsion bars, last seen on the Dodge St. Regis and other R-bodies, had better anchor points. One end was anchored in a beefy cross member. From there it went straight like an arrow forward to the lower control arm or A-arm. The longitudinal torsion bar was not called on to "locate" anything in the suspension geometry.

On the other hand, the transverse torsion bars started out with one L-shaped bend and a series of smaller bends. It had one more mounting point and bushing package per side to fail. The transverse bars also served as trailing locating arms for the lower A-arms.

To make matters worse, they were in the very front of the boxed structure which made them vulnerable to damage. Since each transverse bar was attached at three separate points on the front end, as one Mopar-oriented CHP patrolman complained, "none were ever right after even a minor wreck."

Overall, the consensus was the transverse torsion bars were an acceptable system for light-duty, urban-use, passenger car situations. They did, in fact, sag more easily than Chrysler's original torsion bar design and were much more sensitive to abusive driving. However, periodic ride height adjustments, which were quick and easy to do, were all the F-body and M-body squads needed. It required nothing fancier than a socket wrench and a 12-inch ruler. And it only added five minutes to the oil change.

If that were the only suspension issue, no one outside the National Association of Fleet Administrators would have ever known or cared. The second, and by far most critical problem with the transverse torsion bar suspension, was the K-frame structure to which all of the front suspension was bolted.

Motor pool mechanics and local Dodge and Plymouth dealership service departments got pretty handy at putting the M-body ride height and alignment back into spec. Twist two bolts, and the job was done.

Then as early as 1983, alignment shops ran into trouble getting rid of negative camber. Nor was enough positive camber adjustment possible. At the same time, repeated ride height adjustments were required, even compared to the earlier M-body cars. Cops were complaining more frequently about chronic brake pull and the front end wandering at pursuit speeds.

With signs like this, the transverse torsion bars were immediately suspected. Transverse torsion bars were replaced, the squads were carefully aligned, and front brake calipers were repeatedly rebuilt or replaced. The problem persisted. It became frustrating since these problems were cured in the past by ride height adjustment or replacement of the torsion bars.

This new problem held the key to the overall problem: insufficient positive camber adjustment. This meant literally something in the subframe itself was actually bending. After the standard and expected amount of denial and finger-pointing, the K-frame itself was found to be the culprit.

Sgt. Joe Gavula with the Philadelphia, Pennsylvania Police and an avid Mopar police car enthusiast explains:

"The M-bodies front "K" Member Isolated Crossmember had support brackets that extended upward to support the upper control arms and the tops of the front shock absorbers. These must not have been strong at first, because after a while these "towers" would sag and bend inwards. This would affect the front alignment by not allowing enough positive camber. The wheels would be "in at the top" and the inside of the tires would wear out quickly. You could not adjust the camber enough, because the tower was bent.

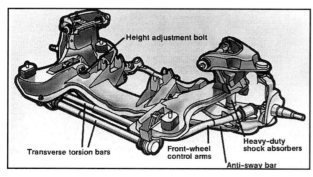

The isolated transverse torsion bar front suspension was developed for the 1976 F-body Aspen and Volare. All M-body Diplomats and Gran Furys used this front spring design. *Chrysler*

"There were a few ways to fix this. One way was to add shims to the support bracket to move it out some. This method was described in a Chrysler Technical Service Bulletin P-4482. Another way was to use offset upper control arm pivot bars. I saw this remedy advertised in our police garage bulletin board. A third way to correct this frame alignment rack was to just bend the brackets back into specifications. This method seemed rather risky to me. How many times could you do this before the metal cracked?

"I believe Chrysler improved this situation with the 1988 model year. We had no more problems with the front ends going out of whack. And when I got a chance to look at a car on a lift, the "K" Member appeared to be slightly different. I suppose that Chrysler beefed up this weak point.

"I myself am still having problems with tire wear on my 1985 Diplomat. The front end is adjusted to its outer limits and is supposed to be within specifications, but I still get tire wear and a little instability. I don't get much satisfaction from the mechanics I go to. I wish I had my own rack to do it right. It is weird. The wheels appear to be straight but on hard turns, you can hear the tires squealing."

Not only did the upper towers bend, sometimes the K-frame itself cracked or split. While this was somewhat evident on 1983 and 1984 M-body cop cars, it happened on large numbers of 1985 and 1986 M-body squads as well.

The reasons for this bending and cracking are as varied as the people recalling the events. Chuck Swift, of Swift Dodge in Sacramento, indicated the K-frames in question were made in Mexico and that they were inferior. Dan Krans, from Chrysler Fleet, pointed to worn-out stamping dies and a batch of questionable steel from Mexico.

The one common thread that over a dozen industry insiders had was this shipment of defective or below tensile strength steel. This would go a long way in explaining a rash of K-frame cracking and splitting complaints. However, neither this defective steel nor the worn stamping die logic explains tower flexing which stole camber adjustments on 1983 through 1987 Mopar squad cars.

All this weak lot of steel did, was further identify the real problem. The K-frame was not strong enough in the first place. This was a combination of not thick enough, not reinforced enough and too sensitive to material strength variations. The A38 police package cars had a reinforced forestructure and additional welding, but obviously not enough.

This problem appeared to be restricted to police cars and taxi cabs—the kinds of cars that get harsh treatment routinely. Since this did not effect passenger cars very much since it was not the cause for any accidents and was not the subject of any law suits, no Diplomats or Gran Furys were "recalled."

Many police departments just put up with the lousy tire wear. After all, it was only a little worse than the already poor mileage most cops get from their squad car tires. The same went for the alignment hassles. New York City has been described as "pot holes surrounded by tall buildings." What was a couple more alignments in this nightmare of fleet management?

If you have read *Dodge, Plymouth & Chrysler Police Cars 1956-1978*, you know who did not put up with the problem: The California Highway Patrol, nor should they have.

For those keeping score in the decades of long shootouts between Dodge Division and the CHP, up to this point, it was 2 to 1, advantage: CHP. The CHP got a Polara cop car in 1961 when there was not officially such a thing. The CHP got 122-inch wheelbase cars in 1965 when the longest Dodge measured 121in. The Dodge division came out on top on the 1980 St. Regis controversy. However, they were gracious winners and "valiantly" assisted to improve the top end.

The front end controversy was decided solidly in favor of the California Highway Patrol. Have we mentioned how influential the CHP was when it came to vehicles? It took the CHP 2-1/2 model years to get Dodge "cuffed and stuffed," but they finally did it.

Chrysler Corp. came up with a two-pronged solution: One to solve the sagging, but intact shock towers. The other to solve the cracked K-frame problem.

In February 1986, and then again in December 1986, Chrysler issued a Technical Service Bulletin. It only dealt with insufficient positive camber adjustment, with the assumption the K-frame was still intact.

The Bulletin called for PN 4014352-front spacer, front suspension upper control arm pivot support; and PN 4014353-rear spacer, front suspension upper control arm pivot support.

Technical Service Bulletin
P-4482 Rev. A 2-5-86

Models: 1983-1987 Gran Fury/Diplomat

Sympton/Condition: Insufficient positive camber adjustment

Parts Required:

PN 4014352-spacer, front suspension upper control arm pivot support-front

PN 4014353-spacer, front suspension upper control arm pivot support-rear

Repair Procedure: This repair outlines the installation of upper control arm support plate spacers.

1. Loosen the caster/camber adjusting nuts (not necessary to remove them).
2. Raise car and remove wheel.
3. Loosen shock absorbed upper not (not necessary to remove).
4. Remove the two (2) support plate bolts at the front end of the plate.
5. Looses the two (2) rear bolts enough to slide the front spacer (longer of two) between the support plate and the frame.
6. Align the holes in the spacer with the holes in the support plate and frame.
7. Insert the two front bolts and start threads. Do not tighten.
8. Repeat Steps 5-7 for the rear spacer (shorter of the two).
9. Torque the four (4) support plate bolts to specification (65lb-ft).
10. Torque the shock absorber upper nut to specification (25lb-ft).
11. Replace wheel on car.
12. Lower the car and adjust the alignment on the side where the spacers were installed according to the procedures and specifications in the service manual.

Note: The upper control arm spacers are to be used only as a set (1 long and 1 short) on the side where they are needed. Under no circumstances are spacers to be stacked to gain additional positive camber adjustment.

NOTE: TSB P-4482 IS CHRYSLER-OWNED MATERIAL, AND IS REPRINTED WITH THE PERMISSION OF CHRYSLER CORPORATION.

This Bulletin estimated it would take 1.8 hours to shim one side and align the squad, and 2.5 hours to align both sides and align the squad. Not all M-bodies ran out of camber alignment. For those that did, not all needed shim on both sides. This Technical Service Bulletin went to all dealerships and all major police motor pools.

The second prong of the 2-prong solution was not open to everyone, only those "wheels which squeaked" the loudest (ie: the departments who complained the loudest). This solution was to . replace the K-Frame.

Some Diplomat and Gran Fury squads suffered from cracked K-frames and sagging shock towers. Chrysler issued a Technical Service Bulletin to cover the problem. *Kevin Gordon and Keith Mesey*

Chrysler is understandably reluctant to discuss exactly which police departments received free K-frames installed, and exactly how many K-frames were involved. Police departments other than the CHP received new K-frames. CHP sources indicated between 300 and 400 1985 through 1987 Diplomats received new K-frames. This amounted to between 5 and 10 percent of the CHP fleet. The K-frame replacement project continued through the 1988 model year, which was the last year the CHP used the Diplomat.

In March 1987, the CHP wrote Motor Transport Bulletin 87-08 to deal with this problem:

Chrysler Corp. determined some "K" members in the 1985 through 1987 Dodges could flex or sag, which resulted in the need for repeated camber adjustment and front end alignment. Also, "K" member replacement had solved instances of chronic brake pull problems, where extensive brake repair procedures did not correct a severe brake pull problem.

Many areas have experienced the following problems with these vehicles:

1. Repeated front end alignment was required. No positive camber adjustment remained. Repeated height adjustments were required.

2. Front end darted or pulled and/or "barreled" at high speed (or combination).

3. Chronic brake pull existed.

To correct these problems, Chrysler Corp. offered new front end "K" members under police adjustment. As a result of this inquiry, the initial response from the field indicated a need for about 150 "K" members. Arrangements were made to ship fifty-six "K" members to the field. Swift Dodge expected to receive about 120 "K" members by March 13, 1987.

Installation of "K" Frame: The installation had to be done by a Chrysler Corp. dealer. Chrysler Corp.'s policy covered the cost of installation and subsequent front end alignment.

In June 1987, the K-frame replacement program was expanded to include brand new, unissued 1987 Diplomat squads, according to another Motor Transport Bulletin.

An agreement had been reached with Chrysler Corp. to replace "K" members on new vehicles, prior to assignment. These "K" members were to be installed by Swift Dodge as work load permits; thus, not all assigned would have a new "K" member.

New units that had a "K" member installed prior to assignment were identified as follows:

1. "New 'K' Member" statement were included on the CHP 57.

2. The "K" member would have a yellow strip painted on the rear of the center section.

3. A white (stick-on) square dot would be located on the front side of the rear view mirror.

The above action was taken to overcome the problem of frequent front end alignment, particularly the "loss" of positive camber, inside wear of front tires, handling problems and chronic brake pull.

In July 1988, the CHP issued a summary of the brake pull and handling problems in their final Motor Transport Bulletin on the subject.

Subject: *Dodge Diplomat severe brake pull and handling problems*

Model: *All Dodge Diplomat Class E Sedans*

This bulletin shall serve as a guide for correcting severe brake pull and handling problems on Dodge Diplomat Class E sedans. The technical information supplied in this bulletin supersedes all previous bulletins. Prior bulletins should be retained for reference and policy information. Due to the inherent sensitivity of the front suspension, vehicle operators should be made aware that abuse has a major impact on handling and braking performance.

This bulletin should not be interpreted as a cure for all brake pull and suspension problems. Basic diagnostic procedures should still be adhered to.

Choosing A Repair Facility *- The Dodge Diplomat is equipped with a unique torsion bar suspension system, which can make obtaining knowledgeable repair service in the field difficult in some areas. This fact should be kept in mind when choosing a repair vendor. Potential repair vendors should be questioned on their knowledge and prior experience with this type of front suspension system. If the potential repair facility is not fully experienced with this suspension system, another vendor should be chosen.*

The repair process should be divided into two categories: Frame and chassis repair and front suspension alignment.

All repairs must be attempted in this order to properly correct the exhibited condition.

In choosing a vendor for frame and chassis repair, look for a reputable collision repair facility. It is not necessary for the shop to have an elaborate frame measuring device, as most work can be performed using a tape measure and knowledgeable skills.

In choosing a suspension alignment facility, look for a shop that has a reputation for performing accurate alignments and thorough front suspension component checks. It is not necessary for the facility to be equipped with a four-wheel alignment machine.

Special Note on Severe Brake Pull *- In the majority of cases, the brake system is not the cause of a brake pull. The brake system should be eliminated as a cause through normal diagnostic procedures. If brake pads and rotors have been replaced and the problem seems to be corrected, you may not have corrected the actual problem. New unconditioned brake pads do not have the same friction characteristics as used condition brake pads do. This has an impact on front suspension action and movement.*

Repair Procedure *- Brake pull and steering wander are influenced by many of the same suspension characteristics. Corrective action should be taken as follows:*

1. The frame or collision repair facility needs to check the following items.

a. Make sure that the rear differential is installed square in the vehicle (thrust angle). If not, this can be corrected by installing the proper thickness shim at the respective front spring mount for the rear leaf springs. The thrust angle should be 0 degrees if in proper alignment.

b. Check the alignment of the K-frame (front subframe) to the chassis to ensure that it is mounted square in the vehicle. This can be checked with a tape measure. Use the chassis reference holes and the center line of the lower ball joints as a guide. Measure in both a forward and an X pattern.

c. Ensure that the steering center link is on place (level) to the ground. This component must be positioned properly to ensure good handling of the vehicle over uneven road surfaces. If the center line is not on place, it will normally be high on the right side of the vehicle. The proper procedure to use in adjusting the place of the center link is to use a porta-power to move the idler arm bracket, which is welded onto the K-frame, into the proper position. In some cases, it may be necessary to shim the power steering gear box to achieve the proper center link plane. The Chrysler Motors method of using a file to elongate the idler arm bracket hole to reposition the idler arm should be avoided.

2. A qualified alignment shop needs to perform the following repairs:

a. Check the power steering gear control valve. To do this, raise the front wheels of the vehicle off the ground and then start the engine. If the steering wheel moves when the engine starts, the control valve needs to be adjusted. At the same time this operation is performed, check the power steering gear sector shaft for lateral movement in the housing. If excessive movement is noted, replace the power steering gear box using the proper police special part number.

b. Check and adjust the front suspension height of the vehicle. Always finish the adjustment process by making an upward adjustment. Ensure that there is adequate clearance between the left side torsion bar and the K-frame. If not, install shims or a bushing kit as necessary. When installing new torsion bar bushings or supports, check the replacement part numbers to ensure that you are using the correct heavy duty replacement part. Set front end height at 12-1/2in + or - 1/4in. A list of part numbers is supplied at the end of this bulletin.

c. Inspect the front sway bar brackets and bushings for wear or breakage. Inspect the K-frame mounting holes for wear. Replace parts as necessary.

d. Perform a thorough and accurate front suspension alignment using the following specifications:

Camber	*0 degrees with no differential between left and right*
Caster	*+2-1/2 degrees with no differential between left and right*
Total Toe In	*1/8in*

It is difficult to align a front suspension and adhere to exact specifications. It is strongly recommended that these specifications be adhered to as closely as possible. The following specifications should be used as the maximum deviation allowed.

Camber:	*Up to -1/4 degree*
Caster:	*Up to an additional +1/4 degree on left side of vehicle*
Total Toe In:	*Up to 3/1in*

If the vehicle has exhibited a repeated deterioration in camber adjustment or has required repeated front suspension alignments to correct a negative camber condition, request a new K-frame from Motor Transport Section.

The consensus of those involved is that the K-frame weakness problem was under control by mid-year 1987 and essentially corrected by the 1988 model year. The 1985 and 1986 model year Diplomats and Gran Furys appear to be the most affected.

The bad news was the problem indeed happened. The good news was two solid solutions to the problem were made by Chrysler Corp. Over 90 percent of the M-body squads could be repaired by the easiest of these two solutions.

By 1988, the Diplomat and Gran Fury were back at Los Angeles County vehicle test site being driven as hard as any vehicle ever was. Skeptical motor pool mechanics, quick to criticize based on the previous year's experience, watched intently.

After sixteen punishing laps at the hands of four different police pursuit instructors, the subjective ratings were one 'good' and three 'good plus.'

The next test was eight 60mph consecutive impending skid stops. This was the maximum deceleration possible. Then the acid test. The ninth stop was a full wheel lock up stop from 60mph.

Evidence of fade prior to locking?	No
Would brakes lock?	Yes
Vehicle stopped in straight line?	Yes
Vehicle stopped within correct lane?	Yes

Some of the responses included: 'A great showing,' 'good fade resistance,' 'No pulling left or right,' 'just one rear wheel lockup one time, but no stability problems nor lane violations.'

And how was the Diplomat with the K-frame problems now behind it? It was generally described by all test drivers as having overall good handling.

Considering the source and with the handling and braking problems of the past still fresh in mind, that was high praise.

References

Insufficient Positive Camber Adjustment," C.R. Klapec, *Technical Service Bulletin*, Chrysler Corporation, December 22, 1986.

K-member Replacement," California Highway Patrol, *Motor Transport Bulletin*, 87-08, 87-18, 88-22, 88-23.

Personal interviews with Chuck Swift, of Swift Dodge, Sacramento, CA; Dan Krans, Chrysler Corp. fleet service engineer; Sgt. Kevin Gordon, Cahokia, IL Police; Keith Mesey, mechanic, Cahokia, IL Police.

"Officer Survey" (see Chapter 46)

"Aspen R/T," staff report, *Motor Trend*, February, 1976

"Dodge Mirada," Rich Ceppos, *Car & Driver*, September 1979

Vehicle Testing and Evaluation Program, Los Angeles County Sheriffs Dept., 1980 and 1988

"Chrysler's Turn, Cornering Mopar's Muscle Cars," Al Kirschenbaum, *Hot Rod*, June 1981

Chapter 9

1984: Best M-body Model Year

In 1984, the full-size, V-8 powered cars started to gain popularity again. The timing could not have been worse. The Dodge, Chrysler and Plymouth car lines were made up of tiny, fuel-efficient, front wheel drive cars. The Dodge Mirada was gone. In fact, the only two V-8 powered, rear-drive cars made by Dodge or Plymouth were the Diplomat and Gran Fury.

Chrysler Corp. bragged they had the highest Corporate Average Fuel Economy (CAFE) in the industry at 27.4mph. Dodge boasted their CAFE rating was right in line with government standards. Big deal. The customers were fed up with

The Dodge Aries K with the AHB police package got more horsepower and better gearing for 1984. It was as fast as the 318ci, 2-bbl Diplomat. *Chrysler*

wheezing, 4-cylinder econo-boxes. They wanted roomy, powerful cars again. This boosted the sales of the V-8 M-bodies if for no other reason than they were the only V-8 cars Dodge and Plymouth had!

For 1984, two engines of significance were no longer available. First, the Slant Six was gone. Introduced as a police engine in 1960, the 225ci in-line 6-cylinder, canted 30 degrees on its side. It missed just one year of police service until being dropped after 1983. This made the Slant Six the longest running of all Mopar police engines.

The Slant Six simply lost the technology race. The OHC 4-cylinder Chrysler and Mitsubishi engines produced as much power as the veteran Slant Six and did it with 25 percent better EPA City fuel economy ratings.

The real crisis for cops was the dumping of the electronic fuel injected 318ci engine. This140hp wedge was never a police engine and was only available in the Chrysler Imperial. However, since its 1981 introduction, cops knew they would eventually get the e.f.i. mill. After all, nearly every great cop engine in history came from the Chrysler luxury cars. There was no reason to think the injected small block V-8 would be any different.

In fact, police fleet managers all but begged for the engine. In 1984, those hopes were dashed. The 4-cyl passenger cars would get throttle body fuel injection later in this model year. However, an injected, Chevy-stomping, Porsche-chasing, Mustang-thumping V-8 for the Diplomat and Gran Fury was not to be.

Dodge and Plymouth had four squads for 1984 and a total of four police engines. This was the leanest police fleet fielded by Chrysler Corp. in years.

Just four car models were available with the police package:

Model Code	Body Style	Car Line	Wheelbase
MGL41	4-door sedan	Dodge Diplomat Pursuit	112.7in
MBL41	4-door sedan	Plymouth Gran Fury Pursuit	112.7in
KDL41	4-door sedan	Dodge Aries Patrol	100.3in
KPL41	4-door sedan	Plymouth Reliant Patrol	100.3in

The four police-spec engines were:

Code	Engine Displ. & Carb.	Availability	Net Torque (lb-ft)	Net HP
EDE	2.2 L (135ci) 2-bbl, 4 cyl	Aries/Reliant	119@3200rpm	96@5200rpm
EEA	2.6 L (156ci) 2-bbl, 4 cyl	Aries/Reliant	140@2800rpm	101@4800rpm
ELD	5.2 L (318ci) 2-bbl, V-8	Diplomat/Gran Fury	235@1600rpm	130@4000rpm
ELE	5.2 L (318ci) 4-bbl, V-8	Diplomat/Gran Fury	240@1600rpm	165@4400rpm

For 1984 Chrysler Corp. adopted a new alphabetic coding system. This replaced the alpha-numeric codes used since the 1960s. See the chapter on VIN decoding. Examples of familiar police codes and the changes are:

	Old	New
Police Package	A38	AHB
318ci, 4-bbl engine	E48	ELE
P215/70R15 tires	U63	TMA
318ci, 2-bbl engine	E45	ELD

These were number and code changes only. The M-body and the K-car squads were almost unchanged from 1983—Diplomat, Gran Fury. The only significant change in the backbone of law enforcement vehicles was in the transmission. The big block A727 trans was used with the 318ci hp through 1983. For 1984, the ELE 318ci, 4-bbl engines received a new small block transmission, code A999.

The A999 was based to a large degree on the proven A904 TorqueFlite. Most of the components are interchangeable. Certainly the physical size of the A999 and A904 are the same. Side by side with a big block A727 trans, the small block A999/A904 trans was obvious.

The A904 trans was not obsolete. The ELD 318ci, 2-bbl engine still used a variation of the A904 called the A998. The A904 had been a durable police trans behind both Slant Six and 2-bbl V-8 engines. By their very class of police work, these taxi-class and patrol-class transmissions get tougher miles than the highway and pursuit cars. The ELD 2-bbl engine and the ELE 4-bbl engine produced nearly the same pounds-feet of torque. The change from a big block to small block trans for the ELE 4-bbl cars was a very low risk.

Specifically, Chrysler modified the basic small block TorqueFlite for 4-bbl police use by:
1. Increasing the number of clutches to five
2. Using double wrapped bands
3. Using a heavier duty main pump

As a general rule, the 3-clutch A904 was used with a Slant Six engine. The 4-clutch or 5-clutch A998 was used with 318ci, 2-bbl engines. The A999 which always had 5-clutches was used with 360ci and 318ci hp engines.

As early as 1975, the four-clutch A998 was used with 360ci, 2-bbl engines in the Coronets. The E57 360ci, 2-bbl pro-duced 180 net hp and 290 net pounds of torque. The additional fifth clutch in the A999 allowed it to easily handle the 165 net hp and 240 net pounds of torque from the ELE 318ci, 4-bbl. The trick drag race setup at the time was to install six, thinner Fairbanks clutches in the five-clutch A999 trans. This could handle any torque a small block V-8 could produce.

The A999 has wide-ratio gears and a lockup torque converter as the A904 had since 1981. For the record, the big block A727 was always set up with the close-ratio planetary gears. The 4-bbl cars did not get wide ratio transmissions until the A727 was dropped. The 1981 through 1983 318ci, 4-bbl cars could certainly have used the quicker gear set. Again, this was a change to the ELE 318ci drivetrain only.

	1983 & Earlier	1984 & Later
First Gear	2.45	2.74
Second Gear	1.45	1.54
Third Gear	1.00	1.00

The 2-bbl V-8 and Slant Six cars had wide-ratio trans gearing since 1981. The wide-ratio trans improved acceleration without any affect on fuel economy. Some argued it actually helped the fuel economy, since the car got to cruising speeds with less throttle. This was the same street based logic used by *Motor Trend* and LASD in the mid-1970s. Gearing too low and gearing too high both wasted fuel.

On the topic of wasting fuel due to improper gear selection, the 318ci, 2-bbl cars still came with 2.24:1 rear gears. Amazing. This produced a three-way frustration of poor city mileage, poor acceleration and low top speeds. The only 318ci, 2-bbl cars that came standard with the 2.94:1 rear gear were the limited-build "oil field special" package cars. Taxis also had the base economy of the 2.24:1 rear gear. As an obscure option, the 2-bbl cars could be fitted with the optional 2.94:1 gears, but the fleet manager had to know how to ask for it.

How slow were these 318ci, 2-bbl M-bodies? At the annual Michigan State Police tests, the ELD 2-bbl Gran Fury had the same acceleration, quarter mile performance and top speed as the Reliant K fitted with the EEA 156ci, 2-bbl. The K-cars had whipped the Slant Six M-bodies each time they faced off. But beating the V-8 cars meant something was wrong with the V-8 cars. There was: poor rear gearing even with the wide-ratio TorqueFlite.

For 1984, Dodge produced V-8 Diplomat and 4-cylinder Aries K police cars. *Chrysler*

This ex-Kansas City, Missouri Police 1984 Diplomat is in California Highway Patrol trim. This is the last year for the Carter ThermoQuad 4-bbl.

The ELE 4-bbl squad cars did well at the Michigan tests again in 1984. They had the quickest zero to 100mph times, the greatest top speed by a close margin, the second strongest brakes and second quickest MIS road course times.

Notice, too, that the competition from Ford and Chevrolet was tough. Less than 1/2 second separated all four eligible patrol cars around the 1.64-mile road racing course at Michigan International Speedway. Once Again the Michigan State Police test procedure declared the Plymouth Gran Fury the best overall squad car of all the models they tested in 1984.

In 1984, the National Highway Traffic Safety Administration funded a study of the air bag as a supplemental restraint system. The California Highway Patrol was among six state police departments to install air bags in squad cars. The CHP installed five air bags in their 1984 Crown Vic squad cars. They retrofitted 100 1983 Dodge Diplomats, already in service, with

The Illinois Secretary of State Police used this slick-top 1984 Dodge Diplomat. *Dave Dotson*

the air bags. The rest, as they say, is history. All Dodge Diplomats and Plymouth Gran Furys came with factory-installed air bags after May 1988.

K-Car. For 1984, the Reliant K and Aries K were still being heavily promoted as roomy 6-passenger cars.

Front headroom and legroom-the most important comfort dimensions in police duty-are actually bigger than the 1984 Ford LTD and Tempo, Mercury Marquis and Topaz. And there's more front legroom than in the 1983 Cadillac Deville and Brougham sedans, according to official MVMA dimensions. Furthermore, the driver's seat adjusts 7.5 inches front to rear in Aries and Reliant for a big range of driver sizes.
(Dodge Police literature)

The Chrysler 2.2L/135ci 4-cylinder engine used in police cars was unchanged for 1984. However, by late in the 1984 model year, the passenger car version of this engine had been upgraded to single-point, throttle-body, fuel injection. The police EDE version remained carbureted through all of 1984 and all of 1985.

In 1986, the police K-cars got e.f.i. These became the first Chrysler Corp. police sedans to ever get a fuel injected engine. And it was only available in 1986 and 1987. The 135ci, e.f.i. engine produced almost exactly the same horsepower and torque as the 135ci, 2-bbl engine.

The Mitsubishi EEA 2.6L/156ci, 4-cylinder engine was upgraded for 1984. A compression boost, and re-calibrated carburetion and ignition increased the horsepower by 8 net hp to 101 net hp. Again, a horsepower increase like that is hard to come by when performance was so readily discarded by all auto makers to get better CAFE ratings.

The K-cars also had a gearing change in 1984 which was for the better. Both 4-cylinder engines got snappier final gears:

	135ci 2-bbl	156ci 2-bbl
1982	2.78	2.78
1983	2.78	3.02
1984	3.02	3.22

With more horsepower and better final gearing, the Reliant K with the EEA 156ci engine was a relative screamer at the Michigan State Police runoffs. It had the same 13 second 0 to 60mph time as the ELD 318ci, 2-bbl powered Gran Fury. It had roughly the same top speed at 105mph. The quarter mile times were just .01sec and .8mph different.

The real challenge came when the similar interior room and different fuel economy were factored in to the equation. The M-body had 53.9cu-ft of interior space compared to the 52.2cu-ft from the K-car. And check out the gas mileage differences:

Vehicle	Engine	EPA City
M-body	318ci, 4-bbl	14.6mpg
M-body	318ci, 2-bbl	16.5mpg
K-car	156ci, 2-bbl	23.2mpg
K-car	135ci, 2-bbl	25.6mpg

The comparison was clear. The 156ci powered K-car was a far better taxi-class squad than both the 2-bbl M-body and the 135ci powered K-car. The 135ci K-car was two full seconds slower in the quarter mile than the bigger engined K-car. The EEA powered K-car also humiliated the 302ci H.O. fuel injected Crown Victoria in straight line performance.

The Dodge and Plymouth K-cars had new and direct competition in 1984: the Chevrolet Celebrity. The Eurosport-based bowtie was powered by a 2.8L/173ci V-6 producing 112 net hp. Not good enough. The performance of the Celebrity was midway between the EDE and EEA K-cars. While the Celebrity had a bit more interior volume, even the big engined K-car got better

gas mileage. Chevrolet dropped the Celebrity police package after 1986.

An "Officers Survey" was sent to over 200 city, county and state police departments nationwide as part of research for this book. See Chapter 17 on this Survey. One of the key survey questions was which Chrysler product was the best overall police car. So far the results have been:

First:	1980 Dodge St. Regis, 360ci, 4-bbl
Second:	1978 Plymouth Fury, 440ci, 4-bbl
Third, tie:	1969 Dodge Polara, 440ci, 4-bbl
Third, tie:	1969 Plymouth Belvedere, 383ci, 4-bbl

Rounding out the Top Five were the M-body squads powered by the 318ci, 4-bbl. Literally every year from 1981 through 1989 received votes. The votes for the Diplomat and Gran Fury were in equal proportion to their sales volume, the edge going to the Diplomat.

The word from the street was the Diplomat and Gran Fury were popular with beat cops. This was inspite of its mid-size interior volume, small-block engine and transverse torsion bar problems. Cops grew to really like the M-body squads!

Many cops mentioned the better suspension and brakes compared to the competition. The M-body squads really were

This 1984 Dodge Diplomat is the best of the breed of M-bodies. This was the first year for the A999 transmission with wide ratio gearing. *Jim Post*

The 1984 M-bodies like this Dodge Diplomat had the most performance of any M-body. This included the quickest quarter mile, the highest trap speed and the fastest top speed. *Jim Post*

Here's an Illinois State Police 1984 Dodge Diplomat with low profile markings. *Dave Dotson*

brick-shaped pony cars. Even the square, no-nonsense profile was strongly favored by many cops. Most cops also knew the 318ci powerplant gave the same overall performance as the 350 and 351ci competition. The M-bodies were not blistering fast, even in 4-bbl trim but then no 4-door squad until the 1990s got over 121mph.

Yes, the Diplomat and Gran Fury were 19 second quarter mile cars. No, this is not quick by drag racing standards. However, with their stiff suspension and phenomenal brakes, these M-body squads could indeed catch 14 second cars given enough time. According to Chuck Swift of Swift Dodge, these were about the most bullet-proof cars ever built. That, too, makes up for the 19 second quarter mile times.

Since the votes for Fifth Overall best Mopar were evenly cast, the authors will decide the winner from the nine years of M-body production. And the winner is...

Fifth: 1984 Diplomat and Gran Fury, 318ci, 4-bbl

The 1984 squads were the first year for some changes and the last year for others. The resulting performance and economy

from these changes were what made the 1984 cars stand out from all other years.

First, this was the last year for the Carter Thermo Quad. From 1985 and on, Chrysler's police cars were fed by GM's carburetor. That rubbed most Mopar enthusiasts the wrong way. Carter has literally meant Mopar performance for decades.

They could tolerate a Holley carb as a substitute. In fact, many enthusiasts (gasp) even favor a Holley carb. But in no way did the Rochester Quadra Jet 4-bbl belong on a Mopar cop motor. It was a purist sort of objection. The 1984 M-bodies were the last 4-bbl cars to use the famous Carter Thermo Quad.

The second reason the 1984 Diplomat and Gran Fury stood out from the other M-bodies was the transmission. This was a bit more controversial. In 1984, the 4-bbl cars went to wide ratio gearing. Acceleration was immediately improved. The wide-ratio cars got to 60mph .6 second quicker on the average than the close-ratio cars. The wide-ratio cars had zero to 100mph times a full 2.1 second faster than the close-ratio cars.

Some of this straightline improvement was in the gearing itself. Some of it was due to the small block A999 trans, also new for 1984. Most cops found the A999 to be as durable as the big-block A727 trans. However, cops in Honolulu in particular, were critical of the switch to a lighter duty automatic. So noted.

The one clear advantage the small block TorqueFlite had over the big block was faster acceleration. Drag racers had exploited this fact for years. Since the A999 was a half scale A727, it had half the inertia and wrapped up twice as fast. At least, that was the concept.

The A999 was durable "enough" and allowed the engine to be much more responsive. Overall, the A999 was a performance improvement, and it first appeared on 4-bbl squads in 1984.

The 1984 small block V-8 engines had a 8.4:1 compression, while the 318ci, 4-bbl starting in 1986 had a lower 8.0:1 compression. We naturally favored the squads with higher compression. Alert gearheads may point out the 1985 M-body 4-bbl cars had 10 more horsepower than the pre-1985 cars, and this rating continued even through the loss in compression. Maybe so.

This brightly-marked, strobe light bar-equipped 1984 Diplomat is a Nassau County, New York Highway Patrol unit. *Ned Schwartz*

The results, however, showed the 1985 cars, even with more horsepower, the same wide-ratio TorqueFlite and 2.94:1 gear, produced the second slowest straight line drag times of all nine years of M-body production.

The 1984 cars were also better than the other years of M-body squads for a more negative reason. The 1984 cars had fewer K-frame problems than other M-bodies in the mid-1980s. This problem peaked in 1985. The 1984 cars seemed to miss that bullet, or at least most of those bullets.

Overall, the 1984 cars get the nod for the best of the M-bodies for the exact reason Mopars in general get the nod—Performance.

The 1984 M-bodies, led by the Gran Fury had:
1. Best 0-60mph time at 10.88sec.
2. Fastest 0-100mph time at 34.43sec
3. Quickest 1/4 mile ET at 18.20sec
4. Fastest 1/4 mile trap speeds at 77.5mph
5. Highest top speed at 121.4mph
6. Second best fuel mileage at 14.6mpg

The straightline performance for 1984 was a unique amount of all years of M-body production. The 1984 cars were the only year a Carter Thermo Quad fed an 8.4:1 engine and transferred the power through a wide-ratio TorqueFlite. There was just one model year for that powertrain combination—1984.

The fuel economy advantage was eye-opening. The change to GM's Rochester Quadra Jet marked a full 2mpg drop in EPA city ratings. With a 1981 peak of 15.5mpg and a 1984 rating of 14.6mpg, the Quadra Jet powered squads managed just 12.2 to 12.7mpg the rest of the 1980s.

The 1984 Diplomat and Gran Fury also produced the first huge drop in Michigan Int'l Speedway road course times. The first three M-body model years starting in 1981 averaged lap times of 92.60 seconds. The 1984 cars sizzled through the course 2-1/2 seconds faster at 90.01 seconds. Swish. One Mississippi. Two Mississippi. Three Mississippi. Swish. That was a fourteen car length lead.

The 1984 M-bodies were the first Dodge and Plymouth squads to be faster around the MIS road course than the leg-

The vented, heavy-duty 15x7in steel wheels are obvious on this 1984 Springfield, Illinois Police Diplomat. *Dave Dotson*

endary 1980 Dodge St. Regis/Gran Fury powered by the 360ci, 4-bbl. Even though brakes and tires would improve for the rest of the 1980s, no M-body model was more than 1-1/2 seconds faster than the 1984 cars.

The Michigan State Police saw these improvements coming. The primary purpose of their tests, like the LAPD/LASD, was to improve the breed. For 1984, the MSP set the standard for 0-60mph times 1 second tougher and the 0-100mph times 3-1/2 seconds tougher. In 1983, the MSP faced reality and did not list a minimum top speed. Top speed was waived in 1982 and the 1981 top speed was a mere 105mph.

Starting in 1984, the MSP reinstated the old 100mph in 3 miles minimum standard. This was in the same league as the 1980 cars because the 1984 M-bodies could run like the 360ci, 4-bbl R-bodies. The 1981 through 1983 model years were bleak. In contrast, 1984 was a great year.

Vehicle	Sales
Dodge Diplomat AHB pkg.	10,330 units
Plymouth Gran Fury AHB pkg.	6,661 units

This green trimmed 1984 Diplomat served the Broward County, Florida Sheriff's Dept. *Dave Dotson*

1984 Police Car Performance Michigan State Police

Vehicle	Engine	0-60 mph	0-100 mph	Top Speed	1/4mi ET	Trap	MIS Road Course	Brake Power
Chevrolet Impala 9C1	350ci, 4-bbl	10.30sec	37.18sec	116.4mph	17.8sec	76.0mph	89.97sec	26.38fps2
Plymouth Gran Fury AHB	ELE 318ci, 4-bbl	10.88sec	34.43sec	121.4mph	18.2sec	77.5mph	90.01sec	25.61fps2
Dodge Diplomat AHB	ELE 318ci, 4-bbl	11.02sec	34.57sec	118.8mph	18.23sec	76.8mph	90.40sec	23.36fps2
Ford Crown Vic Police	351 HOci, 2VV	12.45sec	40.36sec	118.1mph	19.25sec	76.5mph	90.07sec	26.33fps2
Ford Mustang SSP	302 HOci, 4-bbl	7.43sec	20.77sec	129.6mph	15.90sec	89.0mph	n/a	24.64fps2
Ford Mustang SSP	302 HOci, p.f.i.	9.00sec	25.99sec	118.3mph	16.88sec	83.5mph	86.81sec	24.64fps2
Ford LTD Police	302 HOci, p.f.i.	10.29sec	29.89sec	122.6mph	17.76sec	79.5mph	88.41sec	24.36fps2
Plymouth Gran Fury AHB	ELD 318ci, 2-bbl	13.11sec	60.75sec	106.2mph	19.50sec	71.8mph	n/a	25.61fps2
Plymouth Reliant AHB	EEA 156ci, 2-bbl	13.17sec	n/a	105.3mph	19.51sec	71.0mph	92.88sec	23.60fps2
Ford Crown Vic Police	302 HOci, p.f.i.	14.39sec	n/a	100.5mph	19.78sec	69.8mph	n/a	26.33fps2
Chevrolet Celebrity Police	173ci, 2-bbl	13.90sec	61.54sec	110.7mph	19.95sec	71.8mph	93.15sec	24.31fps2
Dodge Aries AHB	EDE 135ci, 2-bbl	14.85sec	n/a	101.9mph	21.50sec	71.0mph	n/a	23.60fps2
Chevroler Impala 9C1	229ci, 2-bbl	18.57sec	n/a	101.0mph	21.93sec	64.8mph	n/a	26.38fps2

1984 Passenger Car Performance

Vehicle	Engine	0-60 mph	1/4mi ET	Trap	Top Speed	Reference
1984 Chevrolet Corvette	350ci, e.f.i.	6.1sec	14.5sec	96mph	155mph	MT July 1984
1984 Pontaic Trans Am	305ci, 4-bbl	7.0sec	15.4sec	92mph	135mph	MT July 1984
1984 Buick Grand National	231ci, turbo	7.5sec	15.9sec	88mph	116mph	MT December 1983
1984 Dodge Daytona Z	135ci, turbo	8.1sec	16.0sec	85mph	122mph	MT September 1983

Plymouth Gran Fury and Chrysler LeBaron M-Body Performance Summary
Michigan State Police

Model Year	Engine	HP	Ratio	1/4mi ET	1/4mi Trap	0-60 mph	0-100 mph	Top Speed	Vehicle Dynamics	Fuel Economy
1981	318ci, 4-bbl	165hp	8.4:1	18.90sec	73.5mph	12.86sec	45.24sec	114.7mph	1:32.54	15.5mpg
1982	318ci, 4-bbl	165hp	8.4:1	19.08sec	76.5mph	12.24sec	39.36sec	116.3mph	1:32.63	13.8mpg
1983	318ci, 4-bbl	165hp	8.5:1	19.10sec	76.5mph	12.38sec	39.68sec	120.0mph	1;32.64	14.0mpg
1984	318ci, 4-bbl	165hp	8.4:1	18.20sec	77.5mph	10.88sec	34.43sec	121.4mph	1:30.01	14.6mpg
1985	318ci, 4-bbl	175hp	8.4:1	19.23sec	73.8mph	12.60sec	42.00sec	119.4mph	1:30.69	12.6mpg
1986	318ci, 4-bbl	175hp	8.0:1	18.80sec	73.8mph	11.58sec	36.58sec	119.4mph	1:29.43	12.2mpg
1987	318ci, 4-bbl	175hp	8.0:1	19.18sec	75.0mph	12.39sec	38.64sec	117.5mph	1:29.77	12.7mpg
1988	318ci, 4-bbl	175hp	8.0:1	19.01sec	74.8mph	12.14sec	40.13sec	117.0mph	1:29.43	12.7mpg
1989	318ci, 4-bbl	175hp	8.0:1	18.63sec	76.2mph	11.77sec	38.02sec	120.2mph	1:28.63	12.7mpg

This 1984 Edinburgh, Indiana Police Diplomat has aftermarket beauty rings to dress-up dog dish hub caps. *Dave Dotson*

References

Standard Catalog of Chrysler, John Lee, Jim Benjaminson, John Gunnell, Krause Publications

Patrol Vehicle Specification, Evaluation and Purchasing Program, Michigan State Police, 1984

Officers Survey

Police and Fleet Vehicles, Chrysler Corporation, 1984

Personal communication, Chuck Swift, Swift Dodge, Sacramento, CA

"Burkhardt on Pursuits," Dale Burkhardt, *Chrysler Power*, January 1993

"Tougher TorqueFlite," Cliff Gromer, *High Performance Mopar*, January 1989

Chapter 10

1985: Rochester QuadraJet Era Begins

In 1985, the Dodge and Plymouth AHB Patrol/Pursuit package was available on just four models:

MGL41	4-door sedan	Dodge Diplomat Pursuit
MBL41	4-door sedan	Plymouth Gran Fury Pursuit
KDL41	4-door sedan	Dodge Aries patrol
KPL41	4-door sedan	Plymouth Reliant Patrol

The Aries K and Reliant K had re-styled sheet metal and upgraded interiors for 1985. The two 4-cylinder front-wheel drive trains, however, were complete carry-overs from 1984. No fuel injection was available on these cop cars yet. They still used 2-bbl carburetors. Once again for 1985, the Chrysler Corp. police fleet was powered by just four engines:

Code	Engine Displacement & Carb	Availability	Net Torque	Net HP
EDE	2.2 L (135ci) 2-bbl 4-cyl	Aries/Reliant	119@3200rpm	96@5200rpm
EEA	2.6 L (156ci) 2-bbl 4-cyl	Aries/Reliant	140@2800rpm	101@4800rpm
ELD	5.2 L (318ci) 2-bbl V-8	Diplomat/Gran Fury	265@2000rpm	140@3600rpm
ELE	5.2 L (318ci) 4-bbl V-8	Diplomat/Gran Fury	250@3200rpm	175@4000rpm

The big changes for 1985 took place with the V-8 powered Diplomat and Gran Fury. Both the ELD 2-bbl and the ELE 4-bbl V-8 were modified.

The 5.2-liter (318ci), two-barrel heavy-duty V-8 police engine was standard on Diplomat/Gran Fury Pursuits. This V-8 engine had been modified for 1985 to deliver the same or better performance with approximately eight percent more miles per gallon compared to 1984. This gain in fuel economy was due to the revision of the combustion chamber, higher compression ratio, and valve gear system changes.

This was "fast-burn" technology spilling over from the smaller 4-cyl engines. The 2-bbl cars had the production volumes to justify these changes. The 4-bbl cars did not, and never received "fast-burn" improvements. The "fast-burn" engines had lower overlap camshafts and were less sensitive to octane ratings.

Again, the 2-bbl police engine used standard, now upgraded, 318ci, 2-bbl heads. The 4-bbl police engine used 360ci HP heads. These were not the 360ci heads used on trucks.

Specifically, the 2-bbl engine received a large increase in compression, from 8.4:1 to 9.0:1. It also received roller tappets. That is right. The hydraulic lifters now had the trick roller cam followers for reduced friction. Finally, the Carter BBD 2-bbl was dropped after 1984. For 1985, the 2-bbl V-8 engines used the Holley 6280-series 2-bbl, for better or for worse.

All these changes to the 2-bbl engine resulted in 10 more net hp. The ELD was now rated at 140 net hp, just like the earlier Chrysler Imperial electronic fuel injected 318ci engine. The torque also increased by 20lb to 265lb.

The change to the 318ci, 2-bbl engine was evident at the MSP runoffs for 1985 model year squads. The old 1984 Gran Fury was still quicker to 60mph and in the quarter mile. The 1984 and 1985 AHB cars had exactly the same quarter mile trap

In 1985, Chrysler Corp. offered the mid-size Dodge Diplomat and Plymouth Gran Fury and the compact Dodge Aries and Plymouth Reliant. *Chrysler*

The Dodge Aries (shown) and Plymouth Reliant got sleeker sheet metal for 1985. Both 4-cylinder engines used 2-bbl carburetors. *Michael Fay and Ned Schwartz*

speeds. The 1985 Gran Fury, however, was a full 7 seconds faster to 100mph and had a 10mph better top end.

Contrary to the 8 percent increase in fuel economy hoped for by Chrysler Corp., the EPA city for the 1985 2-bbl cars were actually 2 percent worse.

Police officers are more likely to select a 2-bbl car for patrol scenarios which emphasize 0 to 60mph times and a maximum fuel economy. Fleet managers are generally less concerned with 0 to 100mph times and high top speeds on a patrol-class, 2-bbl

squad. So, the 1984 318ci, 2-bbl M-bodies, even with less horsepower and less torque might still be considered better squads than their 1985 2-bbl counterparts.

For 1985, the 318ci, 4-bbl engines used Rochester Quadra-Jet carbs instead of the classic Carter ThermoQuad. Chrysler's Bob Lees was a part of the Special Equipment Group's development team during the mid-1980s. He insisted the Rochester was a better carb overall, and a more fuel mixing efficient carb than the Carter.

This Lake George, New York Police 1985 Dodge Aries had a top speed of 100mph with the 2.6L engine. *Michael Fay and Ned Schwartz*

The 1985 4-bbl cars had 10 more horsepower and 10 more pounds of torque than the 1984 4-bbl cars. Lees was positive this increase in horsepower came strictly from the better flow of the Rochester QuadraJet.

As in the changes to the 2-bbl V-8 engines, changes to the 4-bbl V-8 were quite evident at the MSP runoffs. The 1984 cars, however, were better performers in every single test conducted by the MSP. Compared to the 1985 QuadraJet Plymouths, the 1984 ThermoQuad Plymouths had:

    a. faster acceleration to 60mph by 1.7sec
    b. faster acceleration to 100mph by 7.6sec
    c. quicker quarter mile ET by 1.0sec
    d. faster quarter mile trap by 3.7sec
    e. greater top speed by 2.0mph
    f. quicker MIS lap times by .60sec
    g. better EPA city mileage by 2.0mpg

This was not a case of the 1984 Plymouth being a ringer and the 1985 Plymouth a lemon. The 1984 Dodge likewise ran circles around the 1985 Dodge by the same performance margins as the two model years of Plymouth. The changes made to the 1985 ELE 4-bbl engine, specifically the QuadraJet, really appeared to hurt the overall performance.

Lees attributes the poor first-year showing of the QuadraJet to "heat." Late summer in south Michigan can be unbearably hot. Vapor lock can be a significant problem. This was deemed so much of a problem, that Chrysler developed their optional Anti-Vapor Lock Package, Chrysler Part No. 4397613. This was nothing other than a gas tank mounted electric fuel pump. Cars with this package still retained the engine mounted electric fuel pump. The two pumps worked together. The electric fuel pump specifically pushed the gasoline through any areas of vapor lock. It worked.

The 1986 through 1989 QuadraJet-powered, M-bodies did have slightly quicker MIS lap times than the 1984 ThermoQuad

This 1985 Dodge Diplomat was the last Mopar squad used by the Pennsylvania State Police. *Joe Gavula*

cars. However, this improvement was due much more to tires than any other reason. The newer cars used the better performing Goodyear Eagle GT radials. It is no coincidence the best MIS lap times for any M-body car were in 1989. That was the year the Michigan State Police requested super-sticky Goodyear Eagle GT+4 tires for all test cars.

The measure of engine performance is straightline acceleration including top speed. At no time did a QuadraJet-equipped M-body come close to equaling the ThermoQuad-equipped M-body performance when both used the same wide-ratio transmission.

In October 1976, The American City and County trade magazine published this ominous warning regarding Steel-belted Pursuit Radials:

This Pennsylvania State Police 1985 Diplomat is powered by a 318ci V-8 with a Rochester QuadraJet 4-bbl. *Joe Gavula*

AHB Patrol Tires

Model	Code	Tire Type	Tire Size
Diplomat & Gran Fury Pursuit	TMH	Steel-belted radial ply	P215/70HR15raised performance police type black letter
Aries & Reliant Patrol	TJE	Steel-belted radial ply	P185/70HR14 raised performance police type black Patrol letter

Fabric Radial Recommended. Manufacturers recommend specially designed police radial tires or fabric radials for use on pursuit cars. Steel-belted radials are no longer recommended by either the car makers or the Law Enforcement Assistance Administration (LEAA).

An LEAA study to determine the cause of a crash that killed police officers in a high-speed chase found the car's steel-belted radials had shattered, causing the fatal accident. "Any department that puts steel-belted radials on a pursuit car has no room to complain if there's an accident," says auto expert Ray Wynne, Director of Police Transportation for the City of Los Angeles.

Fabric radials, which do not shatter or split at high speeds, were favored by law enforcement agencies over standard tires because of better handling and longer tire life. Most radial manufacturers guarantee their tires for 40,000 miles.

That was 1976. As recently as 1984, all Dodge and Plymouth AHB police package cars came from the factory with Fabric-belted, radial-ply, high-performance, police-type radials. Chrysler Corp. did not forbid the use of steel-belted tires. They did, however, recommend against bias and bias-belted tires, and against non-high performance, police-type tires.

In 1983, the Michigan State Police specified Goodyear Rayon Police Special radials. However, in 1984, the MSP adopted steel-belted, but speed-rated, Goodyear Eagle GT radials. This marked the first of the modern speed-rated radials on police cars. The H-rating was good for speeds up to 130mph.

The tire industry solved the problem of steel belt separation at high speeds by a number of construction changes. The steel-belted tires had a circumferential belt to hold the belts together at high speeds. These tires also received polyester and rayon belt reinforcements. In the form of end caps around the steel belt edges, this diffused the heat generated by the steel belts. The heat was kept from being focused on one area of the sidewall near the tread.

As a result of these improvements, in 1985 Dodge and Plymouth police cars came from the factory with steel-belted pursuit radials. This was also the first year Chrysler Corp. supplied speed-rated tires. The previous 1984 model tires were fabric-belted and did not carry a formal speed rating of any kind.

Important Tire Notice: High-speed radial tires with steel belts are standard with the 1985 Plymouth and Dodge Police Car Packages. These tires have been tested for good handling

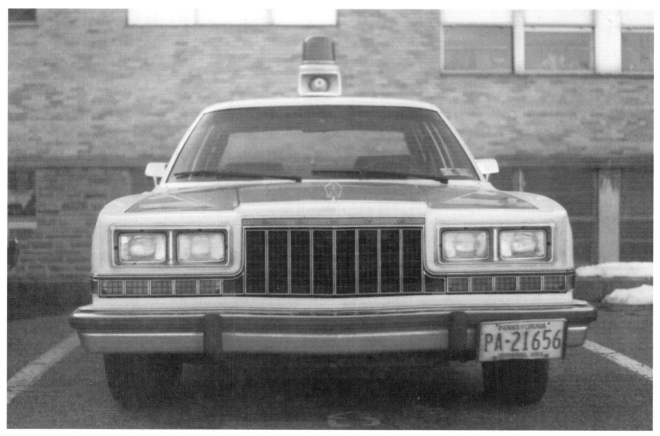

This is the rear view mirror view of a Pennsylvania State Police Diplomat. With a 10hp boost, these cars had top speeds from 117 to 119mph. *Joe Gavula*

characteristics by Chrysler Corporation. Tires other than high-performance police type should not be used for speeds over 100mph.

The suspension system on all Plymouth and Dodge AHB Police Car Packages is designed to provide optimum handling with radial tires. The use of bias or bias-belted tires is not recommended.

The change to speed-rated, steel-belted radials such as the Goodyear Eagle GT, General XP-2000 and Firestone Aerofire was the last significant change in tires during the police career of the Chrysler Corp. squads.

The much-slower-for-1985 M-bodies got beat up at the annual Michigan State Police tests. Of the four patrol-class, 4-door sedans, eligible for the MSP contract, Ford had the best road course times and the quickest acceleration to 100mph. Chevrolet had the best ergonomics and fuel economy. The Diplomat and Gran Fury shared top honors in braking power and top speed.

In spite of a less than awesome showing, the combined overall performance of the Mopar squads was high enough. When the overall performance was figured into the bid price, the MSP contract was issued to the 1985 Dodge Diplomat AHB even though it had a General Motors carburetor. This was the first Dodge-marque squad selected by the MSP process. The California Highway Patrol also selected the Dodge Diplomat as the best overall 1985 squad for their patrol scenarios.

Honorable mention from the 1985 MSP runoffs went to the Chevrolet Celebrity 9C1. The 2.8L engine was available with either a 2-bbl or electronic fuel injection. The injected Celebrity was a screamer. It was too much for the Reliant K to handle, even when equipped with the bigger EEA Mitsubishi engine. The K-cars got shut out in terms of performance this year, even if the EEA K-car could out drag the 2-bbl V-8 M-body. Chrysler Corp. tried to solve this problem by introducing fuel injected K-cars for 1986.

Police sales of the Diplomat and Gran Fury remained strong. The Mopar squads took a bit more than one third of the police market in 1985.

Vehicle	Sales
Dodge Diplomat AHB	14,834 units
Plymouth Gran Fury	7,152 units

ELD 318ci, 2-bbl Gran Fury AHB
Michigan State Police

	1984	1985
Carburetion	Carter BBD	Holley 6280
Net Horsepower	130hp@4000	140hp@3600
Net Torque	235lb@1600	265lb@2000
Test Weight	3853lb	3771lb
Rear Gear	2.24:1	2.24:1
0-60mph	13.11sec	14.20sec
0-100mph	60.75sec	53.27sec
1/4mi ET	19.50sec	20.05sec
1/4mi Trap	71.8mph	71.8mph
Top Speed	106.2mph	116.1mph
EPA City Mileage	16.5mpg	16.1mpg

The Philadelphia, Pennsylvania Police used this 1985 Gran Fury powered by a 318ci, 2-bbl for urban patrol. *Joe Gavula*

This side view of a Philadelphia, Pennsylvania Police 1985 Gran Fury shows the heavy duty, vented 15x7in wheels. This was the first year for OEM steel belted radials. *Joe Gavula*

The 318ci, 2-bbl V-8 used on this "Philly" 1985 Gran Fury uses roller tappets, a Holley carburetor and has more compression than older 2-bbl engines. *Joe Gavula*

ELE 318 ci, 4-bbl Gran Fury AHB
Michigan State Police

	1984	1985
Carburetion	Carter ThermoQuad	Rochester QuadraJet
Net Horsepower	165hp@4000	175hp@4000
Net Torque	240lb@1600	250lb@3200
Test Weight	3888lb	3902lb
Rear Gear	2.94:1	2.94:1
0-60mph	10.88sec	12.60sec
0-100mph	34.43sec	42.00sec
1/4mi ET	18.20sec	19.23sec
1/4mi Trap	77.5mph	73.8mph
Top Speed	121.4mph	119.4mph
EPA City Mileage	14.6mpg	12.6mpg
MIS Road Course	90.01sec	90.60sec

1985 Police Car Performance
Michigan State Police

Vehicle	Engine	0-60mph	0-100mph	Top Speed	1/4 mile ET	1/4 mile Trap	MIS Road Course	Brake Power
Ford Crown Vic 55H	351ci, 2VV	12.30sec	39.78sec	116.9mph	18.80sec	75.5mph	89.6sec	26.34fps^2
Chevrolet Impala 9C1	350ci, 4-bbl	11.66sec	42.24sec	114.3mph	18.85sec	74.8mph	90.8sec	25.92fps2
Dodge Diplomat AHB	318ci, 4-bbl(ELE)	12.42sec	40.15sec	117.6mph	19.10sec	74.5mph	90.8sec	27.11fps2
Plymouth Gran Fury AHB	318ci, 4-bbl(ELE)	12.60sec	42.00sec	119.4mph	19.23sec	73.8mph	90.6sec	26.60fps2
Ford Mustang SSP	302ci, 4-bbl	7.92sec	21.72sec	135.5mph	16.08sec	87mph	85.6sec	25.66fps2
Ford Mustang SSP	302ci, c.f.i.	9.13sec	26.07sec	122.8mph	17.13sec	83mph	86.4sec	25.05fps2
Ford LTD 55H	302ci, c.f.i.	10.53sec	30.74sec	120.6mph	17.98sec	75mph	89.1sec	26.47fps2
Chevrolet Celebrity 9C1	173ci, p.f.i.	12.00sec	42.26sec	115.3mph	18.70sec	71mph	92.8sec	25.56fps2
Ford Crown Vic 55H	302ci, c.f.i.	13.55sec	59.41sec	104.4mph	19.53sec	71.5mph	n/a	26.34fps2
Chevrolet Celebrity 9C1	173ci, 2-bbl	13.87sec	55.31sec	116.1mph	19.70sec	71.8mph	n/a	25.56fps2
Plymouth Reliant K AHB	156ci, 2-bbl (EEA)	14.38sec	n/a	100.2mph	19.98sec	69mph	94.1sec	25.81fps2
Plymouth Gran Fury AHB	318ci, 2-bbl(ELD)	14.20sec	53.27sec	116.1mph	20.05sec	71.8mph	n/a	26.60fps2
Dodge Aries AHB	135ci, 2-bbl (EDE)	16.26sec	n/a	97.0mph	21.03sec	n/a	n/a	25.81fsp2

Here's a Colorado trooper with his 1985 Dodge Diplomat. *Greg Reynolds*

1985 Top Speeds

Car	0-60 mph	Top Speed	Reference
Porsche 928-S	5.7sec	154mph	CD 5/85
Chevrolet Corvette	5.7sec	150mph	CD 12/84
Chevrolet Camaro IROC	7.0sec	140mph	CD 10/84
Pontiac Trans Am	7.6sec	135mph	CD 4/85
Ford Mustang SSP	7.9sec	135mph	MSP-85
Pontiac Fiero GT	8.2sec	125mph	CD 11/84
Toyota Supra	8.4sec	125mph	CD 5/85
Dodge Shelby Charger	7.8sec	124mph	CD 12/84
Buick Grand National	7.5sec	121mph	CD 7/85
Ford LTD 55H	10.5sec	121mph	MSP-85
Plymouth Gran Fury AHB	12.6sec	119mph	MPS-85
Dodge Omni GLH	7.5sec	119mph	CD 5/85
Dodge Diplomat AHB	12.4sec	118mph	MPS-85
Chevy Monte Carlo SS	7.8sec	117mph	CD 7/85
Chrysler Laser XE	8.1sec	117mph	CD 5/85
Ford Crown Vic 55H	12.3sec	117mph	MSP-85
Chevy Celebrity 9C1	12.0sec	115mph	MSP-85
Chevy Cavalier Z24	9.5sec	114mph	CD 3/85
Chevy Impala 9C1	11.7sec	114mph	MSP-85

References

"Fabric radials recommended for pursuit," staff column, *The American City and County*, October 1976

Police and Fleet Vehicles, Chrysler Corporation, 1985

Patrol Vehicle Specification, Evaluation and Purchasing Program, Michigan State Police, 1985

Standard Catalog of Chrysler, John Lee, Jim Benjaminson, John Gunnell, Krause Publications

Personal communication, Bob Lees, Engine Group and Frank Davis, Product Planning, Special Equipment Group, Chrysler Corporation

"Burkhardt on Pursuits," Dale Burkhardt, *Chrysler Power*, January 1993.

Police Parts List, Chrysler Corporation, 1985

Chapter 11

1986: Fuel-Injected Police K-cars

For 1986, Chrysler Corp. repeated the previous two years by offering just four police models and four police engines.

Model Code	Body Style	Car Line
MGL41	4-door sedan	Dodge Diplomat Pursuit
MBL41	4-door sedan	Plymouth Gran Fury Pursuit
KDL41	4-door sedan	Dodge Aries K Patrol
KPL41	4-door sedan	Plymouth Reliant K Patrol

The big news for 1986 was fuel injection for the police package K-cars. Non-police K-cars used fuel injected engines since late in the 1984 model year. By 1986, all Inline 4-cylinder engines had electronic fuel injection.

The Aries K (AHB) and Reliant K (AHB) had annual police sales of less than 1,000 units combined. Introduced in 1982 and discontinued in 1987, many cop car enthusiasts totally overlooked these as the only fuel injected Mopar squads, ever made!

Code	Engine Displacement & Carb	Availability	Net Torque	Net HP
EDF	2.2L (135ci) EFI 4-cyl	Aries K/Reliant K	122@3200rpm	97@5200rpm
EDM	2.5L (153ci) EFI 4-cyl	Aries K/Reliant K	136@2800rpm	100@4800rpm
ELD	5.2L (318ci) 2-bbl V-8	Diplomat/Gran Fury	265@2000rpm	140@3600rpm
ELE	5.2L (318ci) 4-bbl V-8	Diplomat/Gran Fury	250@3200rpm	175@4000rpm

The West Virginia State Police used the Dodge Diplomat in 1986. These were equipped with speed-rated tires from the factory. *West Virginia State Police*

80

These K-cars used a Bosch e.f.i. system, which was a single-point, throttle body injection (t.b.i.). Throttle body injection was not as precise nor as efficient as multi-point injection. However, it was a significant improvement over both the Holley and Mikuni 2-bbl carburetors.

The 2.2L/135ci Chrysler-made 4-cylinder also received a redesigned aluminum head for 1986. This was called the "fast-burn" head. Chrysler caused a controlled turbulence in the head porting which in turn caused the gases to ignite closer to Top Dead Center (TDC).

A more controlled flame front, and one close to TDC, allowed Chrysler to increase the compression ratio on the 2.2L engine without the need for higher octane fuel. Compression was increased from 9.0:1 to 9.5:1 on the 2.2L engine only. A Chrysler-designed Electronic Control Unit automatically adjusted the air to fuel ratio and the spark timing. The end result of the "fast-burn" porting was more rapid and more complete combustion and greatly improved idling.

The peak horsepower and peak torque increased only slightly with the throttle body injection. However, the power curves were both much flatter and the engine was much more responsive at lower engine speeds.

The injected 2.2L engine outperformed the 1985 carbureted 2.2L engine in all areas. The MSP troopers found the 1986 AHB Aries K to have faster acceleration to all speeds and a greater top end, with just a 1mpg fuel economy penalty.

Also in 1986, Chrysler Corp. developed a new 2.5L 4-cylinder engine to replace the 2.6L Mitsubishi engine. The Chrysler-built EDM 2.5L/153ci engine was basically a stroked 2.2L engine. However, it was designed with twin balance shafts for smooth operation. These balance shafts rotated at twice the crankshaft speed and in the opposite direction of the crank to dampen the typical 4-cylinder engine vibrations.

The new 2.5L Chrysler engine also used an overhead cam, "fast-burn" head. And it was also equipped with the Chrysler-Bosch electronic fuel injection. Remember, the 1985 passenger K-cars received the injected Mitsubishi engine, but the cop cars did not. So for the cops, the 1986 2.5L injected engine replaced the 1985 2.6L carbureted engine. The horsepower and torque were almost identical.

The Minnesota State Patrol were loyal to the Plymouth Gran Fury in 1986. These were all 4-bbl cars. *Minnesota State Patrol*

Once again, the MSP troopers confirmed that the change to fuel injection was a good thing. The 1986 Reliant AHB with the 2.5L efi engine did everything better than the 1985 Reliant AHB with the 2.6L carbureted mill. In fact, the flatter power curve allowed the 1986 Reliant AHB to run 2.3 seconds faster around the MIS road course.

As good as the newly-injected K-cars were, the Chevrolet Celebrity in both injected and carbureted versions was still out of reach. This was discouraging. In the end, the K-car beat the Celebrity the same exact way the Aspen/Volare beat the Nova 9C1. Chevrolet dropped the Celebrity police package after 1986, citing sales volumes were too low to justify a special package.

Of course, Dodge and Plymouth knew nothing of Chevrolet's plans for the Celebrity. All they knew was the Celebrity was the front-drive, 6-passenger car to beat. Let's see. If the competition beats your latest fuel-injected engine, what do you do? Why, bolt on a turbo charger, of course!

For 1986, the Nebraska State Patrol (shown), California Highway Patrol and Michigan State Police were among the many to select the Dodge Diplomat. *Dave Dotson*

Chrysler had developed a front wheel drive 1986 1/2 Plymouth Reliant, with a 2.2 liter turbo charged four-cylinder engine, as a prototype for potential police use. The idea was to create a low-cost and fuel efficient vehicle with sufficient power for police use, but it was never widely accepted. While the prototype was a Reliant, Chrysler's police offerings would have been the sleeker Plymouth Caravelle and Dodge 600.—Ed Nowicki

That move, of course, would have solved all performance problems, period. It would also have raised maintenance issues and long-term durability questions. In an ironic move, Chrysler—the front-drive car company—made the decision to pull out of the front-drive police business.

Rather than developing a durable, high-performance, front-drive police car in mid-1986, they decided instead to drop the

This Tennessee State Police 1986 Gran Fury has a Federal Jet-Sonic lightbar and quarter panel mounted antenna. *Dave Dotson*

K-car police package after 1987. Just two years after that, they would decide to get out of rear-drive police cars because all of their technology was in front-drive cars.

DIPLOMAT AND GRAN FURY. The ELD 318ci, 2-bbl engine was a total carry-over from 1985. In a bit of curious marketing enthusiasm, the 2-bbl engines were now called "Pursuit" engines. It had not been that many years since a 2-bbl small block was the basis for a "Patroller" squad and far from a "Pursuit" squad.

The reason for this fleet enthusiasm was much better performance from the 1986 standard equipment cars. In an unusual policy reversal, the 2-bbl police M-bodies now came standard with the 2.94:1 rear gear, again. After three years of bleak performance, due entirely to the 2.24:1 rear gear ratio, the 1986 2-bbl cars with the 2.94 rear gears really moved. Their 18 second quarter mile bracket rivalled some old M-body 4-bbl times.

In comparison to the earlier 2-bbl cars, the 1986 2-bbl cars were pro-stockers. The better rear gear made it to 60mph 2 seconds quicker and to 100mph a full 10 seconds faster. The rear gear alone chopped 1.2 seconds off the quarter mile times and added 2mph to the trap speeds.

Marketing enthusiasm also spilled over to the 4-bbl cars. The top Mopar squad had always been called a "Pursuit." Not glorious enough. In 1986, Chrysler Corp. called the top-of-the-line, 4-bbl engine in the Diplomat and Gran Fury an "Interceptor" engine. Yes, in 1986, the term "Interceptor" became an official Chrysler description for a police engine. Hmmmm. Sounded like the Chrysler fleet folks had been hanging around the blue ovals too much. That was okay. Pontiac called their LeMans police car an "Enforcer" but it didn't run like the original Enforcer either.

In 1986, the ELE "Interceptor" 4-bbl engine suffered a mysterious drop in compression ratio. The reduction from 8.4 to 8.0 is mysterious for two reasons. First, the horsepower and torque remained exactly the same. Must have been more of those "advertised" horsepower readings.

Here's a Mount Prospect, Illinois 1986 Dodge Diplomat. *Greg Reynolds*

Even more mysterious was why a drop in compression would allow the 1986 4-bbl cars to run so much better than the 1985 4-bbl cars. The 1986 M-bodies had one of their best years during the Michigan State Police runoffs. Top speeds and quarter mile speeds were better. Acceleration to 60mph, to 100mph and over a quarter mile was much faster. Even the MIS road course times were quicker. One source said that Chrysler finally figured out how to get the General Motors carburetor to work on a Chrysler V-8.

Chrysler's Bob Lees, Engine Development Team, Special Equipment Group, shed a little light on this mystery. The horsepower loss due to the compression drop was recovered by spark timing improvements and some recalibrations as Chrysler got smarter about emissions. Lees said the combination of the anti-vapor lock package and the more efficient QuadraJet 4-bbl allowed the 1986 cars to turn in some of the best times of all M-body years at the MSP runoffs.

This 1986 Plymouth Gran Fury served the Philadelphia, Pennsylvania Police. *Greg Reynolds*

This Spearfish, South Dakota Police Diplomat is typical of the 1986 model year. *Greg Reynolds*

On the topic of the MSP tests, a review of the results showed exactly how competitive Dodge, Plymouth, Ford and Chevrolet really were when it came to outright performance. Of the eligible 4-door sedans, the quarter mile speeds were all within .45 seconds with trap speeds within .50mph.

The zero to 100mph times and the absolute braking power varied from make to make. However, the overall road course times were separated by just .36 seconds over a 90 second course. And that was an average spread from four different drivers.

By 1986, speed-rated tires took the police market by storm. In 1986, Chrysler Corp. re-phrased their "Important Tire Notice" for the last time. Speed-rated radials were in. All other tires were out.

All Dodge and Plymouth Police Car Packages feature special speed-rated steel-belted radial tires for safe and superior handling at speeds over 100 miles per hour. Non speed-rated tires should not be operated at speeds over 100mph. And, because the suspensions on Dodge and Plymouth Police Cars are designed for use with radial tires for optimum performance, bias and bias-belted tires are not recommended.

In 1986, the V-8 powered Diplomat and Gran Fury were hit with a CAFE-mandated "gas-guzzler" tax. It seems cars with gas economy under 26mpg got penalized. The M-bodies had lockup torque converters which helped mileage quite a bit. What they really needed was a 4-speed overdrive automatic with the lockup converter. Fords and Chevrolets would get them. The Chrysler

This 1986 Plymouth Gran Fury patrolled the roads in Erie County, Ohio. *Greg Reynolds*

Here's a 1986 Vermont State Police Gran Fury Canine Unit with full wheel covers. *Greg Reynolds*

This 1986 Dodge Diplomat houses a Newburgh, New York Police dog. *Ned Schwartz*

police cars would not. Those development dollars were directed to front-drive cars instead.

Production figures for the 1986 M-body police package cars are as follows:

Dodge Diplomat AHB   10,372 units
Plymouth Gran Fury AHB   5,133 units

For enthusiasts who are keeping track, in 1986 the Michigan State Police test methods once again selected the Dodge Diplomat AHB as the best overall squad car. This was the seventh straight time a bid modified by overall performance pointed to a Chrysler product as the best squad. This was also the last time.

Ford, and especially Chevrolet, continued to develop and improve their police package 4-door sedans. With the exception of a driver's side air bag and stainless steel exhaust, further de-

velopment of the Diplomat AHB and Gran Fury AHB stopped cold.

During the last three years of the M-body production, the ruthlessly objective MSP testing selected the Chevrolet Caprice as the better squad. Toward the end of the M-body production, the Chevrolet in fact was the better car. The police market was far too competitive for any auto maker, even Chrysler, to stop the process of continuous improvement.

For the record, the LAPD had not used a Chrysler product for "black and white" cars since 1981. The LAPD bid specs still called for a 114-inch minimum wheelbase and a 350ci minimum displacement engine. No Chrysler product since 1981 met those specs. The M-body cars had 112.7-inch wheelbases and maximum engine sizes of 318ci.

This 1986 Dodge Diplomat is a Troy, New York Police supervisor's unit. *Ned Schwartz*

This 1986 Illinois State Police Dodge Diplomat sports a wide yellow stripe. *Greg Reynolds*

This fuel-injected 1986 Aries K police package car is used by a Miami, Florida Police sergeant. This was a good supervisor's car. *Greg Reynolds*

In 1986, the California Highway Patrol selected the Dodge Diplomat as their heavy-duty, battle cruiser. The CHP selection process involved a straight "low bid" once their minimum performance standards were met. The Diplomat would continue to serve the CHP in the few years to come.

Dodge Aries AHB

Model Year	1985	1986
Engine	EDE Chrysler	EDF Chrysler
Displacement	2.2L/135ci	2.2L/135ci
Induction	Holley 2-bbl	Bosch Throttle Body Injection
Compression	9.0:1	9.5:1
Horsepower	96@5200	97@5200
Torque	119@3200	122@3200
0-60mph	16.26sec	15.50sec
Top Speed	97.0mph	101.0mph
1/4 mi. ET	21.03sec	20.70sec
1/4 mi. Trap	67.8mph	69.0mph
EPA City Mileage	24.2mpg	23.3mpg

Plymouth Reliant AHB

Model Year	1985	1986
Engine	EEA Mitsubishi	EDM Chrysler
Displacement	2.6L/156ci	2.5L/153ci
Induction	Mikuni 2-bbl	Bosch Throttle Body Injection
Horsepower	101@4800	100@4800
Torque	140@2800	136@2800
0-60mph	14.38sec	14.01sec
Top Speed	100.2mph	103.0mph
1/4 mi. ET	19.98sec	19.70sec
1/4 mi. Trap	69.0mph	70.5mph
MIS Road Course	94.1sec	91.79sec
EPA City Mileage	20.4mpg	19.6mpg

ELD 2-bbl Plymouth Gran Fury AHB

Model Year	1985	1986
Engine	318ci, 2-bbl	318ci, 2-bbl
Gear Ratio	2.24:1	2.94:1
0-60mph	14.20sec	12.06sec
0-100mph	53.27sec	43.11sec
Top Speed	116.1mph	110.1mph
1/4 mi. ET	20.05sec	18.88sec
1/4 mi. Trap	71.8mph	73.8mph

1986 Passenger Car Performance

	0-60 mph	1/4 mile ET	1/4 mile Trap	Top Speed	Reference
Chevy Camaro Z28 (5.7L)	6.4sec	14.4sec	94.6mph	n/a	MT 5/86
Buick Grand National	6.0sec	14.7sec	94.0mph	124mph	MT 6/86
Chevy Corvette L98	6.4sec	14.9sec	92.0mph	144mph	MT 11/85
Mazda RX-7 Turbo	6.5sec	14.9sec	91.0mph	145mph	MT 5/86
Pontiac Fiero GT	7.5sec	15.9sec	83.8mph	123mph	CD 2/86
Nissan 300 ZX Turbo	7.5sec	16.0sec	87.9mph	n/a	MT 5/86

1986 Police Car Performance
Michigan State Police

Vehicle	Engine	0-60 mph	0-100 mph	Top Speed	1/4 mile ET	1/4 mile Trap	MIS Road Course	Brake Power
Chevy Caprice 9C1	350ci, 4-bbl	10.92sec	37.96sec	117.0mph	18.25sec	76.0mph	89.73sec	24.20fps2
Dodge Diplomat AHB	ELE 318ci, 4-bbl	114.8sec	36.07sec	121.5mph	18.53sec	76.5mph	89.46sec	25.85fps2
Ford Crown Vic Police	351ci, 2VV	11.74sec	38.49sec	115.1mph	18.53sec	76.5mph	89.37sec	24.68fps2
Plymouth Gran Fury AHB	ELE 318ci, 4-bbl	11.58sec	36.58sec	119.4mph	18.70sec	76.3mph	89.43sec	26.71fps2
Ford Mustang SSP	302ci, p.f.i.	7.59sec	20.55sec	126.1mph	15.80sec	88.5mph	85.49sec	24.31fps2
Chevy Celebrity B4C	173ci, p.f.i.	11.30sec	38.06sec	113.8mph	18.27sec	76.0mph	89.76sec	26.43fps2
Ford Crown Vic Police	302ci, p.f.i.	12.08sec	46.57sec	106.1mph	18.80sec	74.3mph	n/a	24.68fps2
Plymouth Gran Fury AHB	ELD 318ci, 2-bbl	12.06sec	43.11sec	110.1mph	18.88sec	73.8mph	n/a	26.71fps2
Chevy Celebrity B4C	173ci, 2-bbl	12.88sec	48.68sec	113.6mph	19.47sec	73.7mph	n/a	26.43fps2
Chevy Caprice 9C1	262ci, t.b.i.	13.72sec	55.40sec	107.8mph	19.53sec	70.3mph	n/a	24.20fps2
Plymouth Reliant AHB	153ci, t.b.i.	14.01sec	n/a	103.0mph	19.70sec	70.5mph	91.79sec	26.42fps2
Dodge Aries AHB	135ci, t.b.i.	15.50sec	n/a	101.0mph	20.70sec	69.0mph	n/a	26.42fps2

This fuel-injected 1986 Reliant K police package car is seen in-service with the Cook County, Illinois Sheriff. *Greg Reynolds*

References

Patrol Vehicle Specification, Evaluation and Purchasing Program, Michigan State Police, 1986

Police and Fleet Vehicles, Chrysler Corporation, 1986

Standard Catalog of Chrysler, John Lee, Jim Benjaminson, John Gunnell, Krause Publications

"The Great American Police Car," Ed Nowicki, *Police*, December 1989

Personal communication, Bob Lees, Engine Group and Frank Davis, Product Planning, Special Equipment Group, Chrysler Corporation

Chapter 12

1987: M-bodies Move to Kenosha

Chrysler fleet sales also used the same marketing terms of reference from 1986. The K-car engines, regardless of size, were called Patrol engines. The M-body 318ci, 2-bbl engine was referred to as a Pursuit engine. The M-body 318ci, 4-bbl engine was labelled the Interceptor engine. Chrysler kept these terms through the end of M-body production.

The squads and drivetrains themselves were straight carry-overs from 1986 with one exception. All I4 and V-8 engines were now fitted with stainless steel exhaust systems for extended life. The pipe diameters were unchanged. All the cars remained single exhaust. This change significantly lowered maintenance costs for fleets that kept the cars over two years and over 75,000 miles.

This 1987 change to a stainless steel exhaust was one of only two changes that would happen with the Diplomat and Gran Fury through 1989. In May of 1988, these M-body cars came standard with driver's side air bags. That was it. Other than these two, the 1986 through 1989 M-bodies were identical in every regard.

An optional equipment shuffle took place with the ELD 318ci, 2-bbl engine. It was once again banished to a life with 2.24 rear gears. As such, the perky 153ci K-car beat the 2-bbl V-8 M-body by 1-1/2 car lengths in the quarter mile.

The automotive news for 1987 was the purchase of American Motors by Chrysler Corp. for $1.5 billion. No, this did not forgive the LAPD for using AMC Matadors in the early 1970s.

The purchase of AMC is significant to Chrysler police car enthusiasts. Chrysler took over the Kenosha, Wisconsin AMC production facility. Output of the Dodge Diplomat and Plymouth Gran Fury shifted late in the 1987 model year from Fenton, Missouri to Kenosha, Wisconsin. Some 1987 M-bodies were assembled in Kenosha, but by far most were assembled outside St. Louis in Fenton.

M-body Model Year	Assembly Plant
1981 to 1983	Windsor, Ontario
1983 to 1987	Fenton, Missouri
1987 to 1989	Kenosha, Wisconsin

Chrysler spent $200 million to retool the AMC facility for M-body production. They also hinted that AMC might play a role in determining the next generation of police car. All Chrysler Corp. would commit to in 1987 was to keep the M-body in production through 1989. Beyond that, they were not making any promises.

Late in the 1987 model year, Dodge hinted their 1988 Dynasty might be fitted with a police package. The Dynasty was a front-drive, 6-passenger car powered by an e.f.i. V-6.

This was no idle statement. Ford had announced in mid-1986 that a police package Taurus would be at the 1987 Michigan State Police runoffs. Remember that. The Taurus 3.8L e.f.i. V-6, 6-passenger car was not upgraded to police package status for 1987 and as a result did not compete at the MSP vehicle tests.

The police package Taurus was repromised for 1988. It finally showed up for the 1990 model year testing. When the Tau-

This Benton County, Indiana Sheriff's Dodge Diplomat is equipped with a 4 bulb Federal Vis-A-Bar and twin Federal Dash Laser deck lights. Stainless steel exhaust was standard equipment in 1987.

Model Code	Body Style	Car Line
MGL41	4-door sedan	Dodge Diplomat Pursuit
MBL41	4-door sedan	Plymouth Gran Fury Pursuit
KDL41	4-door sedan	Dodge Aries K Patrol
KPL41	4-door sedan	Plymouth Reliant K Patrol

Code	Engine Displacement & Carb.	Availability	Torque (ft-lb)	Net HP
EDF	2.2 L (135ci) EFI 4-cyl.	Aries K/Reliant K	122@3200rpm	97@5200 rpm
EDM	2.5 L (153ci) EFI 4-cyl.	Aries K/Reliant K	136@2800rpm	100@4800rpm
ELD	5.2 L (318ci) 2-bbl, V-8	Diplomat/Gran Fury	265@2000rpm	140@3600rpm
EDE	5.2 L (318ci) 4-bbl, V-8	Diplomat/Gran Fury	250@3200rpm	175@4000rpm

This 1987 Dodge Diplomat serves the special response team with the Benton County, Indiana Sheriff. It is powered by a 175hp, 318ci, 4-bbl V-8.

rus did appear, however, it stole the show. The Taurus re-defined front-drive police cars. It set a pace that no car company to date has been able to match with a front-drive car in terms of performance and durability.

In late 1987, the National Association of Fleet Managers met for their annual Law Enforcement Seminar. These fleet cops were openly critical of the selection of squads available to them. They were generally satisfied with the overall size and durability. However, they were quite unhappy with the overall level of performance.

They do not have the power to overtake many of today's (1987) turbocharged, fuel injected sports cars and sedans. Neither do they handle as well as cars with anti-lock braking and sport suspensions.—Geoff Sundstrom

A review of the "1987 Top Speeds" will show these fleet managers were correct in their complaints. The 1987 cop cars from all automakers really were "slow, old iron." None had ABS. All were shaped like bricks. Only the small-block Ford was fuel-injected and it could not reach the 110mph minimum top speed that was now widely established again.

"Almost everything on the road will outrun a police car," said Jay Emery, manager of transportation service for the California Highway Patrol. I'm afraid that in a few years we won't know what a V-8 is. When that day comes we are all going to be in trouble."

Totally ignoring the exotic Porsche-class sports cars and even the Corvette, the American public was driving all kinds of sport coupes and sedans that could outrun most police cruisers. The cop cars really did "lack the zip to zap new hot cars." Many ordinary performance-oriented passenger cars got to 60mph in half the time it took the 4-door police cruiser. Some had top speeds 25mph faster than the best police package sedans.

It was one thing to get outrun by a Porsche 928. How many of those existed then? It was quite another to be outrun by every Camaro, Mustang, Firebird, Daytona, Regal Turbo and Thunderbird Turbo, not to mention dozens of imported sports cars such as the Mazda RX-7, Nissan 300 ZX and Toyota Supra.

The fleet managers were especially emphatic with Chrysler Corp. They wanted a fuel-injected 318ci V-8, period. Chrysler was the easiest target to shoot at. First, most agencies used either the Dodge Diplomat or the Plymouth Gran Fury. Second, Chrysler had already fuel-injected the 318ci for the Imperial in the early 1980s.

An injected 318ci wedge was seen as the great hope of performance-starved cops everywhere. With the 360ci heads and intake currently used on the 318ci, 4-bbl engine, the injected ELE engine would have been a screamer.

Fuel-injection was seen as such a cure-all, that no one even whispered the age-old solution to better performance—cubic inches. The 360ci, 4-bbl was still an active truck and van engine. California had backed off emission standards to the Federal level.

The 360ci small block and the 318ci small block weigh about the same, so the front suspension would not need to be changed. Both bolt up to an A904/A999 transmission. Both use the same engine mounts. How much could the 360ci, 4-bbl engine effect Chrysler's CAFE rating if they were restricted to the 20,000 police cars per year?

None of that mattered. The 360ci in M-body cop cars was never openly discussed. And the chances of a fuel-injected, 318ci were "slim" according to Chrysler. Once again, all Chrysler development money went into front-drive cars. It did not seem to matter that much of that development work had already been done for the Imperial.

The facts were on the side of the fleet managers. The Diplomat and Gran Fury were slowly being passed by the Caprice and Crown Victoria. Other police cars continued to improve. Reflect-

The Calgary Police Service used the Plymouth "Caravelle" in 1987. This is the Canadian version of the Gran Fury. *Calgary Police Service*

ing this improvement, the Michigan State Police toughened their top speed requirements for 1987. The cars still had to hit 110mph, but now they had only 2 miles to reach that speed. In the past, the 4-door sedans were allowed 3 miles.

In 1987, it happened. The Diplomat and Gran Fury lost fair and square at the MSP patrol vehicle tests. The Caprice took top honors in five of the six test categories. The Gran Fury broke the Chevy sweep by generating the most braking power. The only category captured by a Mopar squad was "best brakes."

For the first time since M-bodies were cop cars, the MSP evaluation process selected another squad. This was not a good sign. Performance and low price had made Dodge, Chrysler and Plymouth police cars the most successful squads in history. Continued engineering advances stopped. The Chrysler Special Bid Group was now all alone in their effort to sell police cars. It was back to the days of "low-bid."

The Michigan State Police have been emphatic from the beginning that the purpose of their testing was to find the best pa-

This Calgary Police Service 1987 Plymouth "Caravelle" is clearly marked as a police car. The front suspension was raised slightly to offset the front pusher bars. *Calgary Police Service*

This Jackson County, Tennessee Sheriff 1987 Diplomat 318ci 4-bbl takes a rest from the EVOC driving course. *Dave Dotson*

trol car for the MSP. In each annual report, they urged other agencies to evaluate their own needs which may be different from MSP needs.

The MSP process selected the best squad based on the minimum performance standards set by the MSP and on the percent weighting given to each test category. Changes in the MSP standards took place over time and so did changes in the MSP weighting. A police department more concerned about fuel economy, braking and interior comfort than the MSP would select a different car than the MSP by using the same raw data.

As such, the Diplomat and Gran Fury continued to be successful squads with numerous city, county and state police departments. Many of these, like the Nebraska State Patrol, merely required the prospective squad to qualify under the MSP standards. Once qualified, the squad was selected by strictly low bid.

This beautiful 1987 Dodge Diplomat AHB has been promoted from police service to daily driver. These 4-bbl cars run a 19-second quarter mile. *Matt Craffey*

Production of the Mopar M-body moved from Fenton, Missouri (shown) to Kenosha, Wisconsin in 1987. Production ceased mid-year 1989.

The Military Police was a major customer for the Reliant (shown) and Aries. This U.S.M.C. version is a perfect restoration. *Mike Keller*

This 1987 Plymouth Reliant used by the U.S.M.C. Military Police has a fuel-injected 4-cylinder engine. This squad car is quicker than the 318ci, 2-bbl M-body. *Mike Keller*

The square-jawed Diplomat and Gran Fury look so much like police cars should look, they are impossible to use as undercover cars. *Chrysler*

Here's an 1987 Put-In-Bay, Ohio Police Aries K police car in its last year of production. *Greg Reynolds*

1987 Police Vehicle Performance
Michigan State Police

Vehicle	Engine	0-60mph	0-100mph	Top Speed	1/4 mile ET	1/4 mile Trap	MIS Road Course	Brake Power
Chevrolet Caprice 9C1	350ci, 4-bbl	10.32sec	34.62sec	118.0mph	17.85sec	77.75mph	88.32sec	26.12fps2
Ford Crown Vic 55H	351ci, 2VV	12.02sec	39.30sec	115.2mph	18.93sec	76.25mph	88.59sec	25.66fps2
Plymouth Gran Fury AHB	318ci, 4-bbl (ELE)	12.39sec	38.64sec	117.5mph	19.18sec	75.00mph	89.77sec	27.44fps2
Dodge Diplomat AHB	318ci, 4-bbl (ELE)	12.72sec	40.53sec	116.9mph	19.35sec	73.50mph	89.95sec	27.24fps2
Ford Mustang SSP	302ci, p.f.i., 5-spd	7.64sec	20.42sec	139.6mph	16.00sec	89.75mph	82.02sec	23.99fps2
Ford Mustang SSP	302ci, p.f.i., auto	8.16sec	21.73sec	139.1mph	16.33sec	86.75mph	83.78sec	23.14fps2
Ford Crown Vic 55H	302ci, p.f.i.	11.85sec	43.47sec	109.2mph	18.55sec	74.00mph	n/a	25.66fps2
Chevrolet Caprice 9C1	262ci V6, t.b.i.	13.94sec	59.22sec	106.0mph	19.90sec	71.00mph	n/a	26.12fps2
Plymouth Reliant K AHB	153ci, I4, t.b.i. (EDM)	15.04sec	n/a	100.4mph	20.38sec	68.50mph	92.90sec	24.88fps2
Plymouth Gran Fury AHB	318ci, 2-bbl (ELD)	14.65sec	52.44sec	113.3mph	20.63sec	71.75mph	n/a	27.44fps2

This was the kind of selection process that allowed Dodge and Plymouth to gain such a respected reputation among cops in the 1950s and 1960s. The California Highway Patrol still uses the "qualify then low bid" approach. The 1987 loss at Michigan was still a genuine loss. Without engineering support from Chrysler, this loss forced the Chrysler Special Bid Group back to the strategy of the 1960s for the rest of the 1980s.

Inspite of the strong 1987 showing from Chevrolet, police all over the country continued to use the M-body squads. From the Vermont State Police to the Honolulu, Hawaii Police and from the Portland, Oregon Police to the Pinellas County, Florida Sheriff's, the Mopars remained popular. Even still, the production figures were down a little for 1987:

Dodge Diplomat AHB	7,426 units
Plymouth Gran Fury AHB	3,632 units

The 1987 model year was the last year for the police package on the Aries K and Reliant K. They would continue to be built as passenger cars through 1989. Fewer than 1,000 AHB police package K-cars were sold each year. Chrysler said "those numbers could not justify the program."

Major Police Departments Using 1987 Diplomats and Gran Furys

Baton Rouge, Louisiana Police
Buffalo, New York Police
Honolulu, Hawaii Police
Kansas Highway Patrol
Miami, Florida police
Montana Highway Patrol
New York City Police
New York State Police
Nebraska State Patrol
Oklahoma Highway Patrol
Philadelphia, Pennsylvania Police
Pinellas Co., Florida Sheriff
Portland, Oregon Police
Prince George's Co., Maryland Sheriff
Tennessee Highway Patrol
Vermont State Police
Calgary Police Service, Canada

1987 Top Speeds

Vehicle	0-60 mph	Top Speed	Reference
Porsche 928	6.5sec	165mph	MT 5/87
Chevrolet Corvette	6.7sec	153mph	MT 8/87
Ford Mustang 5.0 GT	6.5sec	144mph	MT 8/87
Chevy Camaro IROC-Z	6.7sec	144mph	MT 8/87
Ford T-Bird Turbo Coupe	8.6sec	143mph	MT 8/87
Pontiac Firebird GTA	6.9sec	142mph	MT 8/87
Ford Mustang Spl. Svc.	7.6sec	140mph	MSP 9/86
Dodge Daytona Z	8.1sec	135mph	MT 8/87
Jaguar XJ6	10.8sec	128mph	CD 6/87
Buick Grand National	6.1sec	123mph	MT 8/87
Chevrolet Caprice 9C1	10.8sec	118mph	MSP 9/86
Plymouth Gran Fury AHB	12.4sec	118mph	MSP 9/86
Dodge Diplomat AHB	12.7sec	117mph	MSP 9/86
Ford Crown Vic 55H	12.0sec	115mph	MSP 9/86
Plymouth Reliant K AHB	15.0sec	100mph	MSP 9/86

References

"Domestic Dynamite," Ron Grable, *Motor Trend*, August 1987
Scheduled Maintenance and Lubrication Recommendations, Chrysler Corporation, 1987
Plymouth Gran Fury Police Package, Chrysler Corporation, 1987
Dodge Diplomat Police Package, Chrysler Corporation, 1987
Patrol Vehicle Evaluation and Purchasing Program, Michigan State Police, 1987
"Police Say Aging Cruisers Lack Zip to Zap New Hot Cars," Geoff Sundstrom, *Automotive News*, August 17, 1987
Standard Catalog of Chrysler, John Lee, Jim Benjaminson, John Gunnell, Krause Publications

This 1987 Reliant K police wagon served in the Bomb Unit with the Washington D.C. Police. *Greg Reynolds*

Chapter 13

1988: The Last CHP Dodge

For the 1988 model year, the Dodge and Plymouth police fleet shrank to the smallest of combinations ever. A total of two Chrysler Corp. police package cars were available. A total of two V-8 engines were available. That was it.

Model Code	Body Style	Car Line
MGL41	4-door sedan	Dodge Diplomat Pursuit
MBL41	4-door sedan	Plymouth Gran Fury Pursuit

Engine Code	Class	Displacement & Carb	Net Torque	Net Horsepower
ELD	Pursuit	5.2L/318ci, 2-bbl V-8	265@2000rpm	140@3600rpm
ELE	Interceptor	5.2L/318ci, 4-bbl V-8	250@3200rpm	175@4000rpm

The Aries K and Reliant K were no longer available with the AHB police package.

The Gran Fury and Diplomat had been the last rear-wheel drive Dodge and Plymouth passenger cars since the Mirada left the lineup after 1983. The Diplomat and Gran Fury were also the only remaining V-8 powered cars since after 1983.

In 1988, the Diplomat and Gran Fury became real lone wolves. They were now the only carbureted cars in either division. The lowly Omni and Horizon passenger cars received electronic fuel injection for the 1988 model year. This was further evidence that Chrysler Corp. was backing out of the police business. The Chrysler Imperial had a fuel injected 318ci V-8 since 1981 and cops had screamed for it ever since. Not to be.

As the only rear-wheel drive, V-8 powered carbureted cars in all of Chrysler Corp., the M-bodies were not really lone wolves. They were black sheep. And the real wolves in Chrysler Corporate finance and engineering were out to get them. The end would be soon.

The only engineering advancement since 1986 for the M-body cars, except stainless steel exhaust, occurred late in the 1988 model year. Beginning in May 1988, the Diplomat and Gran Fury came standard with a driver's side supplemental restraint or passive restraint system—aka, an air bag.

Since most police cars were made only a couple times a year, and were frequently the first cars in the model year to be made, very few 1988 Mopar cop cars were equipped with the air bag. However, every 1989 Diplomat and Gran Fury was so-equipped. This safety feature became a strong selling point, and rightly so.

The performance tests conducted by the Michigan State Police proved the Diplomat and Gran Fury to be strong contenders. The Chevrolet Caprice emerged the victor, but it wasn't a pretty sight. The Crown Vic tied with the Caprice in the heavily-weighted road course phase and it produced the most braking power. (A Ford with the best brakes!?)

The Diplomat, Gran Fury and Crown Vic were also in a three-way tie for highest top speed. Both the Diplomat and Gran Fury scored better than the other squads in the ergonomic review. However, when the smoke cleared and the pencils were sharpened, the Caprice got the nod. But there was no cockiness as in 1987. The 1988 victory was very close for Chevrolet.

The overall performance and pricing of the Dodge Diplomat was competitive enough that when these same squads faced off

In 1988, the only two police cars available from Chrysler were the Diplomat and Gran Fury. The K-cars were discontinued. *Chrysler*

The 1988 M-bodies, like this KHP Gran Fury, were powered by either the 318ci, 4-bbl 'interceptor' or the 2-bbl "pursuit" engine. *Rick Wilson*

later in the model year in California, the Diplomat won. This became the last CHP Dodge.

The CHP was the first police department to adopt the Dodge police car when it was released in 1956. The prestige associated with the CHP gave the Dodge squads instant credibility. Equipped with either the 230bhp Super Red Ram or the 260bhp dual quad D-500 engines, these Dodges earned respect through their sheer performance.

In turn, Dodge made special engine modifications just for the CHP, juggled wheelbases just for the CHP and even released a special police car model (1961 Polara) just for the CHP. The road was a bit rough at times, but Dodge and the

CHP worked together to smooth things out. Since 1956, the CHP selected Chrysler products as E-class squad cars 28 times in 33 years.

By late in 1988, Chrysler had announced that production of the M-body police cars would cease in mid-1989. Dodge had become such an institution at CHP Motor Transport, they took the time to photograph a farewell picture of the Last Dodge Diplomat, complete with Motor Transport personnel in the background. The era of total dominance in the police market was rapidly coming to a close.

Dodge Diplomat AHB	6,710 units
Plymouth Gran Fury AHB	3,883 units

The 1988 Gran Furys, like this Kansas Highway Patrol unit, were the only rear-wheel drive cars in all of the Plymouth Div. *Rick Wilson*

The 1988 Gran Furys, like this Sparta, Illinois Police detective unit, were the only carbureted cars in all of the Plymouth Div. *Dave Dotson*

This NYC Police vehicle is one of the very rare 1988 Dodge Diplomats. Most NYC Highway Patrol units were the Plymouth Gran Fury. *Ned Schwartz*

Major Police Departments Using 1988 Dodge and Plymouth Police Cars

Buffalo, New York Police
California Highway Patrol
Dallas, Texas Police
Kansas Highway Patrol
Minnesota State Police
Montana Highway Patrol
Nebraska State Patrol
New York City Police
New York State Police
North Dakota Highway Patrol
Oklahoma Highway Patrol
Philadelphia, Pennsylvania Police
Pinellas Co., Florida Sheriff
Portland, Oregon Police
Prince George's Co., Maryland Sheriff
St. Petersburg, Florida Police
Tennessee Highway Patrol
Vermont State Police
Winston-Salem, North Carolina Police
Wisconsin State Police

In mid-1988, M-bodies like this Philadelphia, Pennsylvania Police Gran Fury, came equipped with driver's side air bags. *Joe Gavula*

Here's a 1988 Plymouth Gran Fury used by the New York City Police. All precinct cars were all 2-bbl powered. *Ned Schwartz*

This 1988 California State University, Long Beach Dodge Diplomat 318ci, 4-bbl was still in service in 1995. *John Bellah*

Here's an 1988 North Dakota Highway State Patrol Plymouth Gran Fury. This has a top speed of 117mph. *Jim Benjaminson*

1988 Top Speeds*

Vehicle	0-60 mph	Top Speed
Porsche 928S	6.4sec	165mph
Chevrolet Corvette	6.5sec	156mph
Nissan 300ZX Turbo	7.4sec	153mph
BMW M6	7.9sec	149mph
Chevrolet Camaro IROC-Z	7.2sec	148mph
Toyota Supra Turbo	7.8sec	147mph
Ford Mustang 5.0 GT	7.2sec	142mph
Pontiac Firebird GTA	7.6sec	141mph
Ford Mustang 5.0 LX	8.0sec	135mph
Dodge Diplomat AHB	11.6sec	117mph
Ford Crown Vic 55H	11.9sec	117mph
Plymouth Gran Fury AHB	12.1sec	117mph
Chevrolet Caprice 9C1	10.6sec	116mph

Motor Trend September 1988 and Michigan State Police November 1987.

This Kenosha, Wisconsin-made 1988 Plymouth Gran Fury is shown at Chrysler's Chelsea Proving Grounds. *Chrysler*

1988 Police Car Performance
Michigan State Police

Vehicle	Engine	0-60mph	0-100mph	Top Speed	1/4 mile ET	1/4 mile Trap	MIS Road Course	Brake Power
Ford Mustang SSP	302ci, p.f.i., man.	6.9sec	19.1sec	134mph	15.48sec	91.1mph	82.57sec	25.69fps2
Ford Mustang SSP	302ci, p.f.i., auto	8.0sec	21.8sec	135mph	16.16sec	87.8mph	83.79sec	25.69fps2
Chevrolet Caprice 9C1	350ci, 4-bbl	10.6sec	34.9sec	116mph	18.03sec	77.6mph	88.60sec	25.55fps2
Ford Crown Vic 55H	302ci, p.f.i.	11.4sec	40.6sec	108mph	18.35sec	75.3mph	n/a	26.79fps2
Dodge Diplomat AHB	318ci, 4-bbl	11.6sec	38.8sec	117mph	18.59sec	75.4mph	89.27sec	24.92fps2
Ford Crown Vic 55H	351ci, 2VV	11.9sec	37.7sec	117mph	18.84sec	76.4mph	88.60sec	26.79fps2
Plymouth Gran Fury AHB	318ci, 4-bbl	12.1sec	40.1sec	117mph	19.01sec	74.8mph	89.43sec	23.74fps2
Chevrolet Caprice 9C1	262ci (V6), t.b.i.	13.8sec	52.4sec	109mph	20.08sec	71.85mph	n/a	24.92fps2
Dodge Diplomat AHB	318ci, 2-bbl	14.0sec	57.2sec	110mph	20.08sec	71.85mph	n/a	24.92fps2
Plymouth Gran Fury AHB	318ci, 2-bbl	14.2sec	57.8sec	110mph	20.18sec	71.83mph	n/a	23.74fps2

References

Patrol Vehicle Evaluation and Purchasing Program, Michigan State Police, 1988

Standard Catalog of Chrysler, John Lee, Jim Benjaminson, John Gunnell, Krause Publications

"Fifty Years of Plymouth Police Cars," Jim Benjaminson, *The Plymouth Bulletin*, March-April 1992

Dodge Diplomat/Plymouth Gran Fury Police Cars, Chrysler Corporation, 1988

With few exceptions, the California Highway Patrol used Dodge police cars exclusively from 1956 to 1988. *CHP*

Chapter 14

1989: 10-42 (Ending Tour of Duty)

The September 1989 "Vehicles" column of Law Enforcement Technology told cops everywhere what many fleet managers already knew: Chrysler, manufacturer of the Diplomat and Gran Fury had pulled out of the police car market.

Calling Chrysler "a front wheel drive company," Tom Houston, a sales and parts communications executive for the auto maker, noted that the two police car models were the sole remaining Chrysler rear wheel drive cars. As engineering and design attention shifted away from that technology, Chrysler officials decided to close the factory and pull out of the business.

"Rear wheel drive involves a totally different set of technologies-like drive shafts and differentials," Houston said, "and our engineers were concentrating on other things."

With those words, Chrysler Corp. shut off production of the Kenosha, Wisconsin-built Diplomat and Gran Fury. They stepped out of the police market which they had totally dominated for decades.

In 1989, Chrysler Corp. produced 17 variations of 12 basic engines for all of their passenger cars including police sedans.

1.5L	90ci	Inline	4-cyl	front-drive
1.6L	98ci	Inline	4-cyl	front-drive
1.8L	107ci	Inline	4-cyl	front-drive
2.0L	122ci	Inline	4-cyl	front-drive
2.2L	132ci	Inline	4-cyl	front-drive
2.2L	135ci	Inline	4-cyl	front-drive
2.5L	150ci	Inline	4-cyl	front-drive

PLYMOUTH 1989 PRODUCT LINE

BASIC LARGE	BASIC MIDDLE	SMALL WAGON	COMPACT	SUB COMPACT
Gran Fury	Acclaim	Voyager	Reliant	Horizon
		Grand Voyager	Reliant	Colt
		Vista	Sundance	
		Vista 4WD	Sundance	
		Colt Wagon		

This Plymouth 1989 product line clearly shows why Chrysler Corp. pulled out of the police car business. *Chrysler*

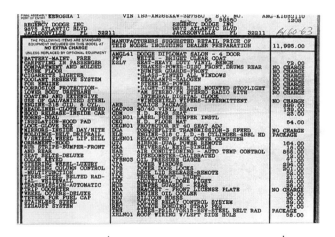

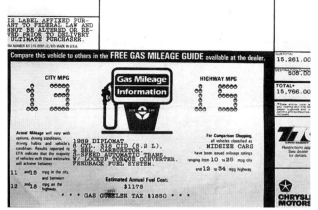

Here's a window sticker from a loaded 1989 Dodge Diplomat used by the Pinellas County, Florida Sheriff. *Robert Helmick*

2.5L	153ci	Inline	4-cyl	front-drive
2.6L	156ci	Inline	4-cyl	front-drive
3.0L	180ci	Transverse	V-6	front-drive
3.0L	181ci	Transverse	V-6	front-drive
5.2L	318ci	Front	V-8	rear-drive

When Chrysler's Tom Houston described Chrysler Corp. as a "front wheel drive company," the above table makes it clear how absolutely correct he was. More than just front drive, Chrysler was a high-technology front-drive company. They had neglected the rear-drive V-8, but had highly developed front-wheel drive engines. Of the 17 engine varieties, the 15 front-drive engines were all fuel injected. In fact, eight of these had multi-point fuel injection. For the most sophisticated power, five of these were turborcharged. Most were overhead cam, SOHC. Two were double overhead cam, DOHC.

The rear-wheel drive, V-8 powered sedan was as foreign to most Chrysler engineers in 1989 as the front-drive, I4 powertrain was in 1975 when development for the Omni/Horizon began.

Chrysler Corp. did not drift into the front-drive business like some other auto makers. Nor did Chrysler get into front-drive compact just to meet the competition. Chrysler went after front-drive vehicles with a vengeance.

In the mid 1970s, when confusion reigned in Detroit, Chrysler made the crucial commitment to its first front wheel drive cars, the Plymouth Horizon and Dodge Omni, targeting them for introduction as 1978 models.

As a result, Chrysler's first two modern, domestic, front-drive cars hit the market two years ahead of the Chevrolet Citation and three years ahead of the Ford Escort.

By the mid 1970s, Chrysler had already gained knowledge of front-drive cars by three different projects dating back to the mid-1930s, according to *Motor Trend*.

The very first Chrysler front drive was an experimental program started in 1934 and completed in 1935. An Airflow-body car was adapted to front-drive.

The corporation did not look at front drive again until after World War II. Armed with a huge amount of wartime materials and construction technology, it made another experimental front-drive project car called the A-227. This was not simply a production car refitted with a front-drive package as in 1934, but a detailed study of total vehicle and vehicle dynamics.

The third front-drive experience set the stage for the "modern" front drive Omni/Horizon. In 1958, Chrysler Corporation bought the French car maker, Simca.

In 1961, three years after Chrysler acquired equity in Simca, the French firm started a development program on a small, front-wheel-drive sedan series. The program started a flow of engineering information back and forth across the Atlantic.

Chrysler engineers actively participated in the development of the Simca 1100, which was a new approach for a company that had for years done a mix of front-engine/rear-drive, rear-engine/rear-drive sedans, sport coupes and roadsters.

Simca went on to merge with Rootes, and the two companies operated as Chrysler France and Chrysler, UK, respectively, until Chrysler sold both to the Peugeot-Citron group in 1978.

Although the Highland Park company has no financial interests left in Europe, it did garner experience in fwd (Front wheel drive) by participating in the design and manufacture of more than 2.5 million fwd cars in Europe. This amounted to 18 years of fwd experience and 12 billion accumulated road miles before the first U.S. front-drives were introduced.

In 1975, Chrysler began development of the L-car which became the 1978 Omni/Horizon.

A most salient byproduct of Chrysler's determination to get 100 percent front-drive by 1984 is fuel economy. Not only had Chrysler led all domestic manufacturers in corporate average fuel economy in the past model year, but also took leadership for 1982 at 26.5mpg .

Strictly speaking, Chrysler had already arrived at the 100 percent fwd figure in the United States, since the Chrysler New Yorker, Plymouth Gran Fury, Dodge Diplomat, Imperial, Cordoba and Mirada are all built north of the border in Canada. The march toward 100 percent front-drive production in North America *[continued into 1983] with the first of six more new products.*

In five seasons of defensive combat, Chrysler has gone from 0 to 85 percent front-wheel-drive, and from being a backmarker to becoming industry leader in the fuel-economy war. When Someday, whether or not Chrysler continues as we know it today, it will be deserving of a chapter on its great adventures between 1978 and 1985.

By the mid-1980's, Chrysler Corp. gave up on V-8 powered, rear-drive cars altogether. The only changes between 1986 and 1989 were stainless steel exhaust systems in 1987 and air bags in late 1988. The engines, transmissions and brakes were not touched at all. Neither was the sheet metal.

Toward the bitter end, the cop cars from Ford, but especially Chevrolet, did in fact overtake the Mopar squads in all areas of performance, economy, comfort and safety.

The New York City Police were loyal to Chrysler Corp. police cars through the end in 1989. *Ned Schwartz*

This 1989 Gran Fury was used by the NYPD Firearms and Tactics Section. *John Cerar*

In 1989, NYPD's Emergency Services Unit used the Gran Fury for supervisors. These were 4-bbl cars.

Ford had fuel-injected the 302 HO V-8 in 1983. Chevrolet added fuel injection to their 262ci V-6 in 1985. For 1989 the Chevy 305ci V-8 and 350ci V-8 received fuel injection. This started out as throttle-body injection, but their cop cars eventually got multi-point fuel injection. That greatly improved performance. The carbureted Dodges and Plymouths could still run with these injected (and variable venturi) cars, but the gap was opening. The Mopars either needed e.f.i. or their old Carter ThermoQuad back.

The competition also worked on brakes. Through 1989, all police package cars had front discs and rear drums. During the 1989 MSP runoffs, the Dodge Diplomat turned in the most braking power. However, by 1990, Ford became the first auto maker to offer rear discs on a fully-duty police package. This was a natural. Fords have historically had awful brakes. The MSP took formal note of this on two separate occasions with the Mustang. At any rate, the 1990 Taurus had four wheel discs. So did the 1992 Crown Vic.

The competition also worked on Antilock Braking Systems (ABS)—the biggest safety improvement in vehicle safety since seat belts. Again, when Chrysler bowed out in 1989, no maker offered ABS. However, Ford again released ABS on the 1990 Taurus and 1992 1/2 Crown Vic. The 1991 Caprice also had full ABS.

Ford and Chevrolet were also busy with 4-speed overdrive automatic transmissions. The Mopar squads ended in 1989 with the proven and durable 3-speed A999 small-block TorqueFlite. Chrysler developed the 4-speed A500 automatic overdrive trans and released it in mid-year 1988. However, this was for use only in rear-wheel drive Dodge trucks.

Cop cars have used all kinds of truck components over the years. Where do you think the rugged Dana 60 rear end was used originally? The 4-speed auto, however, was not to be for cops.

The M-body sheet metal was unchanged since the first M-body squad in 1981. Ford and Chevrolet slicked up the front ends of their cars in the late-1980s. The sleeker more aerodynamic shape helped the Crown Vic to gain 2mph per year starting in 1988. The major restyle of the 1991 Caprice produced a 10mph jump in top speed up to 132mph.

Again, the competition remained competitive. The Chrysler Special Bid Group cannot design improved brakes, bend sheet metal or develop fuel injection. Engineers have to do that, and Chrysler engineers were exclusively restricted to front-drive passenger cars.

Chrysler made a few attempts in the mid and late-1980s to field a front-drive squad car. However, only the 1991 Dynasty

The Wisconsin State Patrol were among the last departments to use the Dodge Diplomat (shown) and Gran Fury in 1989.

Production of the Diplomat and Gran Fury ceased before antilock brakes or four-wheel discs were developed. *Larry Hollingsworth*

3.8L police mule was a serious attempt. None of the earlier attempts were successful if for no other reason than Chrysler's heart really was not in the effort.

If Chrysler was a front drive company, how about a front drive cop car with legendary Mopar performance and durability? In 1989 police asked just that sort of question.

The past non-acceptance of smaller front-wheel drive vehicles was the main reason that Chrysler Motors decided not to market a police package, according to Bob Lees, recently retired Chrysler Motors executive with Fleet Operations. Lees said that Chrysler was strictly a front-wheel drive manufacturer.

Catch-22. Cops didn't like front-drive cars and all Chrysler made was front-drive cars. If they could only have foreseen the wide acceptance of the Lumina B4C and Taurus 55A that would take place in just four years.

On the 75th anniversary of the Dodge Brothers, in 1989 Dodge and Plymouth pulled out of the police business. Production of the M-body rear-drive sedan in Kenosha, Wisconsin ceased. The only other police car made in the 1980s was the K-car. The K-car was dropped from the police fleet after 1987. In 1989, production for the K-car passenger car also ceased, closing production plants on Jefferson Avenue in Detroit and in Toluca, Mexico.

In September 1988, the Dodge Diplomat AHB and Plymouth Gran Fury AHB appeared at the Michigan State Patrol vehicle tests for the last time. All of the eligible 4-door sedans had roughly equal brakes. They all ran the quarter mile in the 18sec bracket except the Caprice which broke out with a 17.6sec ET. The top speed of all four cars was between 119 and 122mph. The road course times were within 2-1/2sec.

The Dodge and Plymouth were competitive in 1989 and the MSP system made allowances in the bid adjustment calculation for being "close." However, the Mopars were not close enough. They captured best brakes and most ergonomic interior. The Caprice got everything else and the final nod.

In the 1950s, the Dodge sold police cars on its performance reputation. Plymouth used the "taxi-tough" approach, but Dodge sold more cop cars even though they were higher priced. Dodge had the huge V-8 engines and the long wheelbases demanded by police specifications.

In the 1960's, Plymouth gained ground in the police market, especially when Plymouth and Dodge shared drivetrains. With equal performance from equal power plants, Dodge and Plymouth even split their share of the police market. Dodge got the exclusive nod only when wheelbase length was critical.

In the depressed economy of the 1970s, low bid was the absolute rule. The more spartan Plymouth squads overtook the higher trimmed Dodge squads. Plymouth led Dodge in police car sales this whole decade.

In the 1980s, and for no clear reason whatsoever, Dodge turned the tables on Plymouth. Dodge outsold Plymouth almost two-to-one every single year. Some sources blamed this switch on the 1981 model year, when the new M-body police car was the Chrysler LeBaron and not a Plymouth. At any rate, even though the M-body cars were identical in nearly all regards, cops strongly favored Dodge.

The only news for 1989 was an improved standard equipment list. In addition to the driver's side air bag introduced in May 1988 as standard, the M-bodies now had tilt wheel, tinted glass, AM/FM stereo with radio delete, and intermittent wipers as standard equipment.

Some police departments were loyal to Dodge and Plymouth right to the very end. We honor a sampling of these city, county and state police departments by displaying their shoulder patches in this chapter. These agencies were the loyalists, the Chrysler enthusiasts.

Each and every one of these departments knew 1989 was the last year for Dodge and Plymouth police cars. Rather than to change their specs, which all could have easily done, they instead enjoyed the last year of America's Police Cars.

1989 Police Car Performance
Michigan State Police

Vehicle	Engine	0-60mph	0-100mph	Top Speed	1/4 Mile ET	1/4 Mile Trap	MIS Road Course	Brake Power
Ford Mustang Spl. Svc.	302ci, p.f.i.	8.60sec	22.89sec	137.2mph	16.59sec	87.03mph	82.51sec	24.45fps2
Chevrolet Caprice 9C1	350ci, t.b.i	9.82sec	29.35sec	122.0mph	17.62sec	79.83mph	86.20sec	26.03fps2
Plymouth Gran Fury AHB	318ci, 4-bbl (ELE)	11.77sec	38.02sec	120.2mph	18.63sec	76.20mph	88.63sec	26.01fps2
Ford Crown Vic 55H	302ci, p.f.i.	12.39sec	42.14sec	110.0mph	18.77sec	74.28mph	89.49sec	26.09fps2
Dodge Diplomat AHB	318ci, 4-bbl (ELE)	11.84sec	38.95sec	119.1mph	18.79sec	75.53mph	88.24sec	26.32fps2
Ford Crown Vic 55H	351ci, 2VV	11.98sec	36.55sec	119.1mph	18.86sec	77.05mph	88.83sec	26.09fps2
Chevrolet Caprice 9C1	305ci, t.b.i.	12.35sec	42.88 sec	114.1mph	19.01sec	73.43mph	n/a	26.03fps2
Dodge Diplomat AHB	318ci, 2-bbl (ELD)	14.38sec	55.58sec	113.6mph	20.23sec	71.55mph	n/a	26.32fps2
Plymouth Gran Fury AHB	318ci, 2-bbl (ELD)	14.98sec	58.13sec	111.2mph	20.23sec	71.55mph	92.51sec	26.01fps2
Chevrolet Caprice 9C1	262ci (V-6), t.b.i.	15.57sec	58.16sec	109.0mph	20.50sec	69.50mph	n/a	26.03fps2

Here's a 1989 Miami, Florida Police Dodge Diplomat *Greg Reynolds*

1989 Top Speeds*

Vehicle	Top Speed
Chevrolet Corvette ZR-1	181mph
Pontiac 20th-Anniv. Trans Am	162mph
Chevrolet Corvette L98	153mph
Dodge Shelby CSX	149mph
Ford Mustang 5.0 LX	142mph
Ford Taurus SHO	141mph
Plymouth Laser RS	140mph
Pontiac McLaren Grand Prix	134mph
Olds Cutlass Quad 4 H.O.	131mph
Chevrolet Caprice 9C1	122mph
Plymouth Gran Fury AHB	120mph
Dodge Diplomat AHB	119mph
Ford Crown Victoria 55H	119mph

*Courtesy of *Motor Trend*, June 1989 and Michigan State Police, September 1988

Police Departments Using 1989 Dodge & Plymouth Police Cars

(Partial Listing)
Buffalo, New York Police
Kansas Highway Patrol
Montana Highway Patrol
New York City Police
New York State Police
Oklahoma Highway Patrol
Philadelphia, Pennsylvania Police
Pinellas Co., Florida Sheriff
Portland, Oregon Police
San Bernadino, California Police
Tennessee Highway Patrol
Vermont State Police
Wisconsin State Police

References

"Chrysler, The First Family of Front-Drive," Jim McGraw, Motor Trend, February 1982
Patrol Vehicle Evaluation and Purchasing Program, Michigan State Police,
Specifications for 4-door full-size police sedan, Los Angeles Police Department, 1989
"The Procurement of Police Cars," Mark Levine and Deirdre Martin, Law Enforcement Technology, September 1989
Standard Catalog of Chrysler, John Lee, John Gunnell, Jim Benjaminson, Krause Publications
Plymouth Press Information, Chrysler Corporation, 1989
"The Great American Police Car," Ed Nowicki, Police, December 1989
"Last of the Chrysler Pursuits," Ed Sanow, Chrysler Power, January 1992

Chapter 15

Galen Govier on VIN Info & Decoding

This chapter will explain how to identify a real Police Car as well as a car with the Police Package.

In the years before 1966, you would find mostly Plymouth's built at the Lynch Road Plant and Dodge's at the Hamtramck Plant. Hamtramck was always referred to as "Dodge Main."

The Body Code Plate (aka Fender Tag) is found under the hood of the inner fender or firewall on most vehicles, but sometimes it is found on the drivers door post near the Serial Number (aka VIN or Vehicle Identification Number).

From 1962-1964 the Body Code Plate differed from Plant to Plant Example: At the Lynch Road Plant-under the uppercase alphabet A or A the code (or codes) found would be referring to the engine, but at the Hamtramck Plant the same location would be referring to the transmission and the engine code (or codes) would be found under QR. If no codes are found under the AB or QR, I have found this to mean that the vehicle is equipped with the standard engine, if it is a 6-cyl vehicle then it is a 225-1BBL, if it is a 8-cyl vehicle then it is most likely a 318-2BBL. And yes they did make some 6-cyl police cars, and I have even found some 2-Door Sedan police cars! When referring to police cars, most people think of a 4-Door Sedan with a big V-8. This is not always true.

1964 Fender Tag Example:

```
1234567890
06   154
ABCDEFGHJKMNNPZRSTVWXYZ
065      45        38      41      91      9
SO       NUMBER    BDY     TRM             PNT
0611     7318      391     K1B             99
```

Serial Number Example: 3941260252

(Built at Lynch Road)

As you can see, I placed the Serial Number below the Car Line on the Body Code Plate. The first 2 digits of the VIN will match the Car Line in most all instances. The 3rd digit on the Body Code plate refers to the Body Style, and the 3rd digit of the Serial Number refers to the Model Year.

The Serial Number is welded (early 1966 and prior) or riveted (mid-year-and 1967) to the left front door hinge pillar (A-Post). The Serial Number is always read from outside the vehicle.

Decoding a 1961-1965 Serial Number;

The serial number from 1961-1965 will consist of a ten (10) digit numeric sequence number.

EXAMPLE: 3941260252
3 = PLYMOUTH 8-CYL
9 = Police
4 = 1964 Model Year

1 = Lynch Road, MI Assembly Plant
260252 = Assembly Plant Sequence Number

FIRST DIGIT: CAR MAKE

1 = Valiant	6-CYL	(1961-64)
2 = Plymouth	6-CYL	(1961-64)
3 = Plymouth	8-CYL	(1961-64)
3 = Belvedere	6-CYL	(1965)
4 = Dodge	6-CYL	(1961-64)
5 = Dodge	8-CYL	(1961-62)
5 = Dodge 880	8-CYL	(1961-64)
6 = DeSoto	8-CYL	(1961)
6 = Dodge	8-CYL	(1963-64)
7 = Lancer	6-CYL	(1961-62)
7 = Dart	6-CYL	(1963-65)
8 = Chrysler	8-CYL	(1961-64)
9 = Imperial	8-CYL	(1961-65)
C = Chrysler	8-CYL	(1965)
D = Polara	8-CYL	(1965)(Also Custom 880)
L = Dart	8-CYL	(1964-65)
P = Fury	8-CYL	(1965)
R = Belvedere	8-CYL	(1965)
V = Valiant	8-CYL	(1964-65)(Also Barracuda)
W = Coronet	8-CYL	(1965)

SECOND DIGIT: CAR MODEL

1 = Low Price Car
2 = Medium Price Car
3 = High Price Car
4 = Premium Price Car
5 = Low Price Wagon
6 = Medium Price Wagon
7 = High Price Wagon
8 = Taxi
9 = Police
0 = Fleet

1 = Valiant V100, 1961-64 Savoy, 1965 Belvedere I, 1965 1961 Dart-Seneca, 1962 Dart, 1963 Custom 880, 1964 880, 1963-64 330, 1965 Coronet Deluxe, 1965 Polara, 1961-62 Lancer 170, 1963-64 Dart 170, Newport, 1961-63 Imperial Custom.

2 = 1961-64 Belvedere, 1965 Fury II, 1961 Dart-Pioneer, 1962 Dart 330, 1963-64 440, 1965 Coronet, 1965 Polara 318, 1964 Custom 880, 1961 Windsor, 1962-65 300, Imperial Crown.

3 = Valiant 200, 1961-64 Fury, 1965 Belvedere II, 1965 Fury III, 1961 Dart-Phoenix, 1962 440, 1963-64 Polara, 1965 Coronet 440, 1965 Custom 880, 1961-62 Lancer 770, 1963-64 Dart 270, New Yorker, Imperial LaBaron.

4 = 1962 Signet 200, 1963-64 Signet, 1964 Barracuda, 1963-65 Sport Fury, 1965 Satellite, 1961-62 Polara, 1963-64 Po-

lara 500, 1965 Coronet 500, 1965 Monaco, 1962 Lancer GT, 1963-64 Dart GT, 300-G, H, J, K, L Latter Series.

5 = WAGON: Valiant 100, Savoy, 1961 Seneca, Lancer 170, Dart, Custom 880,

6 = WAGON: Valiant 20, Fury, Phoenix, 440, Lancer 770, Dart 270, New Yorker & Country.

7 = WAGON: Valiant 200, Fury, Phoenix, 440, Lancer 770, Dart 270, New Yorker Town & Country.

8 = Taxi

9 = Police & 1961 Crown Limo.

0 = Fleet, 1963 300 Pace Setter, 1965 Super Stock

FIRST & SECOND DIGIT = CAR LINE IE: 61 = DODGE V-8 330 (1964)

THIRD DIGIT: MODEL YEAR

1 = 1961	Model	Year	R-SERIES
2 = 1962	Model	Year	S-SERIES
3 = 1963	Model	Year	T-SERIES
4 = 1964	Model	Year	U-SERIES
5 = 1965	Model	Year	V-SERIES

FOURTH DIGIT: ASSEMBLY PLANT

1 = Lynch Road, MI (Plymouth) Assembly Plant
2 = Hamtramck, MI (Dodge) Assembly Plant
3 = Jefferson, MI Assembly Plant
4 = Belvedere, IL (Imperial) Assembly Plant
5 = Los Angeles, CA Assembly Plant
6 = Newark, DE (Delaware) Assembly Plant
7 = St. Louis, MO (Valley Park) Assembly Plant
8 = Wyoming, MI Assembly Plant
9 = Windsor, ONT (Canada) Assembly Plant

LAST 6 DIGITS:

Indicate Assembly Plant Sequence Number

On the Body Code Plate (under or near BDY) only:

THIRD DIGIT: BODY STYLE

1 = 2 Door Sedan
2 = 2 Door Hardtop
3 = 4 Door Sedan
4 = 4 Door hardtop
5 = Convertible
6 = 2 Seat Wagon
7 = 3 Seat Wagon
8 = 6 Pass Hardtop Wagon
9 = 9 Pass Hardtop Wagon

In any model year, I refer to it being a series. For example, S-Series is referring to the 1962 Model Year. Another place this is used is on the Engine Identification Pad, if you were looking at an engine in (or out) of the car, and you located the Engine Boss (aka I.D. Pad). You might find the numbers "V 38." This is telling you it is a 1964 (V-Series 383ci engine, and that is came from a 1964 Model Year vehicle. If it is an "A 383" then it would be a 1965 383ci engine.

1965 was the first year they stamped all 3 digits of the cubic inch displacement on the Engine Boss (388 vs 38 in 1964). Other numbers found on the Engine Boss refer to the month & day the engine was assembled and whether or not it was a HP (4BBL).

One thing I would like to clear up is the difference between the model year and the calendar year, because if an engine is from a 1964 model year car, and it has a July 1963 casting date it tends to confuse.

The 1964 calendar year is from January 1, 1964 to December 31 1964. The 1964 model year is from August 1, 1963 to July 3, 1964.

I have reason to believe the following models were offered from 1962-1964 with a 2nd Digit of 9 in the Serial Number!

Here's a tag from a 1965 Plymouth Savoy with a 225ci, 1-bbl.

DODGE	330	Police
DODGE	880	Police
PLYMOUTH	Savoy	Police
CHRYSLER	Newport	Police

With no known exceptions, in every instance the Police car is found in the lowest model available. For example, a 1964 Dodge Police Car would be a 330 not a 440 or Polara! And a Plymouth would be a Savoy, not a Belvedere or Fury!

In 1965 the Body Code Plate Numbers became universal from plant to plant, which made it a lot easier to understand the meanings.

1965 Fender Tag Example:

1234567890					
4	9	991	9	07	143
ABCDEFGHJKLMNPQRSTVWXYZ					
20	55				3
SO	NUMBER	BDY	TRM	PAINT	
615	58236	R93	K1B	EE1	E

Serial Number Example: 3951305483

In the example above, the 1st digit does not match from Body Code Plate to Serial Number. The reason for this is that the vehicle is a 6-cyl car. And the VIN agrees with that, but the Body Code Plate tells you that it is a Savoy, and leads you to believe it is an 8-cyl car. This is why you need to know your Engine Sales Codes.

Decoding a 1966-80 Serial Number:

In 1966, the 2nd digit was changed from a "9" to a "K" to designate the Police Car. This was continued up through the 1977 Model Year. About 1970 they assigned an A38 Police Sales Code to the Low Price Model and came up with a Police Package.

IE: WL41 + A38 = Police Package vs WK41 = Police Car!

It isn't as if the "L" replaced the "K," it's just that they dropped the "K" as POLICE CARS, and went full into vehicles with the A38 POLICE PACKAGE instead.

A few years ago I called a source at Chrysler and got all of the yearly sales codes from year to year, and the first year for the A38 Pkg was 1970! So with that in mind, 1970 was also the first year that it showed up on a Fender Tag. But the Serial Number would not have had a 2nd digit of "K." An "A38" code would have only showed up on a Fender Tag if the model in mind had the Police PACKAGE-A38, and not if it was a Police MODEL-"K." In all of the Fender tags I have on file, either they have a 2nd digit of K, or they have a 2nd digit of "L: (or "H"), with an "A38," but not both. If the Vehicle Order Number begins with K, that doesn't necessarily mean it is a Police Car, but it does if the Trim Code begins with K.

I believe there was still an A38 Package in 1983, even though it isn't listed on the sheet, but in 1984 the whole Sales Code Alpha/Numeric System was changed to strictly an Alpha System. The Sales Code from 1984 to date is AHB. I just received a 1993 Viper Broadcast Sheet and it still shows the AHB Sales Code as POLICE Package.

The serial number from 1966-1980 consists of a thirteen (13) digit number sequence number.

EXAMPLE: WK21E61227878

W = Dodge Coronet
K = Police
21 = 2 Door Sedan
E = 318 CU IN V-8 Engine
6 = 1966 Model Year B-SERIES
1 = Lynch Road, MI Assembly Plant
227878 = Assembly Plant Sequence Number

FIRST DIGIT - CAR LINE:

C = Chrysler	(1966-78)
D = Dodge exc:	(1966-77)
E = St. Regis	(1979-80)
F = LeBaron	(1977-80)
G = Diplomat	(1977-80)
H = Volare	(1977-80)
J = Gran Fury	(1980)
L = Dart	(1966-76)
M = Horizon	(1978-80)
N = Aspen	(1976-80)
P = Plymouth exc:	(1966-77)
P = Gran Fury exc:	(1975-77)
R = Belvedere/Satellite	(1966-74)
R = Fury exc: ·	(1975-78)
S = Cordoba	(1975-80)
T = Chrysler	(1979-80)
V = Valiant	(1966-76)
W = Coronet	(1966-76)
W = Charger	(1971-74)
W = Monaco	(1977-78)
X = Charger	(1966-70)
X = Charger	(1975)
X = Charger SE	(1976-78)
X = Magnum XE	(1978-79)
X = Mirada	(1980)
X = Imperial	(1966-75)
Z = Omni	(1978-80)

SECOND DIGIT - PRICE CLASS:

E = Economy
L = Low
M = Medium
H = High
P = Premium
S = Special
X = Fast Top
K = Police
T = Taxi
O = Super Stock
N = New York Taxi
G = New York Taxi

THIRD & FOURTH DIGITS - BODY TYPE:

21 = 2 Door Coupe
23 = 2 Door Hardtop
23 = 2 Door Special Coupe
24 = 2 Door Hatchback
29 = 2 Door Special Hardtop
41 = 4 Door Sedan
42 = 4 Door B-Pillar Coupe
43 = 4 Door Hardtop
44 = 4 Door Hatchback
45 = 6 Passenger Wagon
46 = 9 Passenger Wagon

FIFTH DIGIT - ENGINE:

A = 170, 1-1 BBL	6 CYL	(1966-69)
A = 1.7L, 1-2 BBL	4 CYL	(1978-80)
B = 225, 1-1 BBL	6 CYL	(1966-69)
B = 198, 1-1 BBL	6 CYL	(1970-74)
C = Special Order	6 CYL	(1966-69)
C = 225, 1-1BBL	6 CYL	(1970-80)
D = 273ci	8 CYL	(1966)
D = 273, 1-2BBL	8 CYL	(1967-69)
D = 225, 1-2BBL	6 CYL	(1977-80)
E = 273, 1-4BBL	8 CYL	(1967)
E = 318, 1-2BBL	8 CYL	(1966)
E = Special Order	6 CYL	(1970-80)
F = 361, 1-2BBL	8 CYL	(1966)
F = 318, 1-2BBL	8 CYL	(1967-69)
G = 383ci	8 CYL	(1966)
G = 383, 1-2BBL	8 CYL	(1967-69)
G = 318, 1-2BBL	8 CYL	(1970-80)
H = 426ci	8 CYL	(1966)HEMI (or Wedge)
H = 383, 1-4BBL	8 CYL	(1967-69)HP
H = 340, 1-4BBL	8 CYL	(1970-73)
H = 318, 1-4BBL	8 CYL	(1978-80)
J = 440, 1-4BBL	8 CYL	(1966)
J = 426, 2-4BBL	8 CYL	(1967-69)
J = 340, 3-2BBL	8 CYL	(1970-71)HEMI
J = 360, 1-4BBL	8 CYL	(1974)-79)
K = Special Order	8 CYL	(1966)
K = 440, 1-4BBL	8 CYL	(1967-69)
K = 360, 1-2BBL	8 CYL	(1971-80)
L = 440, 1-4BBL	8 CYL	(1967-69)HP
L = 383, 1-2BBL	8 CYL	(1970-71)
L = 360, 1-4BBL	8 CYL	(1974-80)
M = Special Order	8 CYL	(1967-69)
M = 400, 1-2BBL	8 CYL	(1971-76)
N = 383, 1-4BBL	8 CYL	(1970-71)HP
N = 400, 1-4BBL	8 CYL	(1974-78)
P = 340, 1-4BBL	8 CYL	(1968-69)
P = 400, 1-4BBL	8 CYL	(1972-78)
R = 426, 2-4BBL	8 CYL	(1970-71)HEMI
T = 440, 1-4BBL	8 CYL	(1970-78)
U = 440, 1-4BBL	8 CYL	(1970-78)HP
V = 440, 3-2BBL	8 CYL	(1970-72)HP
Z = Special Order	8 CYL	(1970-80)

SIXTH DIGIT - MODEL YEAR:

6 = 1966	Model Year	B-SERIES
7 = 1967	Model Year	C-SERIES
8 = 1968	Model Year	D-SERIES
9 = 1969	Model Year	E-SERIES
0 = 1970	Model Year	F-SERIES
1 = 1971	Model Year	G-SERIES
2 = 1972	Model Year	H-SERIES
3 = 1973	Model Year	J-SERIES
4 = 1974	Model Year	K-SERIES

This plate belongs to a 1966 Dodge Coronet 318ci, 2-bbl.

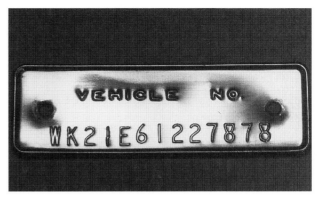

This decodes to mean 1966 Dodge Coronet 318ci, 2-bbl.

5 = 1975	Model Year	L-SERIES
6 = 1976	Model Year	M-SERIES
7 = 1977	Model Year	P-SERIES
8 = 1978	Model Year	R-SERIES
9 = 1979	Model Year	S-SERIES
A = 1980	Model Year	T-SERIES

SEVENTH DIGIT - ASSEMBLY PLANT:
1 = Lynch Road, MI Assembly Plant	(1966-67)
2 = Hamtramck, MI Assembly Plant	(1966-67)
3 = Jefferson, MI Assembly Plant	(1966-67)
4 = Belvedere, IL Assembly Plant	(1966-67)
5 = Los Angeles, CA Assembly Plant	(1966-67)
6 = Newark, DE Assembly Plant	(1966-67)
7 = St. Louis, MO Assembly Plant	(1966-67)
9 = Windsor, ONT Assembly Plant	(1966-67)
A = Lynch Road, MI Assembly Plant	(1968-80)
B = Hamtramck, MI Assembly Plant	(1968-79)
C = Jefferson, MI Assembly Plant	(1968-80)
D = Belvedere, IL Assembly Plant	(1968-80)
E = Los Angeles, CA Assembly Plant	(1968-71)
F = Newark, DE Assembly Plant	(1968-80)
G = St. Louis, MO Assembly Plant	(1968-80)
R = Windsor, ONT Assembly Plant	(1968-80)

LAST 6 DIGITS - INDICATE SEQUENCE NUMBER

From the information I have, most all B-Body Police cars were built at Lynch Road, Michigan until 1971. And most all Dodge & Plymouth C-Body Police cars were built at either Newark, Delaware or Belvedere, Illinois. And all of the Chrysler Police Cars were built at the Jefferson, Michigan Assembly Plant.

1966 Fender Tag Example:
(Built at Lynch Road)

The Serial Number is welded (early 1966) or riveted (mid-year 1966 and 1967) to the left front door hinge pillar (A-Post.) From 1968 to current date the Serial Number is located on top left side of dash panel visible through windshield. The Serial Number is always read from outside the vehicle (not sitting in the vehicle-1967 & older).

1966 DODGE CORONET Deluxe 2 Door Sedan
abcdefghjkmnpqrtuwy
```
+      35      1      +
ABCDEFGHJKLMNPQRSTVWYZ
415
```
SO	NUMBER	BDY	TRM	PAINT
30325925	WK21	KIT	XX1	Y

VIN - WK21E61227878
6130325925 - BODY CODES

The Fender Tag is read from left to right, and bottom to top.
303	Thursday March 3, 1966 Scheduled Production Date
25925	Shipping Order Number POLICE
WK	Dodge Coronet Deluxe Police
21	2 Door Sedan
T K	Police Grade Trim
R 1	Cloth & Vinyl Bench Seat
M T	Tan Interior
P X	Beige Roof Paint
A X	Beige Body Paint
I 1	Mono-Tone Paint Style
N	no accent stripes
T Y	Gold Upper Door Frame Paint
AB 41	318 1-2BBL 230hp V-8 Engine
C 5	Torqueflite Automatic Transmission; radio deleted
e 3	Roof Mounted Light Reinforcement
f 5	Roof Light Wiring/Police
n 1	Spotlight

VIN - WK21E61227878
WK	Dodge Coronet Deluxe Police
21	2 Door Sedan
E	318 1-2BBL 230hp V-8 Engine
6	1966 Model Year
1	Lynch Road, MI Assembly Plant
227878	Assembly Plant Sequential Number

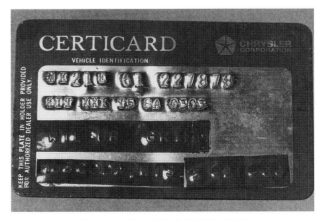

A 1966 Dodge Coronet with a 318ci, 2-bbl had this certicard.

6130325925 - BODY CODES

6	1966 Model Year
1	Lynch Road, MI Assembly Plant
303	Thursday March 3, 1966 Scheduled Production Date
25925	Shipping Order Number POLICE

The Certicards were found on the 1966-1968 Chrysler Products, 1966-67 in a pocket under the hood, and 1968 in a pocket inside the back cover of the owners manual.

This particular certicard is decoded as follows:
WK21 61227878 = SERIAL NUMBER
KIT = Trim Code
XXI = Roof & Body Paint
T5 = Torqueflite Automatic Transmission
SA = Standard axle (SG = Sure Grip)
0303 = Scheduled Production Date

The Owners Name and Vehicle Delivery date will be embossed on a plastic tape and applied to the bottom of the Certi-card.

Here's a VIN tag from a 1976 Plymouth Fury with an "E68" 400ci, 4-bbl.

Other than the VIN all "1's" will be found as "I's"! There are a few exceptions to this rule. And Certicards are available in reproduction.

For further information on decoding VINs, fender tags and certicards on pre-81 Dodge, Plymouth and Chrysler products of all kinds (police and non-police) contact:
Galen V. Govier
Route 1, Box 322K
Prairie du Chien, WI 53821

This plate reads 1977 Dodge Monaco with 440ci, 4-bbl. Special handling refers to shipping, not suspension.

1966 Dodge Coronet Deluxe 2 Door Sedan

B B-Line Broadcast Copy Lynch Road Pit
125476 Job Sequence Number
303 Thursday March 3, 1966
Scheduled Production Date
25925 Shipping Order Number POLICE
WK DODGE Coronet Deluxe POLICE
21 2 Door Sedan
E 318 1-2BBL 230hp V-8 Engine
6 1966 Model Year
1 Lynch Road, MI Assembly Plant
227878 Assembly Plant Sequential Number
X Beige Roof Paint
X Beige Body Paint
1 Mono-Tone Paint Style
Y Bronze Metallic Upper Door Frame
NO Vinyl Roof
NO Stripes
702 BID
K Police Grade Trim
1 Cloth & Vinyl Bench Seat
T Tan Interior
41 318 1-2BBL 230hp V-8 Engine
395 Torqueflite Auto Transmission
Single Exhaust w/Turn Down Pipe
404 3.23:1 Ratio w/8.75" Axle

42 318-2 Auto W/O C.A.P. Dist
1857906 B-Body Front Sway Bar-Strap Type
2582943 22"Radiator Diameter-318 V-8
056 318-2 Engine w/A.T. & Heater Specs
2538331 A727 Torqueflite Auto Trans/POLICE
024 3.23:1 STD 8.75" Axle w/11" Drums
2538933 33 Teeth-Yellow-Speedometer Pinion
14 14 X 5.5" Stamped Steel Wheels
X Beige Painted Wheels
24605R3Hub Caps w/Dodge Emblem
2660717 2.75 X 52.28" Propeller D/Shaft
1857781 LH HEMI Torsion Bar .92 X 41"
1857780 RH HEMI Torsion Bar .92 X 41"
2539795 LH POL. Rear Spring Assembly
2539795 RH POL. Rear Spring Assembly
35B-Body-A.T.-M/B-POL-C1/Brake Brkt
25B-Body-11" HD FT Drum Brakes
32FT Std Ride Shock Absorbers
43RR Std Ride Shock Absorbers
1444564 59 AMP Battery SER 24 Yellow Caps
17B-Body-Column Shift-Manual Strg
V Brown Steering Column
14 2-Spoke w/Full Horn Ring
V Brown Steering Wheel
12 B-Body 318 AUTO Stub Frame

NO Sure Grip
STD Front Heater
STD Radio Deleted
35 7.35 X 14" Black Sidewall Tires (Set of 5 Tires includes Spare)
NO Power Brakes
NO Power Windows
NO Cleaner Air Package
NO Auto Pilot
STD Drum Brakes - 11" Dia (11" std w/POLICE)
NO FT & RR Bumper Guards
NO Electric Clock
NO Console
487 Cigar Lighter
NO Power Deck Lid Release
NO Special Body Style
502 HD FT & RR Floor Mats
509 Glove Box Lock
NO Map & Courtesy Light
NO Brake Warning Light
NO Glove Box Light
NO Ash Receiver Light
NO Trunk Light
STD Clear Glass - all windows
NO Headrests
NO Wide Sill Mouldings
548 Padded Sun Visors
551 Front Foam Rubber Seat Cushion
561 H.D. Seat Springs - FT
562 H.D. Seat Springs - RR
565 Rear Armrests
NO Tachometer
NO Undercoating w/Hood Pad
STD Hub Caps
671 Spotlight
—-Build to Specifications for: USA Order
—-Dealer Stock Order
494 Replaceable Oil Filter
495 Shroud, Engine Fan
591 46 Amp Alternator
645 Calibrated Speedometer
STD Handling Package/POLICE Suspension
663 Roof Mounted Light Reinforcement
665 Roof Light Wiring/Police
REMARKS: HEAVY DUTY FRT & RR Designates Front & Rear HD Seat Springs!

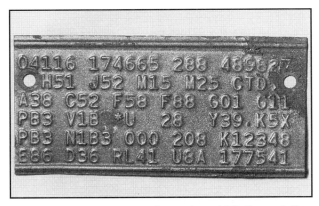

Decoding shows this "A38" police package 1978 Plymouth Fury should have a "E86" 440ci, 4-bbl engine.

1966 Dodge Polara Police 4 Door Sedan

```
abcdefghjkmnpqrtuwy
+        3      9+                      DK41 K63 201911
ABCDEFGHJKLMNPQRSTVWXYZ                 K9A 999 T5 SA
8259    1      CHP B73 5-23-60
SO NUMBER BODY TRIM PAINT 2490 1ST AVE
13088881 DK41 K9A 999 B        SACRAMENTO, CALIF
```

VIN - DK41K63201911

The fender Tag is read from Left to Right, and Bottom to Top

130		Sunday January 30, 1966 Scheduled Production Date
88881		Shipping Order Number
		SPECIAL ORDER/POLICE
D		Dodge Polara Police
41	4	Door Sedan
T	K	Police Grade Trim
R	9	Cloth & Vinyl Seat BENCH
M	A	Gray Interior
P	9	Special Order Roof Paint
A	9	Special Order Body Paint
I	9	Special Order Paint Style
N		No accent stripes
T	B	Black Upper Door Frame Paint
AB	82	440 1-4BBL 365 hp V8 Engine
		DUAL EXHAUST
c	5	Torqueflite Automatic Transmission
D	9	Front Disc Brakes
G	1	26" Radiator Diameter, radio deleted
e	3	Roof Mounted Light Reinforcement
y	9	Special Order

VIN - DK41K63201911

DK	Dodge Polara Police
41	4 Door Sedan
K	Special Order V8 Engine
6	1966 Model Year B-SERIES
3	Jefferson, MI Assembly Plant
201911	Assembly Plant Sequential Number
K9A	TRIM CODE
999	PAINT CODE
T5	Torqueflite Automatic Transmission
SA	Standard Axle
5-23-66	New Vehicle Delivery Date
CHP B 73	"California Highway Patrol"
	2490 1st Ave
	Sacramento, CALIF

As a general rule, this is what identifies a cop car:

1959	9 as third digit in VIN
1960 to 1965	9 as second digit in VIN
1966 to 1977	K as second digit in VIN
1970 to 1983	A38 on Fender Tag
1984 to 1989	AHB on Fender Tag

Further examples of fender tags and decoding are:

+	+				
G31	G33	Y39	28	END	
999	U	B41	F18	F58	F72
999	P2B5	000	224	K10971	
E63	D34	WK41	M3G	170001	

E63	383 4-bbl 8 cyl			
D34	TorqueFlite Transmission			
WK	1973 Dodge Coronet Police			
41	4-door Sedan			
B41	Front Disc Brakes			
F18	65 Amp HD Alternator			
F58	Cross Member Reinforcement			
F72	Single Key Package			
Y39	Special Order			

+	END	+	+	+	
F49	F58	G11	H51	L25	Y39
TX9	U	F14	F33	F38	F43
TX9	K1Y3	KY4	606	K85685	BODY IN WHITE
E86	D34	DK41	U4D	231718	SPECIAL ORDER

E86	440 4bbl 8 cyl HP
D34	TorqueFlite Transmission
DK	1974 Dodge Monaco
41	4-door Sedan
F58	Cross Member Reinforcement
F33	Left Pillar 6" Spotlight
F38	Roof Light Reinforcement
F43	Spotlight Reinforcement
G11	Tinted Glass-ALL
H51	Air Conditioning
L25	Trunk Light
Y39	Special Order

This could have been the Bluesmobile!

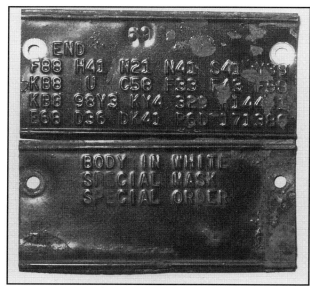

A decoding of this plate reveals a 1976 Dodge Monaco powered by a 400ci, 4-bbl.

	END				
F88	H41	N21	N41	S41	Y39
KB8	U	C58	F33	F43	F58
KB8	98Y3	KY4	329	K14441	
E68	D36	DK41	P6D	171386	

E68	400 4 bbl 8 cyl HP
D36	HD 727-A TorqueFlite

DK	1976 Dodge Monaco
41	4-door Sedan
F88	Engine Oil Cooler
H41	Strato Ventilation
NZ1	Air Pump
N21	Dual Exhausts Without Tips
S41	Rear Sway Bar
F58	Cross Member Reinforcement
F43	Spotlight Reinforcement
F33	Left Pillar, 6in Spotlight
C58	50/50 Bench Seats
Y39	Special Order
	SPECIAL HANDLING

This tag is from a 1978 Plymouth Fury with an "E86" 440ci, 4-bbl engine.

30102	178179	288	488827		
N51	N94	END			
F33	F58	G21	H51	M25	
N41	EWI	*U	28	A38	C52
EW1	N1Y3	000	220	K19566	
E86	D36	RL41	U8A	182271	

E86	440 4 bbl 8 cyl HP
D36	HD 727-A TorqueFlite
RL	1978 Plymouth Fury
41	4-door Sedan
N51	Maximum Engine Cooling
N94	E.S.A. with Catalytic Converter
F33	Left Pillar, 6" Spotlight
F58	Rear Crossmember Reinforcement
G21	Clear Windows with A.C.
H51	Air Conditioning
M25	Wide Sill Mouldings
N41	Dual Exhausts Without Tips
A38	POLICE PACKAGE
C52	Bench Seats

END					
	N37	N41	N75	N94	26
F45	F57	F58	G01	H51	J52
TG6	U	E	D52	A38	F33
TG6	K2T3	000	326	K23376	
E58	D34	HL41	LAF	202508	

E58	360 4 bbl 8 cyl HP/Police
D34	TorqueFlite Transmission
HL	1980 Plymouth Volare

This 1980 Plymouth Volare "A38" police car was powered by an "E58" 360ci, 4-bbl engine.

41	4-door Sedan
N41	Dual Exhausts Without Tips
N75	Auxil. Trans. Cooler
N94	E.S.A. with Catalytic Converter
F57	T-bar Rear Engine Mount
F58	Crossmember Reinforcement
G01	Rear Window Defroster
H51	Air Conditioning
J52	Inside Hood Release
D52	2.93 Axle Ratio
A38	POLICE PACKAGE
F33	Left Pillar, 6in Spotlight

The 2nd Fender Tag usually was off to the right of the basic tag, and shared the same center screw. The Basic tag overlapped the 2nd Tag.

Examples of Secondary Tags I have found next to the Primary Fender Tags are:

abcdefghjkmnpqrtuwy
+   +   +   +
ABCDEFGHJKLMNPQRSTVWXYZ
12345678   AX   TRM   PNT   UBS
MONO BAKE
SPECIAL ORDER
BODY IN WHITE
+   +   +SPECIAL MASK +
SPECIAL ORDER
BODY IN WHITE
SPECIAL ORDER

+   SPECIAL PAINT   +
SPECIAL ORDER

+   +
A38 POLICE

SPECIAL HANDLING
+   +   +   +
BODY IN WHITE   CAR
SPECIAL MASK
SPECIAL PAINT
SPECIAL ORDER

Any Special Order Fender Tags placed on a vehicle designates one of many types of Special Ordered vehicles. I have

found this to be common on most all Police cars.

I believe MONO BAKE means that the paint is only baked once.

Body in White, is self explanatory. Special Mask is common to the police Black & White two-tone scheme. Body in White is not always a White Car, at least the Tag I have is a Dark Blue Metallic.

Special Handling Car has to do with special care in assembly, this 2nd tag is also found in New Yorkers & Imperials.

For further information on decoding VINs, fender tags and certicards on pre-81 Dodge, Plymouth and Chrysler products of all kinds (police and non-police) contact:

    Galen V. Govier
    Route 2, Box 322 K

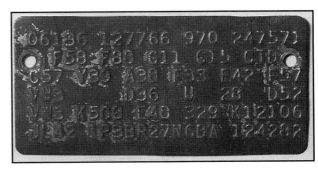

This 1980 Plymouth R-body Gran Fury with the "A38" police package used an "E48" 318ci, 4-bbl engine.

Police-Related Sales Codes

A-Packages	M-Mouldings
B-Brakes	N-Engine Accessories
C-Trim	P-Power
D-Transmission/Axle	R-Radios
E-Engines	S-Suspension/Steering
F-Fleet	T-Tires: 13- & 14-inch
G-Glass	U-Tires: 15-inch
H-Heater/AC	V-Vinyl/Paint
J-Miscellaneous	W-Wheels/Hubcaps
K-Stripes	X-Export
L-Lights	Z-Weight

Order Code	Description
A35	Trailer Towing Pkg.
A37	Taxi Package
AHB/A38	Police Package
A83	New York Taxi Package (1970)
B12	Heavy-Duty Frt. Disc Brakes
B13	Taxi Frt. Disc Brakes
B25	10x2.5" Rear Drum Brakes
B26	10x2.5" Rear Brakes (Taxi)
B28	11x2.5" Rear Drum Brakes
B31	11in Heavy-Duty Manual Drum Brakes
B41	Frt. Disc Brakes
B42	Frt. HD Disc Brakes
B43	Manual Brakes
B51	Power Asst. Disc Brakes
C12	Shoulder Belts
C13	Frt. Shoulder Belts

Order Code	Description		Order Code	Description
C14	Rear Shoulder Belts		G01	Electric Heated RR Window Defroster
C52	Bench Seats		G11	Tinted Glass-All
C58	50/50 Bench Seats		G15	Tinted Windshield Only
C81	Heavy Duty Front Seat Springs		G21	Clear Glass w/AC-all windows
C83	Heavy Duty Rear Seat Springs		H25	Heater Delete
D13	3-speed Manual Trans. Floor Shift		H41	Strato Ventilation
D14	3-speed Manual Column Shift		H51	Single air conditioning w/heater
D30	TorqueFlite Auto. (1982 & Up)		J67	Heavy-Duty Wiring Harness
D31	Light-Duty 904-A TorqueFlite		L25	Trunk Compartment Light
D32	H/D A-727 Torque Flite (Some Years A-998)		L62	AC Hi-Pressure Cutoff
D33	A-999 TorqueFlite		M27	Delete Wheel Lip Mouldings
D34	TorqueFlite Transmission		M93	Delete Body Side Moulding
D36	HD 727-A TorqueFlite		N21	Air Pump
D41	Heavy Duty Clutch		N25	Engine Block Heater
D52	2.94:1 Axle Ratio (1969-74);		N41	Dual exhausts w/o Tips
	2.93:1 Axle Ratio (1975 & Up)		N45	High Capacity Fan
D53	3.23:1 Axle Ratio (1969-74);		N51	Maximum Engine Cooling
	3.21:1 Axle Ratio (1975 & Up)		N65	7-Blade Clutch Drive Fan
D56	3.55:1 Axle Ratio (1969-74)		N75	Aux. Transmission Oil Cooler
D91	Sure Grip Differential		N76	Coolant Recovery System
E11	170 1-bbl. 6 cyl.		N77	Aux. Vacuum Reservoir
E25	225 1-bbl. 6 cyl. (1969)		N81	Fast Idle Throttle
E43	318 5.2L EEC 8 cyl.		N94	E.S.A. w/Catalytic Converter ('75 & Up)
E44	318 2-bbl.8 cyl.		N95	NOx Exhaust Emission Control;
E45	318 2-bbl. 8 cyl. H (1973-74)			California Emission Pkg. (Late 1970s & Up)
E55	360 2-bbl. 8 cyl.		N96	High Altitude Emissions ('73 & Up)
E57	360 2-bbl.8 cyl.		R08	Radio Delete
E58	360 4-bbl. 8 cyl. HP/Police		648/S15/SDD	Police Handling Package, Hemi Suspension
E61	383 2-bbl. 8 cyl.		S41	Rear Sway Bar
E63	383 4-bbl. 8 cyl.		S75	Police Power Steering
E64	400 4-bbl. 8 cyl.		T41	8.25x14" BSW
E68	400 4-bbl 8 cyl. HP		T45	G78x14" BSW
E85	440 4-bbl. 8 cyl.		T52	8.55x14" WSW
E86	440 4-bbl. 8 cyl. HP		T55	H78x14" BSW
F01	Police Engine		T79	FR70x14" O-W-L Aramid
F17	Radio Suppressor Pkg.; 100 Amp Alternator;		T99	Special Order 14" Tires
	114 Amp Alternator (1981 & Up)		U21	8.25x15" BSW
F27/BCC	430 AMP Battery		U28	G78x15" BSW
671/F33/LND	Spot Light-Left Pillar, 6"		U31	8.55x15" BSW
672/F35/LNE	Spot Light-Right Pillar, 6"		U41	8.85x15" BSW
663/F38/XDF	Roof (Light) Reinforcement		U44	J78x15" WSW Fiberglass
665/F41/XHF	Roof Wiring w/Hole		U45	GR60x15" O-W-L. Aramid
652/F42/LDF	Additional Dome Light		U51	9.15x15" BSW
F43	Reinforcement for Spotlight		U57	L78x15" BSW
F46	Roof Light Wiring		U59	GR70x15" BSW Rayon Belted
F52	Manual Low Gear Block Out		U7S	F70x15" B Special Order
F58	Rear Crossmember Reinf. or Welds		U79	F70x15" Special Order
F72/GXB	Single Key Package		U99	Special Order 15" Tires
F82	Power Deck Release		VO1	Mono-tone Paint
F83	Stainless Steel Hose Clamps		VO2	Two-tone Paint
F88	Engine Oil Cooler		VO9	Special Order Paint
F94	P/S Pump Oil Cooler		WO1	Hub Caps
645/F95/JDD	Certified Speedometer		W96	15x7" XHD Wheels
F96	Oil Pressure of Oil/Temp. Gauge		Y33	Fleet Sales
			699/Y39	Special Order

Select 1982 Chrysler Corp. Build Codes

A38-police package
B12-H.D. front disc brakes
B41-power disc brakes front, drums rear
B42-h.d. power disc brakes front, drums rear
C52-bench seat-straight
C57-60/40 split bench seat
D31-A904 auto trans
D33-A999 auto trans
D34-standard duty auto trans
D35-A413 auto transaxle
D36-A727 auto trans
D37-A404 auto trans
D38-h.d. A904 auto trans
D39-A470 auto trans
D52-2.94 ratio rear gear
D69-special order axle ratio
D81-7-1/4in rear axle
D82-8-1/4in rear axle
D92-Sure-Grip differential
D25-h.d. 225ci, 1-bbl
E45-H.D. 318ci, 4-bbl
E62-2.2L 4-cyl, 2-bbl
E72-2.6L 4-cyl, 2-bbl
F17-100 amp alternator
F28-500 amp battery
F33-spotlight, 6in, left
F35-spotlight, 6in, right
F38-roof reinforcement
F42-add'l dome light
F52 low gear blockout
F57-heavy service package
F58-extra heavy service package
F83-stainless screw hose clamps
F84-silicone hoses
F88-engine oil cooler
F94-P/S pump oil cooler
F95-certified speedometer
F96-oil gauge assembly
G01-heated rear window

G11-tinted glass-all
G15-tinted windshield
G16-clear windshield
H53-air conditioning
J16-police relay control
J18-police bonding package
L34-halogen headlights
L55-h.d. stop light switch
N21-air pump
N22-aspirator
N25-engine block heater
N37-catalytic exhaust
N51-max. engine cooling
N55-catalytic heat shield (grass)
N75-auxiliary trans oil cooler
N81-fast idle throttle control-manual
N94-E.S.A. with catalyst
N95-California emissions package
N96-high altitude emissions
SO2-h.d. shocks
S13-h.d. suspension
S14-firm-feel suspension
S16-extra duty suspension, front/rear sway bar, front rear over-size shocks
S41-rear sway bar
S75-police power steering
S77-power steering
T48 P185/70R14 fabric belted pursuit radials BSW
T99 special order 14-inch radial tire
U63-P215/70R15 fabric belted pursuit radials BSW
U99-special order 15-inch radial tire
V09-special order paint
W01-dog dish hub caps
W87-14x6.0 JJ black enamel wheel
W96-15x7.0 JJ extra heavy duty wheel
W99-special order wheel
Y13-test car
Y31-California Highway Patrol car
Y39-special order
Y47-police use

Chapter 16

Officer Survey and Results

Two years to the month after the last M-body police car rolled off the Kenosha, Wisconsin assembly line, a survey was sent out to over 200 city, county and state police departments, nationwide.

The majority of state police departments used their police cars for 2 1/2 years or 70,000 miles. For most agencies, all the Mopars were gone. Certainly most police officers knew the Chrysler Corp. police cars were history. Only the very best connected fleet managers knew that Dodge was tinkering with their Dynasty fitted with an Imperial engine. Of course, the Intrepid was still a dot matrix on some engineer's CAD/CAM system. Only the dreamers thought it would come with the East-West V-6 front wheel drive and the North-South V-8 rear wheel drive.

Front wheel drive and law enforcement just didn't mix well at the time. In 1991, the Ford Taurus was just starting to be accepted for urban-duty, patrol-class work with the Wayne Co. Michigan Sheriff's Dept. The St. Louis, Missouri Police were dabbling with front wheel drive Chevy Celebrities, but most were the non-police package Lumina.

With total sales under 1,000 units a year, the front wheel drive, urban-duty police car did not merit a lot of development. Cops wanted rear wheel drive, V-8 powered battle cruisers. Chrysler Corp. was a front wheel drive-only company. They were out of the police car business, just as they said. This allowed a lot of police personnel of all ranks to comment on the Chrysler products without fear of conflict of interest.

The survey was sent to the public information officer with routing requested to:

Motor Pool Supervisor
Pursuit Driving Instructor
Fleet Manager
Car Enthusiast
Departmental Historian

It gave these specialists an opportunity to reflect on 34 years of Dodge, Plymouth and Chrysler-marque squads. The Diplomat and Gran Fury would be recent in their memory, but still only a memory since most were now out of service. This put all the years of Mopar squads on as equal footing as the passing of time would allow.

The survey was sent to all of the state police in all fifty states including Washington, D.C. and the California State Police and California Highway Patrol. It was also sent to a minimum of three city or county police departments in each state. Additional surveys were sent to the significant city and county agencies in Southern California and New York/New Jersey.

The 1979 thru 1981 R-body Chrysler Newport, Dodge St. Regis (shown) and Plymouth Gran Fury were voted the best Mopar squad cars of all time. *Dave Link*

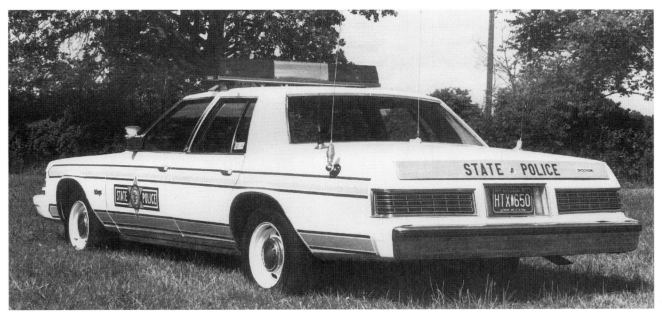

The R-body squad cars, like this Illinois State Police 1980 Dodge St. Regis had the perfect balance of power, handling, size and comfort. *Dave Link*

The first question: Why were Dodge, Plymouth or Chrysler squads selected by your Department? Choices:

Low Bid
Acceleration of Freeway Speeds
Top Speed
Ride Comfort
Handling & Agility at Speed
Interior Room
Ease of Maintenance

Maintenance History
Strong Local Dealer
Officer Preference, Why?
Other

For better or for worse, every responding department checked "low bid" as their top priority. The cold reality of the Dodge and Plymouth police car popularity was these cars were the lowest bid, period. Enthusiasts could hope that top speed, acceleration and durability were keys to the Mopar success story.

A survey of officers ranked the 1978 Plymouth Fury (shown) and Dodge Monaco to the second best of all Mopar squads. *Chrysler Historical*

The 1969 Dodge Polara was the fastest Mopar police car ever made with a top speed of 147mph. It was voted third most popular.

The Mopar squads did have excellent performance and reliability. In some cases, that allowed them to easily qualify for the bid process. But in the final analysis, the dollars and cents bid process was all that mattered.

The "low bid" method most government entities make purchases is why the Michigan State Police method is so encouraging for Dodge and Plymouth enthusiasts. These Mopar squads were not just the lowest bid of any car passing the minimum performance requirements, if there were any. These squads had a dollar and cents advantage that came strictly from their superior performance.

The entire nation may have used Mopar squads because they were low bid, but all along the cops and tax payers were getting the most performance for the dollar. The MSP proved that starting in 1978. Remember that instead of low bid.

Second after the low bid, all the other reasons were given almost equal weight. Some focused on the sheer performance as-

The 1969 Plymouth Fury with the 375hp, 440ci engine is a classic police powerhouse. It runs a 14-second quarter mile. *Virginia State Police*

pects. Other agencies indicated room, ride and comfort. Quite a few indicated a strong local Dodge or Chrysler-Plymouth dealer as a deciding factor. Smaller agencies or those with no motor pool used these dealers for maintenance. Those that did their own repairs checked off maintenance ease and history.

This drives home another point. Car enthusiasts think about cop cars in terms of cubic inch performance. Most cops, however, take a certain minimum level of performance for granted and key in on reliability. The cop car does not have to be fast, but it does have to be reliable.

The last part of the survey was the personal opinions about Chrysler Corp. squads in general. In what ways were the Chrysler squads the best for police use? Some of the answers we expected and some we did not.

Responses included: Withstood constant abuse and hard miles (California Highway Patrol); Usually handled well (Missouri State Highway Patrol); They are rugged and will take much abuse (Delaware State Police); It looked like a police car (Houston, Texas Police); Strong drive train, 727 automatic was best available (Greenwich, Connecticut Police); They were low bid (St. Petersburg, Florida Police); Good handling. Good engines (Chicago, Illinois Police); Cannot think of any reason they were the best (Illinois State Police); Agility and reliability from 1960 through 1971 (Los Angeles, California Police); Diplomat & Gran Fury fit in through school yard fences & down back alleys (New York City Police); Drove them until they died at 150,000 miles plus (Hamtramck, Michigan Police); They were the best vehicles for the money and performance (Indiana State Police); They were fast and cheap (Oregon State Police); None. (Dallas, Texas Police).

The 1980s models had short turning radius and high center for rural roads (Kansas Highway Patrol); Room, acceleration and never overheated (Pinellas Co. Florida Sheriff); Economical (Atlanta, Georgia Police); Excellent acceleration, good handling (Los Angeles, California Police); Power at all speeds (San Gabriel, California Police).

And now the flip side. . .

In what ways were the Chrysler Corp. squads the "worst" for police work? Reponses included: Somewhat small during the 1980s (Michigan State Police); Pushbutton shift (Missouri State Highway Patrol); Not as powerful as Ford or Chevrolet (Delaware State Police); Loose steering and front end problems (Houston, Texas Police); 1980 front end problems and small gas tank (Vermont State Police); Small size in later years (New York State Police); Bent K-frames (St. Petersburg, Florida Police); Small, no power, overheat, fall apart (Illinois State Police); No major problems (Los Angeles, California Police); Front end doesn't hold up (New York City Police, Bronx); K-frames (Reno, Nevada Police); Front end (Portland, Oregon Police); Not good for undercover work! (New York City Police, Brooklyn); 1980s and later poor handling (California State Police); Small trucks and interior (Tennessee Highway Patrol); Front end problems (Dallas, Texas Police); Weak front ends and mystery steering (Winston-Salem, North Carolina Police); After 1978, they were nothing more than a tin can (Maine State Police); Hard to stop with drum brakes (Tulsa, Oklahoma Police); No problems (California Highway Patrol); 1980s and up, too small inside (Los Angeles Co., California Sheriff); Stiff ride and stark Interiors (Pinellas Co., Florida Sheriff); M-bodies had weak K-frames and front suspensions (Philadelphia, Pennsylvania Police).

Next, what was the most miles ever put on a Chrysler squad? Keep in mind, most agencies like Arizona Highway Patrol, California Highway Patrol, Michigan State Police, Missouri State Highway Patrol, Los Angeles Police, Florida Highway Patrol, Indiana State Police, Baltimore Co., Maryland have a maximum number of years or a maximum number of miles allowable on their squads before they are sold. See the chapter on the Police Car Owners of America.

While most squads are usually well-maintained at least mechanically, better than most privately-owned vehicles, the miles they stack up are much harsher. A good rule of thumb is one mile in police use equals two miles of passenger car use.

One of the most popular Mopar squad cars, the 1969 Plymouth Belvedere, has stopped one of the most popular Mopar muscle cars, the 1969 Dodge Daytona. *Roland Osborne*

The squad with a mere 75,000 miles may have the wear of 150,000 normal miles.

Cop cars drivetrains are beefier, and have coolers on everything to extend component wear. Cops expect 100,000 miles of actual duty use from police package cars, and they usually get it. That is 200,000 miles of wear and tear in civilian terms. Even still, it is refreshing to hear this kind of mileage.

The 1969 Plymouth Belvedere was a 4-door Road Runner while the 1969 Dodge Coronet was a 4-door Super Bee. *Chrysler Historical*

The 1984 Dodge Diplomat (shown) and Plymouth Gran Fury were voted to be the fifth most popular Mopar police car.

New York City Police
100,000 plus on most NYPD vehicles
Los Angeles Police
110,000 on 1969 Plymouth Belvedere 383ci, 4-bbl
Tennessee Highway Patrol
120,000 on 1979 Chrysler Newport 360ci, 4-bbl
Pasadena CA Police
125,000 on 1970 Plymouth Fury 383ci, 4-bbl
Vermont State Police
130,000 on 1987 Plymouth Gran Fury 318ci, 4-bbl
(still in service as of July 1991)

Galena, IL Police
133,500 on 1985 Dodge Diplomat 318ci, 4-bbl
Los Angeles Co. Sheriff's Dept.
135,000 on 1973 Plymouth Satellite 400ci, 4-bbl
Prince George's Co. MD Sheriff
140,000 on 1982 Dodge Diplomat 318ci, 4-bbl
University of Southern CA Police
150,000 on 1981 Dodge Diplomat 318ci, 4-bbl
Hamtramck, MI Police
150,000 on 1975 Dodge Monaco 318ci, 2-bbl

Basically unchanged from 1981 through 1989, the M-body Chrysler LeBaron, Dodge Diplomat (shown) and Plymouth Gran Fury were America's Police Car.

Oregon State Police
150,000 on 1979 Chrysler Newport 360ci, 4-bbl
Kansas Highway Patrol
150,000 on 1988 Plymouth Gran Fury 318ci, 4-bbl
Delaware State Police
178,000 on 1982 Dodge Diplomat 318ci, 4-bbl

We don't know if these were the most mileage ever put on squads, but it is expert testimony to the durability of the Mopar small block V-8. The survey gave cops a chance to reflect on their career in Mopar squads. Since most cops used Mopar squads, memorable things that happen in police work just so happen to occur while driving a Dodge, Chrysler or Plymouth.

. . .backing out of a drive, hitting a pole, the career's first accident

. . .the first over 100mph, over 20 mile pursuit of the career

. . .drag racing civilians on Colorado Blvd. in a '68 Dodge Coronet police car

. . .pushing an 80,000 pound double trailer semi off the road with a 440ci wedge powered Polara

. . .stalled engine when slowed down for corner during a pursuit

. . .broke a front torsion bar during a pursuit

. . .catching the squad on fire and burning it to the ground due to leaky valve covers (must have been a big block)

. . .catching the dash on fire, filling the car with smoke when turned on emergency lights to make a vehicle stop

. . .overheating the brakes, over shooting the stopped violator, forced to go down the road, turn around and come back

. . .in a pursuit with a motorcycle, (very tough to keep up) the 1978 Fury 440 finally overtook the bike after a long pursuit, brakes overheated and hit the stopped biker

. . .Diplomat driven into a full ditch, which really "flooded" the engine. All you could see were the red lights.

. . .parking brake released by itself and the squad rolled forward into the violator's car

. . .unit jumped out of park and backed into a fence

. . .Sgt. flipped a 1970 Belvedere in a chase. Landed on wheels and didn't even break the blue light. Only damage was a bent suspension and a flat tire.

The heart of the Officer's Survey was the question, "What is your personal choice for the best Chrysler squad?"

As in any fill-in-the-blank survey, as opposed to multiple choice, the memory can play some tricks on a person, even cops. Some of the answers just could not be counted, inspite of the enthusiasm because:

1. There were no 1980 police Dodge Diplomats.
2. Diplomats never came with 360ci engines.
3. The St. Regis never came with a 440ci engine.
4. The 440 6-pack was not a police engine.

Sometimes the make and model of car was listed but not the year. (Dodge Diplomat). Occasionally the year, make and model were listed but not the engine. (1980 Dodge St. Regis). Frequently the year, make and engine were listed, but not the model. (1974 Dodge 440)

As all cops do, we tried to read "intent" into the vote, but some votes just could not be counted. As a result, while the voting for the best overall Mopar squad may not be able to be certified by Arthur Anderson, here it is for your nostalgic entertainment.

Best Overall: The 1980 Dodge St. Regis with the E58 360ci, 4-bbl. Other cars in the same category were the 1979 Dodge St. Regis, 1979 Chrysler Newport and 1980 Plymouth Gran Fury, all with the E58ci, 4-bbl engine. These were lumped together, but

The 1980 Gran Fury, like this Wisconsin State Patrol unit, is a Mopar police classic. *Greg Reynolds*

the 1980 St. Regis had by far the most votes.

Second Overall: The 1978 Plymouth Fury with the E86 440ci, 4-bbl. Other cars in this same category were the 1977 Plymouth Fury, 1978 Dodge Monaco and 1977 Dodge Monaco, all with the E86ci, 4-bbl engine. These were lumped together, but the 1978 Fury had the clear majority of the votes.

Third Overall Tie: The 1969 Dodge Polara with the 440ci, 4-bbl engine. Also included in this category were a few 1968 Plymouth Belvederes, but not Dodge Coronets from either year. These were the big years for the "beep, beep" Road Runner, 1968 was the first year and 1969 was the best year. The 4-door police Road Runners will be forever cherished as 'muscle with a badge.'

Fifth Overall: The 1984 Dodge Diplomat with the 318ci, 4-bbl. Also included in this category was the 1982 Plymouth Gran Fury and 1981 to 1983 Dodge Diplomat. These squads really were America's Police car. Not the fastest, but fast enough. Not the roomiest or most comfortable, but good enough. They handled well, had great brakes and had "police-spec" durability.

The easiest "analysis" of the voting was that cops used the "last of" method of remembering Mopar squads. The 1969 Polara was the "last of" the high compression big blocks; the last of the 145 plus, incredibly fast Mopar Pursuits. The 1978 Fury was the "last of" any big block Mopar squad.

The 1980 St. Regis was the last of the long wheelbase squad cars, or at least the last one with an engine powerful enough to move it. The 1984 Diplomat and Gran Fury were the last of the 318ci V-8s with the Carter Thermo Quad. That was important. Simply put, after 1984 the Chrysler squad cars used General Motors carburetors.

What was also interesting about the survey was what did not get votes. Not one 400ci engine squad received votes. An excellent engine, this big block was overshadowed every year by the ultimate big block, the 440ci. Not one vote was cast for a Slant Six powered car, nor for a K-car, nor Aspen/Volare. The only 2-bbl car to get votes was the Dodge St. Regis with the 318ci. It was so popular, cops would even accept a 2-bbl engine!

One point of pure speculation: Cops who patrolled in the late 1950s were mostly retired by the late 1970s. If we could have reached their vote, the stormin' D500 Dodges from the 1950s would certainly have displaced the small block M-bodies, and outrun perhaps all but the perfectly balanced R-bodies as the best Mopar squad of all time. In their era, they were as legendary as the 440ci Polara in its era. In the final analysis, however, nothing beats all around balance for this kind of all around the clock duty.

Chapter 17

Michigan State Police Vehicle Tests

In November 1977, the Michigan State Police did something unheard of for any government agency. They did not buy the lowest bid squad car for their officers. Instead they bought the one with lowest adjusted bid. In doing so, the MSP did a great service for their officers and in turn for police officers and sheriff's deputies everywhere. Finally, cost-based performance and comfort were tied to vehicle selection.

Led by then-Sgt., now F/Lt. (ret.) Curtis VanDenBerg, and for every model year since 1978, the Michigan State Police has conducted tests on police cars. These include acceleration to 100mph, absolute top speed, braking power, lap times around a road course, a subjective ergonomic review and EPA city fuel economy. What started off as an internal testing program, has grown to be the most prestigious of all police vehicle testing with the complete involvement of Chevrolet, Ford and Chrysler fleet personnel. Numerous state, county and city bid specifications from across the country now require that any prospective police vehicle pass those MSP tests.

Like the Los Angeles Sheriffs Dept., the MSP serves as an independent test source for all other agencies. A great deal of hard work and detailed testing goes into the evaluation. The MSP makes all of the results available at no charge to other agencies. Each year police officers from other agencies are invited to attend the tests as independent observers. The end result is an objective analysis of performance that goes beyond glossy photos and bravado claims for Dearborn, Warren and Highland Park.

Importantly, under the MSP program, the top performers have a dollars and cents advantage in the bid process. Following

The Michigan State Police vehicle tests are conducted at Chrysler's Chelsea Proving Grounds and at Michigan International Speedway.

the MSP program, one percent of the average bid received is multiplied times the vehicle's weighted score from these performance tests. The result is a dollar adjustment figure that is added to the vehicle's bid price. The contract is awarded to the vehicle with the lowest adjusted bid. The actual price paid, however, is the actual bid price.

The oil embargo and national energy crisis of 1973 and 1974 gave the fleet management at the Michigan State Police "visions of Volkswagen squad cars." New York City police cruised the streets around the First Precinct in Plymouth Horizons in 1980, so the MSP concern was justified!

The MSP was faced with the age old purchasing problem of getting squad cars quoted first and qualifying them second versus pre-qualifying the cars and accepting quotes on only the qualified cars. With the widespread concern with fuel economy and a downsizing trend to smaller cars and smaller engines, the MSP wanted to know in advance how their future cars were going to perform. With the early involvement of the Department of Management and Budget, the Department of State Police determined if the squad wasn't going to perform well, then no bid was acceptable.

Prior to the mid-1970s the MSP tested only the "low bid" squad car. If it met minimum performance standards, then the vehicle was purchased. This bidding process became the focus of attention in 1975. That year Plymouth outbid Chevrolet by $4.45 per car to win the contract. For basically the same price, which was the better car?

The MSP never found out which was the better car (although most readers of this book could tell them) because the MSP followed the bid process to the penny and bought the Plymouths. But it did get them thinking. With the early involvement and help of the Department of Management and Budget, the Department of State Police got this time-honored process reversed. They gave "performance" a dollars and cents value.

In the fall of 1976, a group of MSP troopers tested the 1977 model year squads. The Dept. of Management and Budget had agreed in concept to the MSP plan to purchase a car that was not the lowest bid as long as the performance was high enough. On the 1977 model year cars they made a dry run on the program to see how their proposal would have done. This was a non-published test.

The program was given the green light and became effective on 1978 model year squad cars. In the fall of 1979, this unique test program received funding by the International Association of Chiefs of Police (IACP), through the National Institute of Justice Technical Assessment Program (TAP).

The MSP program is critically important to the history of Chrysler Corp. squad cars. Dodge and Plymouth dominated the police car market in the 1960s and mid-1970s because they were the low bid. However, they also dominated the mid-1970s and most of the 1980s under the MSP program.

This meant, clear and simple, they had the most performance for the money. That is what the MSP program with its nation wide influence set out to prove. Dodge and Plymouth squads were not just "low bid." They were low bid, performers, which no other car company could touch for the money. And sometimes, they couldn't catch them regardless of the money!

Each year the American manufacturers of police patrol package and special service package vehicles are invited to submit to the MSP. They know in advance the minimum performance standards and the priority assigned to each of the performance areas. In May of each year, the minimum performance requirements and the weighting for each performance category are established by the MSP. The zero to 100mph times for example, are based on an average of the previous year's successful vehicles plus ten percent. Other performance criteria come from open discussions with all manufacturers of police patrol and special service package vehicles. Once the performance standards and priorities are set, the MSP is locked into the low bid procedure detailed in their program. The minimum equipment and options required on each car is also made known by mid-year. The MSP tests are restricted to police patrol package and special service package vehicles. This includes full-size, heavy-duty cruisers; mid-size, urban-duty sedans; special service pursuit pony cars; station wagons and 4 wheel drive vehicles.

For the first MSP evaluation conducted on 1978 vehicles, Buick, Chevrolet, Dodge, Ford, Plymouth and Pontiac submitted cars. The Plymouth Fury equipped with one of the last 440ci big block engines took four of the then-seven categories. The bid of $5,485 was adjusted down based on pre-determined formulas and the Fury became the first winner under the new MSP system.

A lot has changed with police cars since 1978. They no longer are available with big block engines like the Chrysler 440, Chevy 454 and Ford 460. Most cars have small V-8s and even V-6s. Nearly all cars are fuel injected rather than carbureted. Instead of 118-inch wheelbase cruisers weighing 4,600 pounds, some squad cars have a 100-inch wheelbase and weigh 3,200lb. The 1978 big block Fury got 10mpg. Today 16 to 18 is the rule. Finally, only Ford and Chevy make official squad cars. Chrysler, who used to be known as the "police car company," pulled out of the business after the 1989 model year.

A vehicle that fails to meet any of the performance standards is disqualified from the MSP bid process. And the MSP has disqualified vehicles every year. Starting in their first year, the Buick 350 LeSabre and the Ford 400 LTD failed to meet minimum acceleration requirements. At times, this seemed harsh. In 1987, the Dodge 318ci, 4-bbl Diplomat was disqualified because it was just 1/4 second slow in the 0 to 80mph test, even though all other goals including 0 to 100mph were met. However, the MSP continues all of the testing as a service to other police agencies whose top speed or acceleration requirements differ from the MSP.

Vehicle Dynamics. The vehicle dynamics test takes place on the road racing course at Michigan International Speedway. This is the test that MSP gives the most weight in the results. The idea is that a police car must have handling characteristics superior to standard vehicles. Superior high speed handling and cornering ability are important both to maintain pursuit with vehicles capable of greater top speeds and to better avoid accidents during pursuit or emergency runs.

The MIS road course is 1.635 miles of hills, curves, sharp corners and a short straight which allows speeds up to 95mph in a full size cruiser. Each car is driven for at least 12 timed laps using a minimum of 3 different MSP road troopers. The final score

is the average of the fastest 9 laps. This is a true test of the overall balance of the car by combining acceleration, braking and cornering. A serious inability in any of these areas would result in a poor lap time.

Acceleration. The second test is for acceleration. The police vehicle must be able to quickly accelerate and overtake the violating vehicle. This "catch time" is especially critical when the squad must stop, make a U-turn and accelerate. These tests took place on the 4.71 mile oval at Chrysler's Chelsea Proving Grounds.

The MSP minimum acceptable acceleration times have fluctuated up and down since 1978. They are dependent on the previous year's performance and on the current year's potential. From 1978 the minimum acceleration performance was relaxed each year because the maximum police engine size got smaller each year. This peaked in 1982. From then on the minimum standards got generally tougher each year.

By 1989, the last year for small block powered Mopar squads, the performance requirements were similar again to the age of the big block. By 1993, the standards were much tougher than in 1978 when cops still had 440ci squad cars. All acceleration tests are run with two troopers on board and without spotlights or light bars.

In 1980 and 1981, the MSP tested full-size cars with wheelbases between 114.4 and 119.9in. They also tested mid-size cars with wheelbases from 105.5 inches to 112.7inches. Each class of squad had its own set of performance requirements. This made for a smooth and orderly transition from the 360ci-powered, 118.5-inch wheelbase St. Regis to the 318ci-powered, 112.7-inch wheelbase Diplomat.

Top speed. The top speed tests are an extension of the last 0 to 100mph run. After the fourth acceleration test, each vehicle

The Michigan State Police began their vehicle tests on 1978 model police cars. Mopars were selected eight times in 12 years.

F/Lt. (ret.) Curtis VanDenBerg developed the MSP testing method where superior vehicle performance was given a dollars and cents advantage.

continues to accelerate around the oval for 3 laps. The highest speed anywhere during this 14 mile run is the vehicle's competitive score. However, each vehicle has to reach a certain minimum top speed and attain that speed within a certain distance.

This is a tough test which many vehicles have failed to pass. The first new "police patrol package" Ford Crown Victoria assigned to co-author Sanow had a top speed of 97mph, period. And the MSP had made the test tougher. They used to give the car 3 miles to reach 110mph. In the mid-80s it changed to 2 miles. The ideal here is that the vehicle must get up to 110mph in order to successfully pursue, overtake and apprehend violators.

For the record, a spotlight lowers the top speed of a squad capable of 120mph by 1.5mph per spotlight.

A compact light bar like the Federal Jetsonic lowers the top speed of the same car by 3mph. More bulky and less aerodynamic lightbars can rob 5 to 8mph.

Brake tests. The MSP conducts both 90 to 0mph tests and 60 to 0mph tests on all vehicles. The idea is that the squad must be able to be repeatedly panic stopped without brake fade or brake locking and remain under total control. A panic stop from 90mph can be quite exciting, especially when the car must stay in its own driving lane.

The MSP does not focus on actual stopping distances like most car magazines. Instead they measure the rate of deceleration. From the rate of deceleration, it is possible to calculate the stopping distance from any speed by using a simple formula.

The MSP brake tests are severe enough to find any flaws in braking performance. The cars are decelerated from 90 to 0mph four times followed by one 60 to 0mph "impending" skid. Impending skid is threshold braking. This is as much pressure as the brakes will take without locking. This sequence is then repeated except the 60 to 0mph becomes a full pedal pressure panic stop. The MSP does not have a minimum rate of deceleration, but does require that the vehicle stay in its own lane. The rate of deceleration becomes the "score" for this stage of the test. The higher the number, the better the braking.

Ergonomics. The patrol car is the cop's office for 8 to 10 hours a day. The job is tough enough without riding in a cramped or uncomfortable car. This is an especially critical issue since all cars have been down-sized compared to the behemoths of the 1960s and 1970s. The squad has to be reasonably comfortable and have the instruments and controls placed conveniently. The squad also must have adequate space for patrol equipment.

Apart from the ergonomics or human engineering aspects of the car, each vehicle is judged by MSP personnel based on its ability to accommodate communications and emergency warning equipment. This includes the difficulty of the installation of the equipment.

To evaluate cars of all sizes and shapes, the MSP used a form developed by the Los Angeles County Sheriff's Dept. Four separate officers judged each car in 29 different areas and the scores were averaged. This evaluation included seat padding, ease of entry and exit, head and hip room, position of window and heater controls and even overall outside visibility from the driver's seat.

Fuel economy. Gas mileage is a major area of concern for any fleet manager, even if the fleet is one vehicle used by a town marshal. In fact, while the MSP gave this area a 10 percent overall weighting, other agencies may rank fuel economy with a much higher priority. This is the advantage of the MSP testing. Each agency can put whatever priority they want on the raw MSP results to select a vehicle tailored just to that agency.

For the fuel economy tests, the MSP wisely referred to the published EPA figures for a comparison. The figures the MSP used as a score were the city fuel economy results out to one decimal place.

It is impossible for any one set of tests to define the best car for overall duty use. Each agency will have its own weightings on individual areas of performance. Each agency will also have different minimum performance standards. The best overall choice can be dramatically changed simply by changing priorities and standards. The MSP methodology makes this easy to do.

When all the criteria are set and the testing is done, all vehicles are assigned a bid adjustment figure. The lower performing cars can still be purchased if the price is low enough. However, the higher bid cars can still be purchased if the performance is high enough. And that is the way it should be.

STATE OF MICHIGAN
DEPARTMENT OF MANAGEMENT AND BUDGET DIVISION
Specifications for
POLICE CARS: PATROL
4-Door Sedan - V-8 Engine
Wheelbase 115.9in, 119.9in
BID REQUIREMENTS:

Prior to bidding, a car dealer, manufacturer, or his representative, will be required to furnish a vehicle for test purposes. All test vehicles shall be 1978 models which are equipped with the drive train, suspension, and brake components, as well as tires and interior appointments and instrumentation as called for in the

In 1980, this MSP Dodge St. Regis 360ci, 4-bbl reached top speeds of nearly 125mph to capture the vehicle tests. *Michigan State Police*

specification requirements on all vehicles in this requisition. Submitters of vehicles shall list any deviations from the specifications at the time of delivery of these test cars. Interior and exterior colors shall be the manufacturer's option. One extra set of four (4) wheels and tires shall be supplied with each car submitted for test. Vehicles submitted shall have undergone sufficient break-in to permit extended periods of maximum acceleration and high speed driving.

The test vehicles will be subjected to a series of initial performance qualification tests. Each vehicle successfully completing these tests will then be subjected to seven (7) competitive performance and acceptability tests. The State of Michigan shall not be responsible for any damage during the tests, or the condition of the vehicle when returned to the submitter after testing. Furthermore, all cars tested will be at the owner's risk for any damage occurring to the vehicles for any reason.

The test vehicles will be tested and driven under the supervision of the Michigan Department of State Police, and will be tested and driven by employees of the department or personnel designated by the department.

SPECIFICATIONS:
Model - 1978 Current New
TO BE STANDARD FACTORY EQUIPPED INCLUDING, BUT NOT LIMITED TO, THE FOLLOWING:
Air Conditioning: Standard nonautomatic temperature control model, factory installed. Tinted glass not acceptable. System to include air conditioning Shutoff Switch to enable rapid disengagement of A/C compressor during high speed pursuit driving and extended idling if necessary for compressor durability. Installation to be approved by Michigan State Police.
Alternator System: Transistorized regulator, 80amp minimum output capacity, minimum curb idle output of 45amp (at manufacturer's recommended idle speed). Shall be of heavy duty design capable of surviving patrol car operation at 110mph. Output ratings are for typical underhood ambient temperatures and not S.A.E. rating method.

Antenna: Standard AM type, externally mounted (radio not to be included).
Battery: 12 Volt; 77amp. hr., min.
Brakes: Power assisted, low pedal position. Disc type in front; drum type in rear. Four wheel disc brakes preferred, if available.
Chrome Strip: To be removed from doors if it interferes with State Police Shield, but shall be furnished if standard. No holes to be on doors for moldings.
Cigarette Lighter and Ash Receiver: On instrument panel.
Cooling System: Vehicle to have maximum size cooling system available; incorporating "coolant recovery" system. Factory installed.
Differential: Heavy duty, limited slip required.
Engine: Cubic inch displacement to be at manufacturers option providing that the car will meet or exceed the vehicle performance requirements found elsewhere in this specification.
Floor Mat: Heavy duty rubber, front and rear. Rubber trunk mat, full floor.
Front and Rear armrests: Rear armrests to be of a style without ash tray or having that may be readily removed.
Front Seat Assembly: Split bench type, 60-40 preferable, or 50-50 acceptable, individually adjustable fore and aft, less center armrests, heavy interior construction designed for rugged police use, comfortably foam padded seat cushions and backs.
Gauges: To be equipped with ammeter or voltmeter, water temperature, and oil pressure gauges, preferably located in instrument cluster, or under dash convenient to driver.
Hoses: Heater and radiator hoses shall be silicone.
Light: Combination Dome and Map, mounted on headliner on longitudinal centerline of vehicle approximately 25in from windshield garnish molding. Dome light controlled by rotating headlight switch to maximum C.C.W. position. Operation to be independent of other lights. Dome jamb switches to be made inoperative. Map Lights, controlled by individual integral switches, to direct a restricted beam of light to the driver and/or to the front seat passenger.

In 1984, the Plymouth Gran Fury took on all comers from Chevy to Ford to win overall the MSP performance tests. *Michigan State Police*

Light: Engine compartment, with mercury switch.

Locks: All locks on a car to be keyed alike, 5 keys to be furnished with each car, different key for each car.

Mirrors, Rearview, Outside: Installed on left-hand and right-hand doors. Left-hand mirror to be remote controlled type. Rectangular design approximate size 5x3in; minimum viewing area of 15sq-in.

Mirrors, Rearview, Inside: Day/night type.

Paint Color: To be same as Dulux 93-032.

Radio Speaker: A permanent magnet speaker, either oval or round, to be mounted in the speaker opening provided on the dash of the unit, voice coil impedance 3.2ohms, power handling capacity 7.0 watts, minimum. Speaker to be of a quality equal to automotive grade. Two speaker leads connected to the speaker terminals, neither grounded, shall be long enough to extend one foot beyond the center of the lower edge of the dash.

Rear Window Defogger Unit: With control within convenient reach of driver, control switch to be clearly marked as to function.

Remote Control Rear Deck Lid Release: Control to be within convenient reach of the driver and labeled as to function. Electric system wired independently of ignition switch, preferred. Bowden cable system not acceptable.

Roof Top Reinforcement and Special Wiring: Install a steel plate 1/8in thick 10in wide, to the underside of top, centered on the longitudinal centerline of the roof panel. Plate is to extend from the windshield header to the first top

cross member support and is to be welded at both ends. Drill one 5/8in hole through roof panel and reinforcing plate, 15in from windshield molding on longitudinal centerline. Feed three insulated stranded wires (one #12 and two #16) through hole in roof and route directly to either side of top at a right angle to the longitudinal centerline, thence to corner post and down the inside of corner post. Wires to extend 18in above roof hole and 48in beyond where they emerge at bottom of corner post. Top hole to be taped to prevent entry of water. Wires to be concealed between headlining and roof panel.

Secondary Ignition Wiring: Resistance type for radio noise suppression.

Special Wiring: One 14 gauge insulated wire running from center under dash to rear center trunk area, leaving 4 feet of this wire extended under the dash and 3 feet extending in the trunk for mounting rear shelf lights.

Speedometer: Shall be calibrated to within 3% accuracy. Preferred Scale graduations to be linear and of 2mph increments. 0-120mph scale.

Spotlights: Unity #225-6, 6in diameter, left- and right-hand mounted, equipped with aircraft landing lamp 4537. Pillar or other approved mount. Left and right spotlights to be individually fused with 10amp capacity. Installation to be approved by Michigan State Police.

Steering: Power steering, manufacturer to provide steering gear which affords maximum firm "feel" and fast return characteristics; designed for high speed pursuit type driving.

126

Steering Wheel: Round or oval with anti-slip surface. Full or half horn ring preferred.

Police Suspension System: To include heavy-duty springs, front and rear, in combination with heavy-duty shock absorbers, and front and rear heavy-duty stabilizer bars.

Tires: Fabric radial, GR 70-15B, minimum. Tires to be Goodyear Police Special Flexten Radial.

Tools: Wheel wrench and jack.

Transmission: To be 3-speed fully automatic, heaviest duty available. Must incorporate low gear lockout to prevent manual shifting.

Upholstery: Seats to be upholstered in cloth, or combination of cloth and vinyl (blue). All vinyl not acceptable.

Wheels: Heavy duty, 15x6.5in minimum.

Windshield Washers: Automatic type.

Windshield Wipers: Multiple speed electric.

QUALIFICATION TESTING

In order to qualify for further testing, all vehicles submitted by manufacturers must meet each of the following performance standards:

1. ACCELERATION

0-60	12.5 seconds or less
0-80	21.0 seconds or less
0-100	38.0 seconds or less

Each vehicle will make four acceleration runs, and the times for the four runs will be averaged.

2. TOP SPEED

A speed of 110mph must be attained within a 3-mile distance. For purposes to be explained in another section of this report, the vehicles will, after attaining the 110mph minimum, be accelerated to the maximum speed attainable within 15 miles.

3. BRAKES

a. Three stops from 90mph with a constant deceleration rate of 22ft per sec/per sec maintained from 90 to 0mph. Actual brake application to be made at two-minute intervals followed immediately by a controlled impending skid stop from 60mph at maximum deceleration rate attainable. (Vehicle to remain stationary between first, second, and third 90mph stops, and before 4th stop from 60mph.)

b. Five minutes after test "a" has been completed, it will be repeated, followed immediately by a panic (all wheel lock) stop from 60mph. Tendency for brake fade and ability of the vehicle to stop in a straight line will be evaluated.

FAILURE OF A VEHICLE TO MEET ANY PORTION OF THE FOREGOING PERFORMANCE STANDARDS WILL RESULT IN THAT VEHICLE'S DISQUALIFICATION FROM FURTHER TESTING, AND ALSO FROM BIDDING.

Squad Car Selected by Michigan State Police Test Methods

1978	Plymouth Fury, 440ci
1979	Chevrolet Impala, 350ci
1980 (full)	Plymouth Gran Fury, 360ci
1980 (mid)	Plymouth Volare, 318ci
1981 (full)	Plymouth Gran Fury, 318ci
1981 (mid)	Chevrolet Malibu, 305ci
1982	Plymouth Gran Fury, 318ci
1983	Plymouth Gran Fury, 318ci
1984	Plymouth Gran Fury, 318ci
1985	Dodge Diplomat, 318ci
1986	Dodge Diplomat, 318ci
1987	Chevrolet Caprice, 350ci
1988	Chevrolet Caprice, 350ci
1989	Chevrolet Caprice, 350ci

The last Mopar squad car to be selected by the exhaustive MSP performance tests was this 1986 Dodge Diplomat. *Michigan State Police*

Michigan State Police MINIMUM Performance Standards

Model Year	0-60 mph	0-80 mph	0-100 mph	Top Speed, Max. Distance
1978	12.5sec	21.0sec	38.0sec	110mph in 3 miles
1979	13.0sec	23.0sec	43.0sec	110mph in 3 miles
1980 (full)	13.0sec	23.0sec	43.0sec	110mph in 3 miles
1980 (mid)	14.5sec	25.5sec	n/a	100mph 3 miles
1981	14.5sec	26.0sec	48.5sec	105mph in 3 miles
1982	14.5sec	26.0sec	48.5sec	no minimum given
1983	14.5sec	26.0sec	48.5sec	no minimum given
1984	13.5sec	24.0sec	45.0sec	110mph in 3 miles
1985	13.5sec	24.0sec	45.0sec	110mph in 3 miles
1986	13.5sec	24.0sec	45.0sec	110mph in 3 miles
1987	12.9sec	23.0sec	42.3sec	110mph in 2 miles
1988	13.6sec	24.3sec	43.2sec	110mph in 2 miles
1989	12.7sec	23.1sec	41.7sec	110mph in 2 miles
1991	12.3sec	20.8sec	37.4sec	110mph in 2 miles
1992	11.7sec	20.3sec	35.1sec	110mph in 2 miles
1993	10.3sec	17.8sec	29.9sec	110mph in 2 miles
1994	10.1sec	17.5sec	29.6sec	110mph (1 mi), 120mph (2 mi)

Note: As a comparison, between 1984 and 1989, the California Highway Patrol had a performance minimum of 0 to 60mph in 13.0sec, 0 to 100mph in 43.0sec and a minimum top speed of 110mph in 2 miles.

Plymouth Fury and Gran Fury Performance Summary
Michigan State Police

Model Year	Engine	HP	Ratio	Exhaust	Rear Gear	0-60mph	0-100mph	Top Speed	Braking	Vehicle Dynamics	Fuel Economy
1978	440ci, 4-bbl	225@4000	7.8:1	dual	2.71:1	92sec	24.40sec	132.7mph	23.29fps2	1:31.05	10.0mpg
1979	360ci, 4-bbl	195@4000	8.0:1	dual	3.21:1	10.15sec	31.34sec	122.9mph	21.44fps2	1:31.65	12.0mpg
1980	360ci, 4-bbl	185@4000	8.0:1	dual	2.94:1	11.31sec	35.45sec	124.6mph	22.48fps2	1:30.84	11.0mpg
1981	318ci, 4-bbl	165@4000	8.4:1	single	2.94:1	12.76sec	42.22sec	115.1mph	25.15fps2	1:33.60	15.5mpg
1982	318ci, 4-bbl	165@4000	8.4:1	single	2.94:1	12.24sec	39.36sec	116.3mph	24.29fps2	1:32.63	13.8mpg
1983	318ci, 4-bbl	165@4000	8.5:1	single	2.94:1	12.38sec	39.68sec	120.0mph	24.92fps2	1:32.64	14.0mpg
1984	318ci, 4-bbl	165@4000	8.4:1	single	2.94:1	10.88sec	34.43sec	121.4mph	25.61fps2	1:30.01	14.6mpg
1985	318ci, 4-bbl	175@4000	8.4:1	single	2.94:1	12.60sec	42.00sec	119.4mph	26.60fps2	1:30.69	12.6mpg
1986	318ci, 4-bbl	175@4000	8.0:1	single	2.94:1	11.58sec	36.58sec	119.4mph	16.71fps2	1:29.43	12.2mpg
1987	318ci, 4-bbl	175@4000	8.0:1	single	2.94:1	12.39sec	38.64sec	117.5mph	27.44fps2	1:29.77	12.7mpg
1988	318ci, 4-bbl	175@4000	8.0:1	single	2.94:1	12.14sec	40.13sec	117.0mph	23.74fps2	1:29.43	12.7mpg
1989	318ci, 4-bbl	175@4000	8.0:1	single	2.94:1	11.77sec	38.02sec	120.2mph	26.01fps2	1:28.63	12.7mpg

Note: Results from 1979 are from the Dodge St. Regis

Note: In 1978 and 1979, the MIS road course was 1.82 miles.
In 1980 and thereafter, the road course was changed to 1.64 miles

References
Patrol Vehicle Evaluation and Purchasing Program, Michigan
    State Police, 1978 through 1993.
"1988 Patrol Vehicle Evaluation and Purchasing Program," (1/2-
    inch VHS video), Michigan State Police
Personal communication, F/Lt. (ret.) Curtis VanDenBerg, Sgt.
    David Storer, Sgt. William McFall, Michigan State Police
    Academy, Lansing, MI
Attendance at 1992, 1993, 1994, 1995, 1996 model year MSP
    vehicle tests

Chapter 18

California Highway Patrol Experiences

In the past, the words "Highway Patrol" and "Dodge" were synonymous, as Dodge sedans patrolled the highways of many of our United States.

Dodge was added to the California Highway Patrol's fleet of Buicks and Oldsmobiles in 1956. The 1956 Dodge Pursuit Car selected by the CHP was the Coronet series 2 door sedan. Included with the Pursuit package was a heavy-duty frame, heavy duty springs and shock absorbers, 30amp generator and 60amp/hour battery, heater and defroster, a map light and variable speed electric windshield wipers. The D500 V-8 engine was utilized, connected to the PowerFlite 2 speed automatic transmission. The D500 engine had hemispherical combustion chambers, displacing 315ci. With two 4-barrel carburetors, the D500 produced 260bhp.

In 1957 the Automobile Manufacturers Association, (AMA), withdrew from auto racing. In effect, this meant that American automobile manufacturers would no longer participate or officially sponsor cars in stock car racing. After this resolution went into effect, Dodge switched it's racing efforts toward capturing the police market.

Also in 1957, Chrysler Corp. departed from the traditional coil spring front suspension design and had introduced "Torsion Air" front suspension. This design used torsion bars, which instead of bulky coil springs, connected the front suspension to a point near the middle of the car. When the front wheel went over a bump, the torsion bar would twist, thus absorbing the shock. Torsion bar suspension also provided sufficient room under the hood for a large engine. Routine maintenance and repairs could be performed without difficulty.

The main advantage in this new suspension design is that Chrysler Corp. cars had superior handling characteristics. Automotive writers of that era praised Chrysler products for their ability to go around corners without excessive body roll and sway, which most Detroit products seemed to do in the interest of a soft ride.

Along with a quantity of 1957 Pontiac Chieftains purchased by the CHP, 275 Dodge 2-door sedans were also acquired. These Dodges were probably powered by a 325ci V-8 engine, and the new 3-speed TorqueFlite automatic transmission.

Patrolmen found the TorqueFlite to be an improvement, especially in mountain regions. The PowerFlite, along with other two speed automatics, was becoming obsolete. The gap between low and high range was too great. There was an "over-rev" situation in low range, and the engine would lug when shifting into high.

The reason that two different makes of cars were purchased each year is that the CHP, during that time period, tested, selected, and purchased cars twice a year. There was also a theory that if the CHP purchased cars from all the manufacturers, then nobody would become angry. 1958 brought Dodge and the 430ci Mercury Turnpike Cruiser into the fleet.

The Dodge was equipped with the D500 engine, which displaced 361ci and produced 320bhp when fed by two 4-barrel WCFB Carter carburetors. This was the first year for the "B" block, or "Wedge" engines.

Motor Trend tested a 1958 CHP car and compared it against a stock 1958 Dodge Custom Royal sedan equipped with a single 4-barrel version 361ci D500 engine.

The stock sedan with power brakes and steering was somewhat easier to drive, and the stock suspension gave a smoother ride. The CHP car with two four-barrel carburetors had slightly quicker acceleration times, accelerating from 0-60mph in 9.3sec. The standing start quarter mile was accomplished in 17.3sec with

The California Highway Patrol is the country's most influential police department on the topic of police vehicles.

This CHP 1959 Dodge Coronet with the Super D-500 dual quad 383ci V-8 had a top speed 15mph over the CHP's 110mph minimum. *Chrysler Historical*

Here's a 1959 CHP Dodge Coronet. This 3800lb car ran a 16sec quarter mile. *Darryl Lindsay*

an 84mph terminal speed. These times were similar to 1957 Dodge performance figures. *Motor Trend* did not list what top speed was. However, something in excess of 120mph is a safe assumption. *Motor Trend* also liked the handling for both cars. The CHP version, with stiffer torsion bars and rear springs had a somewhat harsher ride, but showed practically no lean while cornering.

1958 was also the year that the CHP began formal driver training for it's patrolmen. (The word "patrolmen" is used, because at that time, the CHP did not employ female traffic officers).

The Emergency Vehicle Operating Course, (EVOC), headed by Sergeant Robert M. Phillips, a former race car driver, became a part of the curriculum of the basic Highway Patrol Academy. Cadet officers who did not pass the EVOC segment would not go on to graduate and become State Traffic Officers. Line CHP officers return once every three years for an EVOC refresher.

EVOC training consumed about four days of the CHP's then 12-week basic academy. Cadet officers were taught a mixture of classroom theory and practical experience. Driving the 1.7-mile road course and skid pad training were also included. The training vehicles were retired CHP cruisers outfitted with roll cages and racing type seat belt/shoulder harnesses.

Instructors "stacked the deck" by using special tires without tread, and hidden switches operated ignition cut-outs, horns, or spray water at the cadet driver's face to simulate some of the distractions which could occur under an actual pursuit. On the skid pad, the surface was coated with oils, then sprayed down with water. The students were then told to chase the instructors about the track. The instructors sometimes ended up chasing the students instead.

The EVOC course was based on the theory that a patrolman chasing a car at 100mph was just as dangerous as dealing with an armed criminal. Highway Patrolmen are trained in the use of firearms, so why not teach them how to handle a car at high speed?

Today's EVOC course is located at the CHP Academy in Bryte, a suburb of Sacramento, the state capitol. The course includes a mock-up of an actual freeway, and residential area.

EVOC training today is taught by most major law enforcement agencies throughout the world. Much of the training material comes from the CHP EVOC program, which is one of the first programs of its kind ever developed. It is also considered one of the best.

In 1959, the CHP tried to purchase one make of car each year, rather than different makes. This made sense, as stocking replacement parts and maintenance was simplified. The 2-door Dodge Coronet was again selected, powered by the single 4-barrel version of the D500 engine, which was now increased to 383ci and produced 320bhp. The push button TorqueFlite automatic transmission was used. Borrowed from Chrysler's big parts bin, were huge 12x2-1/2-inch "Total Contact" drum brakes. The cars were equipped with special, fade resistant, organic linings with a swept braking surface area of 251sq-in. The Highway Patrol now had a cruiser which had handling and stopping ability matching its engine performance.

Dodge downsized their cars slightly for 1960. However, the Dodge Polara, supplied by John Drew Motors of Sacramento, won the bid for the CHP contract. 1960 was the first year that the CHP moved away from the 2-door sedan to the 4-door models. The 1961 cars acquired by the CHP were essentially similar, powered by the 320bhp 4-barrel 383ci engine.

By now a strong working relationship had developed between Chrysler Corp. and the California Highway Patrol. Com-paring a stock Dodge Polara with a CHP cruiser will show 244 special items which are not fitted to the stock Dodge. Some of these modifications were visible to the naked eye, such as the chrome trim which was deleted from the front doors so the CHP insignia could be affixed, and the inside rear view mirror which was hung from the top of the windshield, rather that affixed to the dash on the stock models. Other modifications which were not as visible, including heavy duty suspension, 15-inch road wheels, with thicker spider sections for extra strength, and heavy duty driveline components.

One source indicates that extra care was used in engine assembly. This made for a somewhat factory "blueprinted" engine. The camshafts fitted to engines designated to the CHP, on paper, showed the same specifications as a stock 383 camshaft. However, it actually had more lift and duration. Ignition and carburetion also had some subtle changes.

By 1962 there was no Dodge in the lineup which could meet CHP's wheelbase specification of 122in, or 3,950lb weight requirement, due to Dodge's downsizing. In 1961 the CHP tested smaller patrol cars and found that they did not meet the Department's standards for handling, and offered less comfort to the officer. Thus, the 1962 Chrysler Newport wore the CHP insignia that year.

One Chrysler Corp. source indicated that Dodge upper management was unhappy that Dodge no longer had a large car. After careful consideration, Chrysler brass gave the nod to again produce a large car. Over the 1961 Christmas production line break, large amounts of midnight oil was burned in order to complete this project. The older Chrysler body was utilized. New front end sheet metal was produced along with various new trim pieces. Dipping into Chrysler, Dodge, and by now, defunct DeSoto parts bins, supplied the rest of the necessary materials. The result was the Dodge 880. (It was interesting to note that the Dodge 880 just happened to meet CHP wheelbase and weight specifications)!

Dodge could not provide the 880 in time to meet the CHP contract for 1962. However, by 1963 the 880 was more than ready to serve the State of California.

Replacing the faithful 383 engine was the RB series "B" engine. RB, meaning 'Raised Block,' to accommodate a longer stroke, enlarged this engine to 413ci. Fed by a single Carter AFB 4-barrel carb, the 413 produced 360bhp. Additional changes for 1963 also showed the "Total Contact" brake system replaced by the more conventional "Bendix" type drum brakes. The Bendix

In late-1959, the CHP added the HIGHWAY PATROL lettering over their door shield. *John Bellah*

This 1960 Dodge Dart is undergoing CHP handling and top speed tests. It reached 129mph. *CHP*

brakes used smaller diameter drums. However 3-inch wide shoes were fitted in the front and rear. This considerably increased surface area.

As the reader might assume, the State of California did not specifically purchase CHP vehicles strictly on the basis of low bid. Ever since the mid-1950s, the Highway Patrol conducted comprehensive vehicle tests to determine what was the best car for highway patrol duties. An eleven man vehicle evaluation team reviewed vehicle specifications and consulted with factory representatives. A prototype meeting CHP specifications was manufactured and submitted for testing.

A 1,600-mile course which covered most of the types of terrain and climates that a CHP cruiser may encounter was driven. Starting in Sacramento and heading for Southern California, the course covered altitudes of over 8,700 feet, mountainous "S" turns, freezing cold, cobblestones, dirt roads, high speed high-

ways and extreme desert heat. Upon arrival in Southern California, acceleration, handling, braking and speed tests were conducted at Riverside Raceway. The cars were then driven back to Sacramento.

Some of the specifications required for California Highway Patrol cars during the late 1950's were as follows:

ENGINE
Overhead valve V-8 engine, minimum displacement of 380ci, compression ratio of at least 9.75 to 1. Carburetion shall be a single unit, however, multiple barrel designs are permitted.

COOLING SYSTEM
Heavy-duty, pressurized design to provide adequate engine cooling when the vehicle is driven under severe loads, and in severe heat conditions. The cooling system must be able to withstand the additional heat generated by an air conditioning unit if it were to be added at a later date. (CHP units operated in desert regions were fitted with an aftermarket air conditioning unit).

HOSE CLAMPS
Must be a positive-closure type, consisting of a stainless steel band and worm screw drive device.

CHASSIS
122-inch wheel base, minimum length. Heavy duty suspension and shock absorbers to give maximum roadability at high speeds, and to minimize brake dive and spring wrap up during acceleration and braking.

REAR AXLE
Designed to give best overall performance.

TRANSMISSION
Heavy duty automatic transmission

ROAD WHEEL RIMS
15-inch heavy duty. Must have the maximum rim width for the tire installed. Must have heavy duty rim and spider material to withstand high speed operation. A safety ridge must be rolled into each horizontal bead to prevent the tire from coming off the wheel in the event of a blowout.

This 1961 CHP Dodge Polara is powered by a 383ci, 4-bbl. All other police departments ran the Dodge Dart in 1961. *George Caravas*

In 1962, the CHP selected the only 122-inch wheelbase car made by Chrysler Corp., the Newport Enforcer. *CHP*

TIRES
Minimum size of 7.60x15in high speed construction to permit continued speeds of 100mph. 6 Ply, black sidewall design.
BRAKES
Heavy duty with oversize drums and heavy duty linings.
FRONT END COMPONENTS
Heavy duty hubs, spindles and bearings.
GLASS
Laminated safety glass windshield with the upper band to be tinted.
WINDSHIELD WIPERS
Variable speed electric wipers, with windshield washer.
HORN RING
Full circumference, 360-degree type.
HEATER AND DEFROSTER
Factory fresh air unit.
SPEEDOMETER
Certified to be accurate within 2mph.
SEATS
Minimum 1in of foam rubber padding. Seat springs to be heavy duty.

Examples of other makes competing for the CHP contract during the 1950s were Buick, Oldsmobile, Pontiac and Mercury. Ford, Chevrolet and Plymouth weren't eligible as they did not meet CHP standards for minimum weight or wheelbase length.

Only after the cars had passed CHP's testing procedures would they be eligible for bidding. Selected police vehicles were purchased by whichever vehicle had the lowest bid.

The 1964 cruisers were similar to the 1963 413ci Dodge 880's. 1964 was the last year for Chrysler's pushbutton controlled TorqueFlite, and for the dashboard mounted "Police" speedometer.

It seems that some of the factory speedometers were temperature sensitive, and indicated speeds would vary during temperature variations. Traffic courts throughout the state became aware of this fact and soon dismissed speeding citations written by CHP installed "police" speedometers on the dashboards of it's cruisers. These speedos were made by Stewart-Warner, Barbour-Stockwell and Jones Motorola. These state of the art aftermarket speedometers used centrifugal measurement of speed, rather than the magnetic method used by most automotive speedometers. These speedometers also were temperature compensated. By 1965 the factory police certified speedometers were accurate enough to meet with the CHP's and the court systems approval. The patrolmen welcomed the factory speedometers back too, as the aftermarket speedometers were somewhat noisy.

1964 was also the year that the CHP tested disc brakes. Two test cars were equipped with disc brakes. One car was equipped with a prototype Budd front disc/rear drum brake set up, which was later to be optional on large bodied Chrysler Corp. cars. The other car was set up with a Airheart-4-wheel disc brake system. It is unknown exactly what the test results were, but a large percentage of the 1965 cruisers were equipped with the factory 4 piston Budd front disc brakes.

Patrolmen who worked in the desert regions in the older units with drum brakes welcomed the new disc brake equipped cars. It seemed that the drum brakes would accumulate sand and grit inside the brake system. A sufficient build-up of this grit would cause the brake lining material to glaze. The result was no brakes. A patrolman attempting to stop a violator under these conditions, upon finding his linings had glazed, would pull around the violator and, with both feet standing on the pedal, pa-

The CHP experimented with pusher bars on its Enforcement-class vehicles as early as 1962. *CHP*

tiently wait until the cruiser ground to a stop about a half mile down the road. The patrolman would wave the violator to approach him and issue the citation. For the next thirty minutes the brakes would crackle. The next thing was to bring the car back to the shop to have the grit removed from the brake system.

The 1965 Polaras purchased by the CHP had the conventional steering column mounted automatic transmission selector lever, rather than Chrysler's pushbutton system, which had been in use since 1956.

This perfect 1963 Dodge 880 is powered by the 413ci wedge. *John Bellah*

Some patrolmen may have welcomed the new system, since sometimes the pushbuttons had a tendency to stick. Even today, there are several theories as to why Chrysler abandoned the old "typewriter set-up." One reason was the upcoming Federal requirements requiring a standardized transmission shift range sequence. Another was that Chrysler, attempting to sell more vehicles to high school driver training programs, was encountering some resistance as the pushbutton arrangement was deemed "unconventional," by some.

Another interesting fact for 1965 was that Dodge shortened the wheelbase on its 1965 Polara models to 121in. This was one inch less than CHP specifications called for. Not to worry! Dodge lengthened the wheelbase on the CHP version to meet specs.

The 413ci engine received a large cylinder bore and was increased to 440ci for 1966. 1966 was the first year for exhaust emission controls for new American cars first sold in California. (CHP cars were not exempt from these requirements either!) The 1966 Dodge CHP car was supposed to be powered by a 365bhp version of the 440ci engine. It seemed that several CHP units ended up being powered by the 426ci "Street Wedge" engine, which was fed by a Carter AFB 4-barrel carburetor and produced 365bhp at 4800rpm. The 426ci only appeared in CHP cars and was not an "official" police package engine. About 1966, all units began to be equipped with pump shotguns. Previously, only units patrolling in high crime rate areas were equipped with shotguns. A Remington 870 riot gun was installed in an electronic shotgun rack mounted vertically to the dashboard in every unit.

By now, the other automakers were accusing Dodge of "sleeping" with the California Highway Patrol. For 1967 Oldsmobile won the Contract, after the CHP purchased a 1966 Oldsmobile to test as an actual cruiser.

On paper the Olds seemed impressive. The 425ci V-8 engine was rated at 365bhp when fed by the Rochester Quadra Jet Carburetor. This carburetor had small primary barrels for good fuel mileage and controlling exhaust emissions. It also had large secondary barrels to facilitate engine breathing. A Delco electronic ignition was utilized. Power was transferred through G.M.'s excellent, recently introduced three speed Turbo Hydramatic transmission. The police suspension was assisted by anti-sway bars front and rear.

Tom McCahill, of Mechanic Illustrated tested a 1968 version of the Oldsmobile Police Apprehender, and stated that "it was the greatest American car I have driven since 1960."

Reality, and theory can be two different stories, however. Some officers described the 1967 Olds as "The worst thing the State ever did to us!" Officers complained of weak brakes and poor handling. Maintaining a full tank of gas and adding three or four boxes of flares in the trunk aided handling, however, extended periods of idling would cause the Olds to "load up." The Olds accumulated considerable "down-time" awaiting repairs.

Swift Dodge of Sacramento supplied cars to the CHP for 1968. It was during this time period that the CHP began to experiment with roof mounted warning lights and electronic sirens. It had long been CHP practice to install Unity spotlights on both sides of the car. The driver's spotlamp used a red sealed beam bulb, and the passenger side spotlamp had a white bulb. A flashing red sealed beam, and a flashing amber lamp was mounted on the left side of the rear package tray. This provided warning illumination to the rear of the car. A similar system is still used currently on some cruisers, with an additional blue lamp installed on the right package shelf which flashes in conjunction with the amber bulb.

A Federal "growler," or mechanical type siren was installed under the hood. Patrolmen of that era remarked that it was necessary to use the siren sparingly. Even though a heavy duty alternator was utilized, (in some cases a 60amp Leece-Neville), the siren would draw so much current that eight long blasts of the siren would drain the battery.

The early two-way radios were another source of battery load. These radios used vacuum tubes which consumed huge amounts of current. A dynamotor was used to power the transmitter. The dynamotor is a generator powered by an electric motor. The patrolman had to key the transmit button on the microphone, and wait for the dynamotor to "wind up" before he was able to speak.

By the 1969 the 440 V-8 engine had been increased from 365bhp to 375bhp. The 1969 Dodge Polara were similar to the 1968's, only faster. Many patrolmen considered the 1969 Dodge the fastest CHP cruiser. Many stories still abound of 140+mph "romps" of 1969 CHP cruisers. Young, aggressive patrolmen loved to "egg-on" violators by turning on the red spotlight while about 1/4 mile behind the violator. This would almost guarantee a pursuit!

One patrolman relates how he and his partner were chasing a late model Pontiac GTO going down Cajon pass, which is a downhill freeway running for several miles. Looking back on the incident, he feels that maybe he and his partner were just a little too relaxed. During this chase, he was driving with one hand on the wheel, smoking his pipe and his partner slumped in the seat half asleep. The Dodge was steady a as a rock. The speedometer "pegged." The actual speed was estimated by the patrolman as approaching 160mph.

Separating fact from fiction can be difficult. Contrary to popular belief, CHP cars were not set up for driving at maximum speeds. A rear axle ratio of about 3.23 to 1 and fuel economy with 3.23 to 1 being the ratio of choice for Chrysler Corp. cars. Fuel mileage on CHP cruisers averaged to about 8mpg, with Union 76, (now UNOCAL), premium gasoline being the fuel of choice. Most CHP cruisers of that era would easily exceed 120mph. A car which was properly broken in and in a proper state of tune would do close to 140mph.

Black and White 428ci Mercury Monterey sedans wore the CHP insignia for 1970. Riding on a 124-inch wheelbase, equipped with disc brakes and police suspension with front and rear anti-sway bars, the Mercury looked good "on paper."

The CHP still specified manual steering on it's cruisers. As the large majority of Mercurys—almost all of them—came equipped with power steering, officers found that steering was difficult. Ford had to fit large steering wheels to the CHP cars to make steering easier.

Officers found the Mercury to be comfortable, and straight line performance to be good, however, not as good as the 1969 Dodge. Air conditioning, adopted a couple years previously, helped in the hotter regions.

The Mercs had different handling characteristics which the officers didn't like. Brakes were another story. The first three panic stops were OK. After that, as one officer described, "It would take all available feet pressing the pedal to the floor, and the car went faster!"

The 122-inch wheelbase Dodge Polara returned in 1971. However, emission controls reduced the 440's output to 370bhp.

For 1972, CHP made serious efforts to experiment with power steering and ordered half of the 1972 Polaras so equipped.

This 1963 Dodge 880 is being readied for CHP duty by Motor Transport Div. *CHP*

Here's a 1964 Dodge 880 braving the snows of Northern California. *CHP*

Cars equipped with power steering had a placard advising the driver of this. Emission control concessions and a more conservative method of measuring engine horsepower dropped the 440's horsepower to 276 SAE net hp. (California version).

To offset some of the power losses brought on by the tightening of emission standards, Chrysler Corp. fitted Carter Thermo Quad 4-barrel carburetors on it's high performance V-8 engines. These carburetors replaced the Holley, AFB and AVS carbs which were utilized during the late 1960s. (The term AFB stands for Aluminum Four Barrel, and AVS stands for Air Valve Secondary, a variation of the AFB). The Thermo Quad used the same theory as the Rochester Quadra Jet carburetor, which General Motors was currently using. The primary barrels provided good fuel economy and helped to control emissions. Huge secondaries provided power and performance under full throttle operation. The float bowls of the T.Q. were made of plastic to provide a cooler fuel mixture, which in turn produced higher engine efficiency.

Dodge won the contract in 1973, and again in 1974. However, Dodge changed the name of it's big car from Polara to Monaco. In addition, power steering was fitted to all CHP cruisers.

In the past, both the CHP and individual officers distrusted power steering on police cars. One of the reasons was that it was felt that power steering felt "numb," and little feel of the road was transmitted back to the driver. Some felt that this was dangerous on a police car. Another reason for not installing power steering was cost. An extra $100 per car on 1,600 cars was a lot of tax payer's money.

By now, Chrysler's "Firm-Feel Pursuit-type power steering" had been developed. This was a special power steering setup for police cars. The units are assembled using selected gears for the minimum amount of free play, and different internal springs provide a firm feel to the steering. Power steering also had a faster ratio, and it only took 3 1/2 turns lock to lock, compared to the manual steering ratio of 5.3 turns lock to lock.

The CHP also found that money spent on power steering was well spent. When the cruisers were sold after CHP service, models with power steering were more desirable to the buying public, and therefore could command a higher price.

CHP Motor Transport maintains two outlets for surplus CHP vehicles. Northern California vehicles are sold at Motor Transport in Sacramento, and the Torrance Office handles Southern California vehicles.

Cruisers are currently surveyed out at 95,000 miles. Equipment such as radios, push bumpers, spotlights, shotgun racks, sirens and emergency lights are stripped from the units and the car is repainted. An exception is when the car is sold to another law enforcement agency. Certain equipment may be sold with the car, and the car can remain black and white.

Who buys surplus CHP cars? In some cases these cars are sold to other police departments. People looking for a heavy-duty sedan to tow a trailer are also prospective customers. Currently, taxicab operators purchase quite a few cars from the CHP. Cars in poor mechanical condition are sold "as-is." Many of these cars are sold to movie companies, and eventually are wrecked.

A used CHP car in good condition can be an excellent buy. Most of the mileage is freeway-type mileage, and the cars don't usually receive the abuse that a city police car must endure. The CHP also maintains their cars carefully. In many cases, the cars are maintained by a local dealer.

The catalytic converter made it's debut in controlling emissions in 1975. The 1975 Dodge Monacos utilized by the CHP had a dual exhaust system, thus two catalytic converters were used. By now the 440ci engine's output had diminished to 210 SAE net hp. (California version). Officers considered the 1975 to be the slowest Dodges yet! By now, many of the units were equipped with light bars, which also reduced top speed by 10mph.

These are the experimental Airheart REAR disc brakes on a 1964 CHP Dodge. *CHP*

136

Legend has it that even though the 1975 model was a dog, a 440 is a 440! And, any 440 had the ability to push a Semitrailer with doubles, fully loaded at 80,000lbs, out of the roadway if necessary.

Radial tires and a rear anti-sway bar improved handling considerably on the 1975 models. To handle the additional electrical demands, Chrysler developed a 114amp alternator for police and other heavy duty applications.

Additionally, the CHP purchased 100 Dodge Coronet sedans to evaluate a smaller car as a patrol vehicle.

The CHP selected the Dodge Coronet sedan for 1976. Resting on a 117-1/2-inch wheelbase, and weighing almost 500lb less than the Monacos, the Coronets regained some of the performance lost due to emission controls. In the aftermath of the fuel and energy crisis of the early 1970s, the lighter Coronets gave better fuel mileage.

It was around this time that the first female traffic officers went out on patrol. The Department began looking at using split front seats, with fabric upholstery. The fabric upholstery was more comfortable on hot days, and added to the resale value when the car was re-sold after service. The 60/40 front seats made it comfortable for two officers of different size and stature to occupy the front seat. An almost intolerable situation could develop where the driver was short and the passenger was tall. With a bench front seat, the driver would be in an unsafe situation by moving the seat back to allow room for the passenger officer and not be able to properly control the car or have a proper view of the roadway. And the passenger would have to spend several hours of an eight hour shift scrunched up in misery.

The bottom line was that adding creature comforts improved officer morale. Resale value was enhanced, too, as that was factored into the budget money allotted for the purchase of new patrol vehicles.

Dodge dropped the large body in 1977 and the intermediate bodied Coronet was renamed the Monaco. For 1977 and 1978, the CHP utilized the 117-1/2-inch wheelbase Monaco sedan. Sadly, 1978 was the last year for Chrysler's "B" series engine, in any displacement.

A victim of Government pressure to produce more fuel-efficient cars, the mighty "King Kong" 440 engine, which ruled California's highways, as well as over 50 percent of the rest of the United States, was doomed.

The mighty E86 Police engine produced 255 SAE net hp and 360lb-ft in the 49 state "Federal" version, and for California usage produced 240 SAE net hp and 330lb-ft. Also included were numerous modifications to provide additional performance and reliability, such as double roller timing chain and gears, an antiturbulence windage tray, a lubrite-treated camshaft, heavy duty valve train components, molybdenum filled top piston rings and specially inspected connecting rods. Both the Federal and California engines were fed by the Carter Thermo Quad 4-barrel carburetor, and had dual exhaust systems, including dual catalytic mufflers.

Car and Driver conducted a road test of the 1977 440ci Monaco Police Pursuit, equipped with the Federal emissions package, and called it the "Fastest American Sedan." The 440 propelled the 4480lb sedan from 0 to 60mph in 8.1sec, and went on to cover the standing quarter mile in 16.3sec at 88.2mph.

Top speed was recorded at 126mph. This was impressive performance, considering the weight of the car, and the fact that it was equipped with the 2.71 to 1 rear axle ratio. If equipped with the 3.23 gearset, acceleration times would be even better. Gasoline mileage was also impressive, about 9.5mpg in the city, and 11.5mpg on the highway. In actual police service this would be closer to 6mpg.

The brake system on the police version used 11.6in vented discs up front and 11x2-1/2-inch drums in the rear. The difference between the civilian Dodge and the police version was a dual diaphragm power booster for increased power assist and semi-metallic front brake pads. Included with this package were hub caps with cooling holes to dissipate the extra heat generated by the semi-metallic friction material. *Car and Driver* recorded .78G stops, bringing the car to a stop from 70mph in 209 feet.

In addition to the heavy duty suspension components utilized on police models, Chrysler, in manufacturing it's police vehicles, incorporated structural strengthening throughout the body. This was in the form of extra welds and bracing which reduce body flexing. This in turn made for better handling, and was one of the reasons that a police car must be ordered as such. Taking a standard sedan, and adding extra equipment does not make a police car.

For 1979 the CHP selected the Dodge St. Regis. This "R" bodied Dodge rode on a 118.5-inch wheelbase and was powered by a 360ci, 4-barrel V-8 which produced 190 SAE net HP. (California version). The top speed of a 1979 CHP St. Regis was in the neighborhood of 117mph.

By this time the future for high performance police interceptors looked bleak, especially in California. Some engines were unavailable due to California's emission standards, which were more restrictive than the rest of the United States. Police vehicles at that time had to meet the same emission requirements as civilian vehicles.

The CHP began an 18 month study to look at different types of patrol vehicles. Included in this test were 12 Plymouth Volare Station Wagons, 12 Ford Fairmont Sedans, 12 Chevrolet Malibu Sedans, and 12 Chevrolet Z28 Camaros.

The CHP observed that the 4-barrel 318ci Volare would reach a top speed of 109mph. Acceleration of the 3,533lb wagon was considered disappointing. Some officers considered the acceleration, or more correctly, the lack of acceleration to be dangerous, since it took in excess of 14sec to accelerate to 60mph from a standing start.

A look at the specifications quickly explained the reason. The final rear axle ratio was 2.41 to 1. According to the CHP, this ratio was selected for fuel economy. It also may have been that ratio was selected in order to meet emission standards. Automotive experts have long felt that a ratio in the neighborhood of 3.3 to 1 was the best compromise for a V-8 American sedan with

The CHP experimented with 4-piston Budd FRONT disc brakes on their 1964 Dodge 880. *CHP*

In 1965, the CHP forced Dodge to alter the wheelbase of this Polara to meet their 122-inch specs. *Darryl Lindsay*

an automatic transmission. An extremely high ratio such as 2.41 looks good "on paper" for good mileage. Perhaps a traveling salesperson, who constantly drives at 55mph and does a minimum of city driving, will get good results from such a ratio. In "the real world," a ratio of around 3:3 to one provides the best compromise for economy and performance. The 2.41 ratio may have explained the transmission failures experienced by the Volare.

The Chevrolet Z28 Camaro provided the best performance of all of the test vehicles. The truth of the matter was that the Camaro did not hold up well under CHP service. As history will later tell, the CHP eventually selected a high performance "pursuit" vehicle in 1982, and that was the Ford Mustang.

It seemed that all twelve Chevrolet Camaros with the 350ci experienced major engine problems. A reliable source told this writer how several years ago he interviewed an assembly line

Each year, vintage CHP squad cars like these 1965 and 1966 Polaras gather at the CHP Academy. *John Bellah*

138

This 1966 CHP Dodge Polara features an experimental revolving beacon top light. *CHP*

worker at the General Motors Assembly plant in Van Nuys, California, where Camaros are assembled. It seems that when the twelve black and white Camaros rolled down the assembly line it was obvious that the cars were intended for some type of police service. A decision among the workers was made to "mess with the police!," and the cars were deliberately sabotaged. If this story is true, then the line workers certainly got their revenge against the cops! Ford eventually got the CHP contract, and the General Motors Van Nuys Assembly plant was closed down, forever! "CHP Unloading its 'Dog Cars,'"stated the full page headlines of one Los Angeles newspaper.

The Dodge St. Regis was selected again in 1980. However, for 1980, the 360ci engine available in California, (in either a police or civilian version), was the 4-barrel 318ci, which produced 165 SAE net hp.

It was soon apparent that these cars had a top speed of about 85mph where it was flat and level, and about 65mph on hills. Officers complained that VW Bugs could out-run them. The term "318 Syndrome" became a part to the CHP jargon.

Chrysler and State officials put their collective heads together in order to find a solution to this problem. Any vehicle modifications would have to be made with the blessing of California's Air Resources Board, and meet California emission standards.

The CHP made plans to sell part of the 900 cars purchased in 1980, to help offset the cost of 1981 models, which promised better performance.

Even to this day, CHP Officials are reluctant to openly discuss this situation. However, it was strongly indicated that part of the problem was a personality clash between one particular CHP Official and Dodge. (This individual wanted to see a different make of car wear the CHP insignia).

In later years, this official attempted to persuade state purchasing officials not to pay for the 1985 and 1988 CHP cars.

The CHP had anticipated that there would be performance deficiencies on the early 1980s police cars offered for sale in Cal-

ifornia, and deliberately omitted certain performance specifications during the test and bid process. State purchasing officials concluded that the St. Regis met specifications, and the contract was honored.

The CHP sold about 100 of its Dodge St. Regis "dog cars" to other law enforcement agencies at their cost, $7,091.00 per car.

"Officially" the remaining cars were modified by installing transmission shift kits and removing the muffler, letting the catalytic converter handle the silencing of the exhaust system. These cars were designated for use in urban areas where top speed wasn't important, and in areas where they would quickly accumulate high mileage and be sold quickly after the required mileage.

Unofficially, however, was a different story. Rumor has it that one area, upon discovering a serious engine problem such as a flat camshaft, pulled the engine out and sent it to a rebuilder to be rebuilt. Somehow, these 318 engines were returned with a different camshaft and early drive gears, which did not allow any timing retard. It was stated that these "rebuilt" engines would "smoke the tires" upon acceleration.

CHP Motor Transport officials reported that some cars that came in for service had been illegally modified. These changes ranged from disconnected emission systems, to aftermarket, high performance camshafts and carburetors. Nevertheless, the CHP could not condone these activities. Tampering with emission equipment violated the law and the CHP was not exempt from the law.

The only cars which the CHP deliberately removed emission equipment was on cars used for EVOC training. These cars were considered "off road vehicles," and thus are exempt from smog requirements.

The problem was finally resolved in 1982 when the state law was changed and allowed emergency vehicles to meet only Federal emission requirements. This considerably improved the law enforcement vehicle situation in California.

This 1968 Dodge Polara is the car of which legends are made.

Two Dodge Diplomats were submitted for testing by the CHP in 1981. Among a crowd of reporters, CHP personnel, and nervous Chrysler executives, the Diplomats were put through their paces at Mather Air Force Base. With a wheelbase of just under 113in, the Diplomats accelerated from 0 to 60mph in 12.8sec, and reached a top speed of 115mph. This was a speed which was 6.5mph faster than the "official" top speed recorded by the 1980 St. Regis during the 1980 tests. The Diplomat being 14-1/2in shorter and 240lb less than the St. Regis also delivered better fuel economy.

The 350ci Chevrolet Impala won the bid for 1982. However, the Diplomat returned in 1983. The Ford Crown Victoria won the contract for 1984. Then the Diplomat returned every year through 1988, except in 1987 when the Chevrolet Caprice Classic won the bid.

Described as "One of the most bullet-proof cars ever built," by Sacramento Dodge Dealer, Chuck Swift, the Diplomat as a Highway Patrol car generated mixed emotions. Part of the prob-

lem was the only available V-8 engine for the Diplomat was the 318ci. The 360ci was only available in trucks and vans. Nevertheless, the Diplomats would still accelerate from 0 to 60mph in 11.55sec and top out at 117mph. The Chevrolet Caprice Classic with 32 more cubic inches and a 4-speed automatic transmission would cover 0 to 60 in 9.4sec and top out at 118mph. The Chevrolet would accelerate from 0 to 100mph about 10sec quicker than the Diplomat.

Who was the dealer that sold over 15,000 cars to the California Highway Patrol? Swift Dodge, of Sacramento. Located a convenient distance from CHP Motor Transport, Swift Dodge developed and maintained an efficient working relationship between the State of California and Dodge.

This relationship progressed to the point where Dodge shipped cars designated to the CHP painted in one color and Swift Dodge would conduct the Pre-Delivery Inspection and paint them the additional color.

Swift Dodge had been one of the top one percent Chrysler Dealers in the United States for the past 25 years, and the number one retail dealer for Northern California in 1988. Swift Auto World North, also a Dodge Dealership in Sacramento, was rated number three retail dealer for Northern California in 1988. Swift also had a Chrysler-Plymouth Dealership, and franchises to sell Rolls-Royce, Jeep, Eagle, and Lotus vehicles.

Additionally, Swift Dodge had received numerous other awards including sixteen Chrysler Awards for Excellence, which Swift Dodge had received over a period of many years.

Born in Ogelsby, Texas, Charles O. Swift graduated from Gila Bend High School in Arizona. From there he attended Pasadena City College. A World War II Veteran, Swift served 33 months with the U.S. Army Infantry and held the rank of Technical Sergeant upon completion of his military service, at the age of 21.

Swift then went on to establish a Hudson Dealership in Gila Bend, and over the next 19 years owned and operated several dif-

In 1968, Chrysler Corp. bragged about 440ci engines and 437sq-in brakes. *CHP*

ferent dealerships in Arizona. His dealerships sold Ford, Mercury, Edsel, Desoto and Plymouth vehicles.

In 1966 Swift moved to Sacramento and bought out John Drew Motors, an existing Dodge Dealer. He opened Goldie and Swift Dodge in April 1966. The following year, Swift bought out his partner, Immanuel Goldie, thus changing the name to Swift Dodge. That same year Swift Dodge won the contract to supply the CHP with 1968 Dodges.

In addition to being involved in numerous automotive industry affairs, Swift was also involved in community affairs. He was president of the Chamber of Commerce, past director of the Arthritis Foundation, and an advisory board member of Resources for Independent Living, and Mercy Hospital Foundation.

A spinal tumor in 1976 left Swift partially paralyzed from the waist down. Even though he was confined to a wheelchair, Swift still took an active role in running his dealerships. Part of this included appearing in television advertisements for his dealerships several times a week.

In 1977 Swift was named National Retailer of the Year by the National Brand Names Foundation at an awards ceremony in Washington, D.C. Swift also received the Prestigious Time Magazine dealer award in 1987. Last, but not least, Chuck Swift was awarded a commendation for service to the California Highway Patrol.

The CHP Diplomats were fitted with the 4-barrel version of the 318ci LA engine. Unique in the fact that this engine was only available in the police version of "M" bodied cars, Chrysler went once more into "it's bag of tricks" to produce the E48 police engine.

The civilian 318ci engine was rated at 130 SAE net hp, and was fed by a 2-barrel carburetor. The 4-barrel version was equipped with engine reliability modifications which included double roller timing gear and chain, forged connecting rods, Lubrite treated camshaft and heavy-duty valve train components. An anti-turbulence windage tray was fitted between the crankcase and oil sump. This not only improved engine lubrication at high speeds, but it is also slightly improved horsepower, to the tune of about 5hp. The big horsepower gain came from the 360 heads and 4-barrel Thermo Quad carburetor. The E48 engine was rated at 165 SAE net hp.

Attached behind this engine was Chryslers famed 727 TorqueFlite 3 speed automatic transmission. Final drive ratio on the police versions was 2.94 to 1.

The suspension system on the police Diplomats consisted of heavy-duty transverse front torsion bars and rear springs, a heavy duty front sway bar, and tucked above the rear axle rested the rear sway bar. Heavy-duty shock absorbers completed the S16 extra duty pursuit suspension.

While many manufacturers were downsizing their cars during the late 1970s and early 1980s, Chrysler did not downsize the brake system of the police cars. Heavy-duty front disc brakes with semi-metallic linings and 11x2-1/2-inch rear brakes handled stopping chores. Essentially, these brakes were the same size brakes used on the large Monaco/Fury series, and 3/4 ton vans and trucks.

The 1985 Diplomats were given a 10hp increase, bringing the rating to 175 SAE net hp. Among other changes were the transition to the Rochester QuadraJet 4-barrel carburetor, as Carter ceased production of the Thermo Quad.

The "bullet-proof" 727 TorqueFlite automatic transmission was also phased out of production in passenger cars after the 1982 model run. By 1985 a wide ratio version of the 904 TorqueFlite with a lock-up torque converter was used in the police version. While this was still a good, reliable transmission, even in police service, (given proper care and maintenance), it was not

This beautifully restored 1969 CHP Dodge Polara has been used as a movie car. *Rhonda Madden*

recommended that this combination be used in attempting to push disabled 18 wheelers off the roadway. Call a tow truck!

A front suspension problem which first became apparent on the 1986 Diplomats, reappeared on the 1988s. The problem was traced to some front suspension "K" members which were manufactured in Mexico. The "K" member, which supports the front suspension, would begin to sag after about 20,000 miles of service. This would cause difficulty in maintaining front wheel alignment. As the problem became worse, the steering would lock up. Replacing the "K" member solved the problem.

1988 was the last year the CHP used the Diplomat. After the last Diplomat went through CHP's Motor Transport Services to be outfitted, a ceremony commemorating the event was held, thus culminating a 32-year relationship between the California Highway Patrol and Dodge.

While the Diplomat was not the most popular sedan in the CHP's fleet, it wasn't hated either. Considering that the Diplomat was in the middle of the fierce competition between Ford and Chevrolet to corner the police market, the Diplomat served the State of California credibly. Had the 360ci engine been available, it would have been more evenly matched against the competition.

CHP specifications required that vehicles be purchased through a dealer located in the Sacramento area. The reason for that was the vehicles were then delivered to CHP Motor Transport Service, located at the old CHP Academy in Sacramento.

Upon arrival at Motor Transport, the vehicles were run through an eight step process to outfit and equip them as CHP cars. They were properly marked. Radios, scanners, shotgun racks, emergency lights and sirens were installed. The cars were then shipped to various parts of the state to begin service. Motor Transport also received units which had ended their service and removed police equipment. The cars were repainted and sold to the public on a bid basis. A similar operation in Torrance handled and disposed of squad cars from Southern California.

The California Highway Patrol is considered to be one of the nations leading law enforcement agencies. Part of the reason is due to the Department's vast research and development in determining the best patrol automobile. The CHP, along with the Michigan State Police, Los Angeles Police Department, and the Los Angeles County Sheriff's Department have set the standards

This 1969 Dodge Polara remains 27 years later as the fastest 4-door sedan ever used by the CHP. *Ned Schwartz*

for law enforcement vehicles. Many other agencies purchase their vehicles based upon the vehicle tests and evaluations established by one or all of these agencies.

The CHP's research and development has paid off with better and more reliable vehicles than the general public drives. Twenty years ago CHP vehicles were sold after 75,000 miles of patrol service. Later that was upped to 85,000 miles, and is currently 95,000 miles. Part of the reason the cars are allowed to be in service longer is because of the state's current financial situation. Another part of the reason—I feel—is that Detroit is building a better, more reliable car.

The CHP also saw a need for safer automobiles. As a one of the pioneers in using and testing safety belts almost 40 years ago,

the CHP also saw a need for better brakes and better handling automobiles. The Department asked for better handling and stopping performance, and Detroit listened.

CALIFORNIA HIGHWAY PATROL VEHICLE SELECTION
1956
PONTIAC Chieftain 2 dr. sedan. 317ci V-8.
DODGE Coronet 2 dr. sedan. 315ci V-8, 2-4-barrel carburetors, 260bhp. PowerFlite 2 speed automatic.
1957
PONTIAC Chieftain 2 dr. sedan. 347ci V-8 engine.
DODGE Coronet 2 dr. sedan. 325ci V-8 TorqueFlite
1958
DODGE Coronet 2 dr. sedan. 361ci V-8, 2-4-barrel carburetors, 320bhp. TorqueFlite
1959
DODGE Coronet 2 dr. sedan. 383ci V-8, 4-barrel carburetor, 320bhp. TorqueFlite.
1960
DODGE Polara 4 dr. sedan. 383ci V-8, 4-barrel, 320bhp. TorqueFlite.
1961
DODGE Polara 4 dr. sedan, 383ci V-8, 4-barrel, 320bhp. TorqueFlite.
1962
CHRYSLER Enforcer 4 dr. sedan. 383ci, 4-bbl V-8 325bhp. TorqueFlite.
1963
DODGE 880 4 dr. sedan. 413ci V-8, 4-barrel, 360bhp. Torque-Flite.
1964
DODGE 880 4 dr. sedan. 413ci, 4-bbl V-8. 360 bhp. TorqueFlite.

This is current CHP Commissioner Maury Hannigan with a 1974 Dodge Monaco from his Sergeant days. *Darryl Lindsay*

1965
DODGE Polara 4 dr. sedan 413ci, 4-bbl V-8. 360 bhp. Torque-Flite.
1966
Dodge Polara 4 dr. sedan. 440ci, 4-barrel V-8, 350bhp.
Special note: Some came equipped with 426ci "Street Wedge" engines, 365bhp, 4-barrel carb.
1967
OLDSMOBILE Delmont 88 4 dr. sedan. 425ci V-8, 4-barrel, 365bhp. TurboHydramatic transmission.
1968
DODGE Polara 4 dr. sedan. 440ci 4-barrel, 350bhp. TorqueFlite. Disc brakes.
1969
DODGE Polara 4 dr. sedan. 440ci 4-barrel, 375bhp. TorqueFlite. Disc brakes.
1970
MERCURY Monterey 4 dr. sedan. 428ci V-8, 4-barrel 360bhp.
1971
DODGE Polara 4 dr. sedan. 440ci V-8, 4-barrel, 370bhp. TorqueFlite

1972
DODGE Polara 4 dr. sedan. 440ci V-8, 4-barrel, 276 SAE net hp TorqueFlite. (1/2 of the fleet equipped with power steering).
1973
DODGE Polara 4 dr. sedan. 440ci V-8, 4-barrel. 280 SAE net hp TorqueFlite.
1974
DODGE Monaco 4 dr. sedan. 440ci, 4-BBL, 275 SAE net hp TorqueFlite. ("Firm Feel" power steering included in all cars).
1975
DODGE Monaco 4 dr. sedan. 4-barrel 440ci V-8, 210 SAE net hp TorqueFlite.
1976
DODGE Coronet 4 dr. sedan. 440ci. 4-BBL V-8, 250 SAE net hp TorqueFlite.
1977
DODGE Monaco 4 dr. sedan. 440ci, 4-BBL V-8, 230 SAE net hp TorqueFlite.
1978
DODGE Monaco 4 dr. sedan. 440ci, 4-BBL, 240 SAE net hp, TorqueFlite.

This 1980 CHP Dodge St. Regis was powered by a mere 318ci, 4-bbl, much to their dislike. *CHP*

The lighter 1981 Dodge Diplomat still powered by the 318ci saved the day for Dodge. *CHP*

1979
DODGE St. Regis 4 dr. sedan. 360ci 4-barrel V-8, 190 SAE net hp TorqueFlite.
1980
DODGE St. Regis 4 dr. sedan. 318ci 4-barrel V-8, 155 SAE net hp TorqueFlite.
1981
DODGE Diplomat 4 dr. sedan 318ci 4-barrel V-8, 165 SAE net hp A727 TorqueFlite.
1982
CHEVROLET Impala 4 dr. sedan. 350ci 4-barrel V-8. TurboHydraMatic.
FORD Mustang 2 dr. 302ci. 2-barrel V-8, 157 SAE net hp. 4 speed manual transmission.
1983
DODGE Diplomat 4 dr. sedan. 318ci 4-barrel, 165 SAE net hp. A904 TorqueFlite.
FORD Mustang 2 dr. 302ci 4-barrel V-8, 175 SAE net hp. 5 speed manual transmission.
1984
FORD Crown Victoria 4 dr. sedan. 351ci 2-barrel, Variable Venturi carburetor, 180 SAE net
hp. 4 speed overdrive, (AOD), automatic.
FORD Mustang 2 dr.

1985
DODGE Diplomat 4 dr. sedan. 318ci 4-barrel V-8, 175 SAE net hp TorqueFlite
FORD Mustang 2 dr. sedan.
1986
DODGE Diplomat 4 dr. sedan. 318ci 4-BBl, V-8, 175 SAE net hp TorqueFlite.
FORD Mustang 2 dr. sedan. 302ci V-8, fuel injected, 200 SAE net hp
1987
Chevrolet Caprice Classic 4 dr. sedan. 350ci V-8. 4-speed overdrive automatic.
FORD Mustang 2 dr. sedan.
1988
DODGE Diplomat 4 dr. sedan. 318ci, 4-BBL, V-8, 175 SAE net hp TorqueFlite.
FORD Mustang 2 dr. sedan.

References

Standard Catalog of American Cars
1946-1975 (1st edition)
1946-1975 (2nd edition)
1976-86
The California Highway Patrolman
The Fleetest Fleet 4/84 Hal Rubin
Readying Our Cars and Motorcycles for Patrol Duties 3/93 Hal Rubin
TV'S Original Highway Patrol 8/92 Sam Knight Misc issues.
Motor Trend Magazine
'58 Dodge on Trial 3/58 James E. Potter
Seat Belts Pro & Con 6/57 William Carroll
Wanted by the Califorinia Highway Patrol 2/59 Lester Nehamkin (Published in M.T.'s Western Edition)
Schools for Tin Stars with Lead Feet 8/66 Steven Kelly
What Police Cars are Made of 6/66 Steven Kelly
What's Black and White and Can Save You Money? 6/71
Popular Mechanics
Final Exam Day for Patrol Cars 6/58 Ewart Thomas
Car Life Magazine
How the Best Drivers Get That Way 5/61 Robert Lee Behme
Cars the Automotive Magazine
We Test a Factory Rod the Dodge Police Cruiser 7/60 Joe H. Wherry
Sports Car Graphic Magazine
SGG Joins the CHP 12/84 Jack R. Nerad
Driver Magazine
130mph Professional 6/67 Bob McVay
Car and Driver Magazine
In the Name of the Law 3/65 Jesse L. Alexander
Civilian Bear Spotters Guide 12/77
Fastest American Sedan: Dodge Monaco Police Pursuit 7/77
Rodder & Super Stock Magazine
Dodge 413 Patrol Pursuit (Circa 1965) Martyn L. Schorr
Classic Chrysler Quarterly

1978 Super Cars (Spring, 1988) Tom Quadrin
Mechanix Illustrated
The Truth About Police Cars 1/68 Tom McCahill
Police Product News
C.H.P. Goes Racy With the Camaro Z/28 (Circa 1983) Bob Hagin
Car Craft Magazine
Chipp Off the Old Block 12/79 Niel Britt
Chrysler Power Magazine
Last of the Chrysler Pursuits 1/92 Ed Sanow
California Highway Patrol Various Annual Reports
Motor Transport Service-various documents and photographs
The California Highway Patrol . . .Yesterday and Today 1989 Robert A Wick

INTERVIEWS

Maury J. Hannigan-CHP Commissioner
D.O. Helmick, Deputy Commissioner
Jim Rogaski, Motor Transport Section
Reginald "Bo" Bohanan, MTS
Chris Morgan, MTS
George Caravas, Traffic officer
Warren Clark, CHP ret'd.
Judd Strong, CHP ret'd.
Jim Turnin, CHP ret'd.
Joe Schlecter, Traffic Officer
Frank W. Wylie, (Ret'd. Chrysler P.R.)
Charles O. Swift, Sacramento Dodge dealer.
Darryl Lindsay-P.C.O.O.A.
Greg Marsh-Santa Monica Fire Dept.
Philip Moser-San Mateo County Sheriff's Department
Ronald Derderian-Beverly Hills P.D.
Marvin Ruffin-CHP MTS
LOS ANGELES TIMES Various issues
POPULAR HOT RODDING MAGAZINE
HOT PURSUIT 4/93 Scott Oldham

Chapter 19

Police Package Test Mules

In 1982, as a result of a 1979 CHP experiment, the pursuit-class squad car was re-discovered. To the shock of some and the glee of others, a small-block V-8 powering a 100-inch wheelbase pony car fully filled the patrol shoes of the big-block V-8, powering a 122in cruiser.

The 302ci equipped Mustang easily out-accelerated, out-top ended and out-cornered all the full and mid-sized squad cars. The Mustang never could out-brake the bigger cars, but that was the fault of Ford. It took Ford another decade to correct the problem.

After 1981, the only A38/AHB police package cars offered by Chrysler Corp. were the Diplomat and Gran Fury. Powered by various versions of the 318ci, 4-bbl, these M-bodies could keep 350ci Chevrolets and the 351ci Fords at bay. But nothing from Dodge or Plymouth could touch the outright performance of the Mustang.

Each year at the Michigan State Police runoffs it was the Mustang first, and all other police vehicles as "also rans." Of course the Diplomats and Gran Furys did well in the 4-door sedan class, which was where the contract was placed.

Even still, getting your best police car beat in heads-up competition by a Ford any kid could own, was a humbling experience for the auto makers who at one time made America's Fastest Car. The facts were, neither Dodge nor Plymouth had anything in the Mustang's class. Until 1987.

Actually, the Dodge Daytona Turbo Z was introduced in 1983 as a passenger car. This was Chrysler Corp.'s performance leader, "an all-out sports car, built to take on the best of its kind in the world." That meant the Camaro 5.0L and Z28 and Mustang 5.0 GT. The Daytona Z was powered by a 2.2 liter, multiport fuel injected and turbo-charged 4-cylinder engine producing 142 net hp.

Motor Trend witnessed Dodge do the backhand with driving gloves to both Chevrolet and Ford, so they gathered all three cars at the Laguna Seca road racing track for a 3-way shootout.

The powerful and balanced Camaro simply out-classed the other two cars. It had the highest power-to-weight ratio and "almost flawless handling." It was 1/2 to 1 second faster in the quarter mile and a full 3sec quicker around the Laguna Seca road course. Chevy had to have known the Camaro could easily knock off the Mustang if they ever decided to get in the police car business. Camaro did when Chevrolet did—in 1991.

Second place, however, went to the Dodge Daytona Turbo Z. It was 1/2 second slower in the quarter than the Mustang, but had better braking (what police car doesn't?) and better cornering g-forces. When the tire smoke cleared, the hair-dryer Dodge beat the Mustang around the road course by one full second. Swish. One Mississippi. Swish.

	1/4 Mile ET	1/4 Mile Trap	Skid Pad	Laguna Seca Rd Crse
Camaro Z28	15.6sec	90.5mph	.88g	1:25.4sec
Daytona TurboZ	16.5sec	81.6mph	.83g	1:28.8sec
Mustang 5.0	6.1sec	87.5mph	.77g	1:29.9sec

Motor Trend called the Daytona TurboZ "The best-handling, front-wheel drive production car we have tested."

Okay, fine, Dodge knew they could take out the police Mustang anytime they wanted. That gave Dodge the self-assurance to ignore the Mustang at the MSP runoffs for the next four years.

By 1987, Chrysler Corp. was even more committed to front drive cars. They survived the rumors of the M-body being dropped by 1985. However, by 1987, rumors surfaced again that the M-body would disappear after 1989. This time the rumors were better founded. And the fire was fueled when in 1987 Dodge released a police test mule in the form of the Daytona Shelby Z.

If Dodge was going to stay in the police business, they had to have a "proven" test car. Typically this meant two 6-month trials in actual police service. It also meant the competition got

tipped off to the plans.

In 1987, Dodge released their Daytona Shelby Z. If Dodge was ever going to field a pursuit-class car, this was it, they decided. The engine was the same as earlier turborcharged fours except for the intercooler. This alone boosted the horsepower to 174 net hp.

Carroll Shelby, known most more for suspension tricks than engine modifications, added gas-shocks, larger front and rear sway bars and 50 series Eagle GT pursuit tires on wider wheels. The Shelby Z ran the quarter in 16.2sec at 88.1mph with a cornering force of .89gs.

In preparation for the shutdown of M-body production, Dodge promoted the Shelby Z to "police test mule" status. This made instant headlines in the hard-core cop magazine, *Police*. The following column written by Ben Crookshanks appeared in the February 1988 issue of *Police*. The column is printed without edit, in its entirety and with the written permission of *Police* magazine.

West Virginia State Police troopers praised the 1987 Daytona Shelby Z for its speed and handling. *Ben Crookshanks/Police magazine*

The Shelby Z Experiment

You can't outrun the long arm of the law." That's an old and work cliche' but there are two West Virginia State Troopers who would be hard to outrun. They are road testing two Dodge Daytona Shelby Z's, the Chrysler Corporation's entry into the sports car field. Powered by 2.2 liter engine, this car is capable of a top speed of 150mph.

Since 1977, the West Virginia Department of Public Safety (State Police), along with the Michigan State Police and the Illinois Toll Road Authority, has participated in a program testing state police cars. The testing takes place at two sites in Michigan, one of which is the Chrysler Providing Grounds in Chelsea.

From time to time, Chrysler leases cars to police departments to conduct long-term endurance tests on new designs, as police work puts a lot of rough miles on vehicles in a short time. If a car holds up under police treatment, it will certainly hold up for the average car buyer. This type of testing is more practical than just taking a car out and running it around the track of the proving ground.

When West Virginia State Police Superintendent Col. W.F. Donohoe heard that Chrysler wanted a police department to road test two 1987 Shelby Z's, he immediately said, "Send 'em on down."

In due time, the cars arrived and were assigned to Sgt. D.P. Lake and Trooper C.R. Mankins of the Turnpike Detachment of the State Police. Chrysler leased out the two cars for $1 each per year for two years and agreed to perform all maintenance, with the stipulation each car be driven at least 50,000 miles a year. Two tests are being performed simultaneously: one is an endurance test for Chrysler, the other is a feasibility study for the State Police to determine if a small-bodied, high performance car would fill a niche in the department's vehicular arsenal.

The two Shelbys are stock, except for the addition of normal police equipment and decals. One uses a blue "fireball" dash light, and as an experiment, the other car was recently fitted with a light bar to see what effect it would have on the vehicle's aerodynamics.

Some of the stock features include disc brakes, performance rubber and tuned suspension, rack and pinion steering, front and rear spoilers, air, a complete set of analog gauges, an AM/FM cassette with six speakers and a five-speed stick shift.

The new 2.2 liter 174-horsepower, intercooled turbo engine can move the Shelby from 0 to 60mph in 6.9sec. Sgt. Lake was surprised with the car's smooth acceleration and the fact that there was no sudden surge of power or loud noise when the turbo kicked in.

In one high-speed chase, Lake had the Shelby up to 138mph. "I didn't realize I was going so fast, it was handling so well," he said. "I was fine until I looked down and saw '138'. Then I got a little nervous." His collar, driving a Hurst Olds 442, topped out at 115mph.

After six months and more that 24,000 miles of driving, the faults and virtues of the Shelby are obvious. Getting in and out while wearing a fully equipped gunbelt is a little difficult, and the car is not very practical for transporting either personnel or prisoners. Because of low ground clearance, a Shelby is limited to paved roads which can be a problem in predominately rural areas. On the other hand, a Shelby Z is entirely functional for Interstate or turnpike patrol. It will outrun and outmaneuver an ordinary, general purpose cruiser and mileage averages 20 to 22 miles per gallon, nearly double that of other patrol cars.

Despite its shortcomings as a general purpose vehicle, Sgt. Lake said the Shelby Z has far exceeded his expectations. When asked if he would miss the car when the test was over, his answer was an emphatic, "Yes, sir!"

The Tennessee Highway Patrol also took part in the durability testing of the Shelby Z. In the final analysis, however, the Shelby Z did not make it past the "mule" stage. It had the performance. Even though cops dread a turbo-charged squad car due to turbo maintenance, this did not surface as a problem.

What stopped the Shelby Z was overall size. Even in the restricted Prima Donna role as a pursuit-only vehicle, the 97-inch wheelbase Daytona was simply too small. At least that was the official version from Chrysler fleet officials.

This author still feels the need for the maintenance-heavy turbo to deliver the pursuit performance was the real issue. We will never know. But to this day, not one police package or special service package squad car from any domestic car maker has ever had a turbocharger. Not one. Fuel injection? Yes. Front-wheel drive? Yes. Overhead cam? Yes. Turbo? No way. The Daytona Z was dropped from consideration as a special purpose police vehicle in 1988. In 1989, Chrysler Corp. went out of the police car business completely. No more cop cars from the Corporation that one time made 80 percent of all cop cars. Chrysler was definitely conspicuous in their absence at the LASD/LAPD and Michigan State Police vehicle tests in 1990. No Chrysler-made cop cars and no plans for cop cars. Hmmmmm.

Then in 1991, Dodge once again tipped its hand with three different front drive police test mules. One was a modified Dodge Dynasty. The others were standard Dodge Spirit R/T and Acclaim LX passenger cars.

<u>Dodge Dynasty</u> In 1991, Dodge proving ground personnel put together three specially-modified Dynastys. One went into police service with the Stevens Point, Wisconsin Police. Another patrolled the Ann Arbor, Michigan area with the Washtenaw County, Michigan Sheriff's Dept. The third was kept by Dodge for internal testing.

These Dynastys had beefed-up suspensions, anti-lock brakes, 60-series pursuit tires and engine oil coolers. Most significantly, the 3.3L V-6 had been replaced by the 3.8L Imperial V-6. By 1991 the UltraFlite electronic 4-speed automatic had been de-bugged. The Dynasty was ready to crush crime. The world read about it in the November 1991 issue of *High Performance Mopar:*

Chrysler is back in the police car business! For decades, Chrysler was America's Police Car Company. In the 1960s, they brought us the Fury and Coronet 440 4-barrel freeway interceptors that ran 140mph all day long. In the 1970s even with full smog gear, the Chrysler big block police cars ruled the streets. In the 1980s, the reliable Diplomat and Gran Fury were the backbone of law enforcement making up 80 percent of the cop cars. Chrysler put teeth in their Patroller, Enforcer, Pursuit and Interceptor police packages.

The most recent Chrysler cop cars were the 318 4-barrel M-bodies. These squared-off and carbureted workhorses still ran from 117 to 120mph, according to independent tests by the Michigan State Police. After the 1989 model year, Chrysler discontinued production of the M-body. According to Chrysler's Tom Houston, Chrysler was gearing up to be only a front wheel drive company.

In 1989, every police package and special service package squad car on the market was rear wheel drive. And yet the Diplomat and Gran Fury were the only rear wheel drive cars in the entire Chrysler fleet. As engineering and design attention shifted away from RWD technology, Chrysler decided to get out of the police car business and close the Kenosha, Wisconsin manufacturing plant.

This left a large number of agencies out in the cold. The state police in Wisconsin, Tennessee, Nebraska, New York, California, Vermont and the New York City police have used Chrysler squads since anyone could remember. Records dating back to the 1950s proved their Pentastar loyalty right to the end.

The Washtenaw County, Michigan Sheriff found this 1991 3.8L Dodge Dynasty test mule to be fast and reliable.

Many police and sheriff's' departments gave the 3.3L-powered Dodge Dynasty a try for both uniformed and detective use. *McCreary Chrysler*

It was not a happy scene at donut shops all over the country when Mopar-lovin' cops had to settle for a bowtie or blue oval. So when the cops got a chance to bend the ear of Chrysler president Bob Lutz, they did it. Lutz lives in Washtenaw County, Michigan. As the story goes, one disgruntled deputy took Lutz to task. At the very least, the cops wanted a competitor to the Taurus.

Things have changed since the police pullout decision in 1989. Front wheel drive cars were hot and getting hotter. Corporate fleet people were originally not impressed with what they saw as a 5000-car, front wheel drive police market. Lutz, however, had better vision than that. Most of the FWD cars being used as cop cars are not police package cars.

The facts are a great deal of urban patrol is done by mid-size FWD squads. Many passenger cars were purchased from local car dealers and just pressed into police service. Of course the reliability and durability of a non-police package car are not as good. The demand became stronger for FWD police package. Ford was the first one out with their 55A Taurus 3.8L for 1990. Chevy just released their 1992 B4C Lumina 3.1L. Toyota has formal plans for a 1993 Camry police package. But even releasing a police package in a car does not get it any more. It has to perform.

Since the first Michigan State Police tests in 1977, the MSP has tied performance to the bid price. The low bid no longer gets the business to those using the MSP method. The bid price is adjusted by a performance factor. As we found out in the 1992 MSP cop car tests, the Lumina is no match for the Taurus in terms of acceleration, top speed and road course lap times

Since the MSP tests are conducted each year at Chrysler's own Chelsea Proving Grounds, Chrysler fleet people certainly knew what performance they needed to beat. The Mitsubishi 3.0L V-6 and the Chrysler 3.3L V-6 available in the Dodge Dynasty

were simply not powerful enough. Chrysler solved that problem just like they had done dozens of times before. when faced with the same problem. They used whatever engine was in the Imperial at the time.

This time the Imperial engine was a Chrysler-designed 3.8L sequential multiport fuel injected V-6 made at Chrysler's Trenton, Michigan engine plant. This 3.8L engine was based on the 3.3L V-6, but produced more horsepower and more torque. And the 3.8L did it at lower rpms.

The 3.8L uses a cast iron block, nodular iron crank, forged rods and aluminum heads. The roller lifters use pushrods to reach the overhead valves which were controlled by variable rate, semi-conical valve springs. The 2-piece cast aluminum intake uses18-1/2in tuned runners and a single plenum chamber. A distributorless direct ignition system sets the whole works on fire.

Actually, the 3.8L police engine produces slightly more power than the Imperial version thanks to better exhaust and computer calibration. The factory is reluctant to put an exact horsepower number on the police 3.8L, since the engine has not yet formally been released. The Imperial 3.8L puts out 150hp and 203lb-ft of torque. The police version puts out 160hp and 225lb-ft of torque. We know because The Dynasty police engine has to equal the Taurus police engine. Simple as that.

The Dynasty squad car uses the A604 Ultradrive EATX transaxle. Introduced in 1989, this electronic 4-speed automatic overdrive shattered the Chrysler reputation for bulletproof drivetrains. On the A604, upshifts, downshifts, internal clutching, kickdown at WOT, and torque converter lockup are all controlled by a microprocessor fed by a series of switches, solenoids and sensors. That is the bad news.

The good news is the pump and clutch failures from 1989 have been resolved. The computer software problems from 1990

The Dodge Spirit and Plymouth Acclaim (shown) are replacements for the K-cars but boast more power and better brakes.
Scott Zane

have been fixed. The Ultradrive no longer cycles between gears when climbing a grade. The kitchen shift is faster, as is the overall response to WOT. Finally, the response is also faster when going from Park to Drive and from Reverse to Drive. The police A604 has been calibrated for police work with higher rpm shift points and firmer shifts.

The Dynasty AHB police package also includes beefed up shocks, larger diameter coil springs and heavier front and rear anti-sway bars. The police package includes 4-wheel disc brakes with ABS. The latest Chrysler cop car also comes with external coolers for the engine oil and transaxle fluid. Overall handling is greatly improved by the use of 60-series, V-rated Michelin tires on wider 15-inch wheels.

The AHB Dynasty 3.8L police package is currently under test by the Washtenaw County, Michigan Sheriff's Dept. and the Stevens Point, Wisconsin Police. These agencies are using the Dynasty as a full-service, heavy duty squad car, not as a mere light-duty traffic watcher. These police cars will go through two 6-month in-service trials and all the police input will be considered before the final production release.

We caught up with the AHB package Dynasty at the 1992 Michigan State Police cop car competition. The MSP requires that the cars they test be actual production models, so the pre-production Dynasty 3.8L was not given the chance to burn up the track. But the way the Dynasty has been equipped, it could very well sweep next year's MSP cop car tests for mid-size cruisers. Dodge is back. (end of article)

Dodge, however, did not release the Dynasty for police use after all.

The prototype squad was whip-quick, handled well at all speeds and had enough room for the urban patrol duties. This time the problem was related to the marketing of the Dynasty passenger car itself.

It would take until the end of the 1991 model year, or perhaps the start of the 1992 model year to complete all of the durability tests and in-service police field tests. The soonest the Dynasty would be ready to be released was 1992. Yet the Dynasty was already scheduled to go out of production after 1993. It was

being replaced by the mystery "LH" car, aka Intrepid.

Dodge correctly decided not to market a police package car knowing it would only last 1 to 1-1/2 model years. The Taurus 55A and Lumina B4C got a reprieve. The Dynasty 3.8L would have taken them both out. The results were that good.

Spirit R/T and Acclaim LX. During the same time the 1991 Dynasty 3.8L police mule was crushing crime in Wisconsin and Michigan, unmodified Mopar passenger cars were being tested for police duty in Texas and North Dakota.

One of these was the 224 net hp Dodge Spirit R/T. The other was the more sedate Plymouth Acclaim LX 3.0L. Again, these were passengers cars seeing limited police service. This was the first step before "police mule" status, which helps to define the police gear the "mule" will carry.

The Spirit and Acclaim were upscale replacements for the Aries K and Reliant K. These were again classed as 6-passenger cars based on their 103.5-inch wheelbase. They were direct competitors to the Chevy Corsica, Ford Tempo, Honda Accord and Toyota Camry. So, 6-passenger cars were the trend. The Spirit and Acclaim were more aerodynamic, more plush and made a better use of passenger room than the older K-cars.

Both new cars were now available with anti-lock brakes. Rear discs were standard on the Spirit ES and R/T and Acclaim LX as was a driver's side air bag. A sport handling suspension was standard on these models. The Spirit ES and Acclaim LX used a 16:1 ratio rack and pinion power steering. The Spirit R/T had a quicker ratio, 14.2:1 steering gear.

The real difference between the Spirit/Acclaim and Aries/Reliant was in the powertrain. The K-cars were never available with V-6 engines. The Spirit/Acclaim came standard with a 2.5L In-line, 4-cylinder and had a turbo version as an option. The police interest however, was in the more powerful optional DOHC In-line 4 and the SOHC V-6.

Vehicle	Spirit ES, Acclaim LX	Spirit R/T
Engine	3.0L SOHC V-6	2.2L DOHC I4
Induction	Multipoint Injection	MPFI, Turbo III
Bore x Stroke	3.59inx2.99in	3.44inx3.62in
Compression	8.9:1	7.8:1
Manufacturer	Mitsubishi	Chrysler/Lotus
SAE Net HP	141hp @ 5000rpm	224hp @2800rpm
Transmission	EATX 4-speed auto	Getrag 5-speed manual
Final Drive	3.43:1	3.85:1

The Plymouth Acclaim LX was equipped with the 3.0L V-6. This was a perfectly acceptable combination for light, urban police work. The Mitsubishi-made, fuel-injected V-6 had the same peak horsepower as the 3.1L V-6 in the Lumina squad.

This was a little disappointing since the Mitsubishi engine had SOHC heads compared to the pushrod Lumina engine. However, the lighter weight of the Acclaim and the flatter torque curve of the SOHC design allowed the Acclaim to perform better than the Lumina B4C.

This was significant. At the time, the Lumina B4C had the distinction of being the slowest of the true police package squads. This was a very uncomfortable reputation, even though the squad may have successfully performed all its police duties. The SOHC-powered Acclaim avoided this "slowest but acceptable" title. The Spirit ES was also powered by the same 3.0L SOHC V-6 engine.

The non-police package Acclaim LX and Spirit ES have been used by various city police agencies as light-duty, urban patrol vehicles. These cars were never upgraded to police package status.

By far the most exciting of the 1991 passenger cars used by Dodge and Plymouth to test the police waters in civilian trim was the Dodge Spirit R/T. Plymouth did not have a similar extreme performance version of the Acclaim.

The Spirit R/T was available only in 1991 and 1992. It was an absolute land rocket. Chrysler designed the Spirit R/T "to out-perform the world's finest performance sedans." The Spirit R/T ran the quarter mile in 14.5sec at 97mph and had a top speed of 141mph. This made it the quickest American-made, 4-door sedan. More than that, the Spirit R/T was the quickest 4-door sedan in the world, including the Volvo.

Cops who got to try out the Spirit R/T had a genuine opportunity to humiliate Corvettes, Trans Ams, Mustangs, Camaros and all other lesser cars. With an incredible 224 net hp, the Spirit R/T could keep up with all these sport coupes even though the Spirit had the aerodynamics of a brick.

All this straight line performance was made possible by the most powerful 4-cylinder engine made in America. Chrysler and Lotus got 224 net hp out of 135ci. That was 1.67 net hp per ci. Remember when 1.0 brake hp per ci was a pure-bred race engine? The Spirit R/T had doubled that power.

All this power came from Lotus-designed head, pistons, intake manifold and exhaust manifold in combination with a Garrett intercooled, water-cooled turbocharger. The Spirit R/T engine was Chrysler's first engine to use 4 valves per cylinder. This 16-valve engine had a 6500rpm redline and a block based on the durable 2.2L VNT Turbo IV engine. The bore, stroke and basic engine casting were the same.

For 1991, Chrysler worked on the Spirit and Acclaim front Iso-Strut suspension. They raised the front roll center for faster response, reduced the bump steer, increased the caster for better tracking and reduced the flex in some steering components. This, combined with the extra-stuff, sports suspension, seemed to do the job.

Even at speeds well above 100mph, this car felt solid and stable, proving the basic suspension design was a good one.

Car & Driver put the Spirit R/T in a three way shootout with the arch-rivals Taurus SHO and Lumina Z34. Pay attention here. These DOHC V-6, 4-door, front wheel drive cars may be the dominant squad cars of the future. Car & Driver had pages of praise for the Spirit R/T engine, but was a little disappointed in the overall handling. Again, for cops also, straightline performance was fun, but road course lap times were the best measure of a squad.

Though Dodge beefed up the Spirit's basic underpinnings for R/T duty including increased spring rates and tighter shocks, the suspension quickly revealed its famile-sedan lineage when the corners came up fast.

Fitted with standard 205/60R-15 Michelin XGT V4 tires, the R/T recorded the group's highest roadholding figure (0.80g), yet out in the real world where few turns are as steady and smooth as a skid pad the R/T felt nervous, unsettled, even clumsy.

Incredibly, despite the car's grip and enormous straightline speed advantage, whoever was driving the R/T inevitably fell behind the other two clippers through the challenging curves of Ohio's southeastern quadrant.

"It's easily upset by potholes during brisk cornering," one tester wrote. "And the steering loses precision above 70mph."

"Not enough feedback through the wheel for accurate cornering," added another.

By far, the Spirit R/T's best asset was its performance-to-dollar ratio. At a base price of $17,820 (including air conditioning and power mirrors), the R/T packed more wallop than any other four-door you can buy for the money.

In spite of the Spirit R/T's lack of an advanced suspension, Patrick Bedard summed up the R/T best when he called it a "haul-hiney sedan." Like the Acclaim LX, the Spirit R/T never made it to "police mule" status and the R/T option was dropped after 1992. And the fleet folks at Ford and Chevrolet breathed a sigh of relief.

This 1991 Winfield, Illinois Police Dodge Spirit is powered by a 3.0L SOHC V-6. *Greg Reynolds*

The 1992 Dodge Spirit R/T test mule ran a 14sec quarter mile. *Chrysler*

The 1992 Dodge Spirit R/T test mule was powered by a 2.2L turbo to a top speed of 141mph. *Chrysler*

Dodge Dynasty AHB Police Package
GENERAL
body style	4-door, 6-passenger
drive train	front engine, front drive

DIMENSIONS
wheelbase	104.4in
track, f/r	57.6in/57.6in
length	192.0in
height	53.6in.
curb weight	3175lb

ENGINE
type	V-6, transverse mounted
bore x stroke	3.78inx3.43in
displacement	230ci/3.8L
compression	3.0:1
valvertrain	overhead valve, 2-valves/cylinder
induction	sequential, multiport fuel injection
horsepower	160hp @ 4400rpm, SAE net
torque	225lb-ft @ 3200rpm, SAE net
fuel required	unleaded regular

DRIVETRAIN
transmission	A604 Ultradrive 4-speed automatic overdrive, electronic

GEAR RATIOS
1st	2.84:1
2nd	1.57:1
3rd	1.00:1
4th	0.69:1
transaxle	3.42:1

SUSPENSION
front	heavy-duty, gas-charged, position-sensitive MacPherson struts; heavy-duty coil springs; heavy-duty anti-sway bar
rear	trailing arm, rigid axle with track bar; heavy-duty coil springs; heavy-duty gas charged shocks; heavy-duty anti-sway bar

STEERING
type	power-assisted, rack & pinion, precision-feel
ratio	18.0:1
turns	2.85, lock to lock

BRAKES
front	power vented disc, 10.08in
rear	power disc, 10.04in
ABS	standard

WHEELS & TIRES
wheel size	15x6in
tires	P205/60VR15 Michelin XGT V4

Dodge Spirit R/T
(non-police test mule)

Dodge Dynasty AHB Police Package
GENERAL
body style	4-door, 6-passenger
drivetrain	front engine, front drive

DIMENSIONS
wheelbase	103.5in
track, f/r	57.6in/57.2in
length	181.2in
height	53.5in.
curb weight	3162lb

ENGINE
type	Inline 4-cylinder
bore x stroke	3.44inx3.62in
displacement	135ci/2.2L
induction	Turbo III (Garrett), inter-cooled
valvertrain	dual over head cam(DOHC), 4 valves/cylinder
fuel injection	sequential, multiport
horsepower	224hp @ 6000rpm, SAE net
torque	217lb-ft @ 3200rpm, SAE net
compression	7.8:1

DRIVETRAIN
transmission	5-speed manual, close ratio, Getrag
final drive	3.85:1
gear ratios	
1st	3.00:1
2nd	1.89:1
3rd	1.28:1
4th	0.94:1
5th	0.72:1

SUSPENSION
front	heavy-duty, gas-charged, position-sensitive MacPherson struts; heavy-duty coil springs; heavy-duty anti-sway bar.
rear	trailing arm, rigid axle with track bar; heavy-duty coil springs; heavy-duty gas-charged shocks; heavy-duty anti-sway bar.

STEERING
type	power-assisted, rack & pinion, precision-feel
ratio	14.2:1 quick-ratio
turns	2.4, lock to lock

Mid Size Police and Passenger Car Performance

Vehicle	0-60mph	0-100mph	Quarter Mile ET	Trap	Top Speed	Reference
Dodge Dynasty 3.8L V-6 OHV AHB Mule	9.8sec	29.6sec	17.6sec	78mph	128mph	Chrysler Fleet
Ford Taurus 3.8L V-6 OHV 55A Police	9.88sec	29.62sec	17.58sec	79.7mph	129.4mph	MSP-91
Chevrolet Lumina 3.1L V-6 OHV B4C Police	12.08sec	41.87sec	18.67sec	74.1mph	111mph	MSP-92
Dodge Spirit R/T 2.2L I-4 DOHC non-police	5.8sec	15.6sec	14.5sec	97mph	141mph	CD 3/91
Plymouth Acclaim LX 3.0L V-6 SOHC non-police	9.9sec	29.8sec	17.6sec	80.3mph	124mph	MT 9/91
Chevrolet Lumina Z34 3.4L V-6 DOHC passenger car	7.1sec	20.8sec	15.5sec	90mph	113mph	CD 3/91
Ford Taurus SHO 3.0L V-6 DOHC passenger car	6.6sec	18.2sec	15.2sec	93mph	140mph	CD 3/91

Here's a Plymouth Acclaim 3.0L V-6 with a Jetsonic lightbar being used by the Military Police. *Greg Reynolds*

BRAKES

front	power vented disc, 10.08in
rear	power disc, 10.04in
ABS	standard

WHEELS & TIRES

wheel size	15x6in
tires	P205/60VR15 Michelin XGT V4

References

"All American GT's," Ron Grable, *Motor Trend*, July 1983

"Dodge Daytona Shelby Z," Daniel Charles Ross, *Motor Trend*, July 1987

"The Shelby Z Experiment," Ben Crookshanks, *Police*, February 1988

"1993 Dynasty Cop Car," Ed Sanow, *High Performance Mopar*, November 1992

Patrol Vehicle Specification, Evaluation and Purchasing Program, Michigan State Police, 1991, 1992, 1993

"Dodge," Jay Koblenz, 1991 Sneak Preview, Harris Publications

"Dodge Spirit R/T," Patrick Bedard, Car & Driver October 1990

Dodge Performance Catalog, Chrysler Corporation, 1991

'92 Dodge Chrysler Corporation, 1992

"Yankee Clippers," Arthur St. Antoine, Car & Driver, March 1991

"Technical Highlights," Nicholas Bissoon-Dath, Car & Driver, October 1990

Motor Trend's Guide to Chrysler-Plymouth 1990, Fred M.H. Gregory, Petersen's Custom Publishing, January 1990

Chapter 20

1992: Jeep Cherokee AHB Police Package

In 1992, Chrysler officially returned to the police car business after sitting out for all of 1990 and 1991. The squad was powered by a 190 net hp 6-cylinder with the top speed limit removed and a maximum engine cooling package. The AHB police package vehicle had anti-lock brakes, 4-speed overdrive automatic trans with auxiliary trans oil cooler, 15x7 extra heavy duty wheels with speed-rated, 70 series radials, and a 120mph certified speedometer.

The latest police package Chrysler squad had the square-jawed look of a Chrysler police car. It certainly accelerated, braked and cornered like a Chrysler police car. The only catch was the emblems on the squad clearly read "Jeep Cherokee 4x4."

Chrysler Corp. tinkered with front-wheel drive police package cars for all of the eighties and the first part of the nineties. As such it was a mild shock to see the new generation of Chrysler police vehicles were four wheel drive, not front-wheel drive. However, it made sense.

Jeep was the most respected name in four-wheel drive. Police departments had already used Jeeps for various forms of patrol. The Cherokee in particular was being used, in non-police trim, as a supervisors or sergeants squad, as a K-9 squad, as an all-weather squad in the snowy north and as an all-terrain squad in many rural areas.

In 1992, Jeep made it official. Led by fleet engineer Mike Smith, Jeep put together a genuine AHB police special service package. Jeeps had always been police spec-durable, so the basic Cherokee needed only minor attention to the suspension, wheels and wiring.

The powerplant was a 4.0L/242 ci Inline 6-cylinder with overhead valves and electronic fuel injection. This mill put out an astonishing 190 net hp and 225 pounds of torque. Those figures completely out-shine the Ford Explorer, Olds Bravada, Chevy Blazer, GMC Jimmy and British Range Rover. On the AHB police engine, the engine controller had FRI shielding and the top speed limiter removed. The final drive ratio was 3.55:1.

The police suspension differs from the AWE Off-Road suspension mainly in the sway bar size. Both suspension package get gas shocks and steel wheels (instead of cast aluminum). However, the cops get thicker front and thicker rear sway bars. The transfer case is a "special service" unit and the tires are 70-series instead of 75-series. The cop vehicles get upgraded wiring, H.D. alternator and a high CCA battery.

Built around a 101.4-inch wheelbase, the AHB police package Cherokee was available as a 2-door or 4-door and either rear-wheel drive or four-wheel drive layouts. On its release, Chrysler Corp. Fleet Operations flatly stated: The Bloodhound Just Became Obsolete

It was one thing to make the claim. It was another issue to back-up the claim. That was where the Michigan State Police tests came in. The MSP test only police package squads, but they test all police package squads. In 1992, the MSP tested the Cherokee AHB.

In straightline tests, the Cherokee ran in the same 17 second quarter mile bracket as the Crown Vic, Taurus and 350ci Caprice Wagon. The Cherokee was quicker than the Caprice 350ci and the Lumina which were in the 18 second bracket.

When it came time to shut down, the Cherokee showed its Chrysler heritage here, too. It out-braked the Caprice, the Crown Vic, the Lumina and of course, the Mustang.

Cops at the MSP runoffs could not hardly believe their eyes. It was surprising for a "Jeep" to have such good straight line performance. Sure, the Cherokee screamed like a banshee in a straight line, but just wait until the road course, the skeptics thought. Wait, indeed!

The end of the front stretch at the MIS road course is a tight, uphill, blind, left-hand curve. The squad has to slow down from speeds over 85mph—the tough task of braking while going downhill. On broken pavement, the left turn will only allow speeds of 35mph or so. This puts the turn in the wrong power band for all but the 5-speed cars.

Some cops expected the "too-tall" Jeep to be on its side mid-way through this awkward turn. Not so. At the hands of MSP pursuit drivers, the Cherokee braked hard, went into a perfectly controlled drift and powered out of the turn with a vengeance. In fact, a few times the Cherokee lifted it inside front tire an inch or so off the pavement doing a Porsche 911 impersonation. It was great.

The 1992 Jeep Cherokee astounded cops by its speed and agility around the MIS road racing course during MSP tests.

In 1992, around the MIS road course the Cherokee police 4x4 outran the Lumina B4C, Caprice 9C1 305ci and Caprice Wagon 350ci. Even more humiliating for the competition, the Cherokee was just 0.16 sec behind the SOHC Crown Vic 55H and 0.68 sec behind the Taurus 55A. Chrysler fans took great pleasure in seeing the in-line 6, high-centered, brick-shaped 4x4 right on the bumper of the sleek new Crown Vic, equipped with the much-heralded "modular" V-8 engine.

Some cops shook their head in disbelief while others cheered and clapped. Chrysler was back in the police car business for sure. The Cherokee wasn't what anyone had expected, but that too was part of police work. The Cherokee did not perform like a Jeep 4x4. Instead it performed like a Chrysler police package.

The Cherokee was an amazing king of squad car. Not only could it out run some of the conventional squads on a road racing course, the Cherokee scored well in overall comfort, too. The "Ergonomics and Communications" phase of the MSP vehicle analysis considered front seating comfort, rear seating comfort, instrumentation, vehicle control placement, overall visibility and accessibility for communications gear.

In this phase, the 1992 Cherokee tied with the Crown Victoria and was judged superior to the Mustang, Camaro and Lumi-na. The Cherokee was used primarily by supervisors, sergeants, and K-9 officers. It was very important to keep supervisors and dog handlers comfortable!

In 1992, law enforcement really did not have anything in the 4x4 class with which to compare to the Cherokee. Jeep solved this problem. They advertised the Cherokee comparing it directly against the conventional squad cars using MSP data, much to the horror of the other car makers. It was embarrassing that a "Jeep" blew the best police package cars into the weeds.

Motor Trend once again solved this informational dilemma in a four-way, mud-slinging contest: Cherokee v. Explorer v. Bravada v. Range Rover. Of the Cherokee non-police package 4x4 they said:

"The design is senior but is blistering, youngster-quick in this class; nimble, predictable and fun to drive. The torque Jeep 4.0 liter inline six-cylinder of 190 horsepower always offered great blasts of power. The simple suspension was commended for nice performance handling. This is the Mustang/Camaro/Fire-bird of 4x4s."

Overall, *MT* gave the nod to the Cherokee for superior on-road performance stating it was a "fun hot rod."

	Jeep Cherokee 4.0L	Ford Explorer 4.0L	Range Rover 4.0L	Olds Bravada 4.3L
0-60mph	9.8sec	11.8sec	12.1sec	12.1sec
1/4 mi. ET	16.9sec	18.1sec	18.3sec	18.5sec
1/4 mi. Trap	79.4mph	75.7mph	75.4mph	73.4mph
60-0 mph	151ft	174ft	150ft	171ft
Handling	.78g	.66g	.65g	.69g

Locked in 4-wheel drive, the Cherokee lifts the inside front tire around the MIS road course, just like a Porsche.

The 1992 Jeep Cherokee with the AHB police package includes heavy duty coolers.

To show the 1992 MSP performance was not a fluke, the Cherokee police 4x4 returned to the Michigan State Police tests for 1993 and did it all over again. In fact, in every category, the 1993 Jeep actually ran better: quicker acceleration, faster trap speeds and top end, more braking power and faster road course lap times.

Unlike 1992, in 1993 and 1995, the Ford Explorer stepped in the police boxing ring to challenge the Cherokee. Big, big mistake.

This gave the Cherokee a direct competitor to pound in the pavement in front of cops everywhere. It was as if Ford did not know this was heads-up competition. Ford dipped their toe in the police 4x4 market and was promptly bushwhacked by the Cherokee.

The Cherokee was 2-1/2sec faster to 60mph, 20sec faster to 100mph and had a 11mph greater top speed. The Cherokee had better brakes, of course. In the final analysis, the Explorer was a passenger vehicle, while the Cherokee was a police vehicle.

The 1993 Jeep Cherokee Special Service Package uses a 4.0L 6-cylinder engine with the speed limiter removed.

The police Cherokee 4x4 is faster around a road racing course than some conventional police cars.

As of the 1996 model year, the Jeep Cherokee AHB remains the only Chrysler Corp. police vehicle.

Police Special Service Package
4x4 Comparison

	Jeep Cherokee AHB 1992 (MSP)*	Jeep Cherokee AHB 1993 (MSP)*	Ford Explorer 4.0L 1993 (MSP)**
0-60mph	10.64sec	9.84sec	12.47sec
0-100mph	40.39sec	34.15sec	54.67sec
Top Speed	113.3mph	115.0mph	104.1mph
1/4 mi. ET	17.9sec	17.47sec	18.71sec
1/4 mi. Trap	76.3mph	78.53mph	74.87mph
Brake Power	25.73fps2	26.91 fps2	25.36fps2
MIS Road Course	87.79sec	87.00sec	n/a

*In all Michigan State Police tests, the Cherokee was driven in full-time, 4-wheel drive at Chrysler's request.

**These are unofficial, hand-timed results supplied by Chrysler Fleet and were not published by the MSP.

1993 Chrysler Jeep Cherokee
Police Special Service Package

2-door, 4-door, rear-wheel, all-wheel:101.4in wheelbase (26Z) 4.0L/242ci, OHV, 190 net hp, 225lb torque, electronic fuel injection, Inline 6-cylinder

H.D. 4-speed overdrive automatic
3.55:1 final drive
Police Special Service Package:
90 amp alternator/500 CCA battery
Anti-locking brakes
Column shift
Electronic noise suppression
Floor covering-black rubber front & rear
Dual manual remote mirrors-black
Max. engine cooling (incl. aux. trans. cooler)
Manually controlled extended idle switch
Heavy duty seats (front & rear)
Selec-trac transfer case (4-wheel drive only)
Tilt steering column
Goodyear P225/70HR15 SBR blackwall all season tires (5)
Styled steel wheels 15x7in with black hub
120 mph certified speedometer cluster (with trip odometer)
Gauge package
Dual note horns
Cowl-mounted, foot-operated parking brake
10 wire (cold) roof wiring harness, installed
Police suspension package: 28mm front sway bar, 16mm rear sway bar, gas shocks, front & rear
Speed limiting delete

Standard Equipment

Armrest-front hockey stick style
Carpeted Kick Panel
Fender Flares & front air dam-black
Fuel Tank-20.2 gallons (approx.)
Glass-light tine
Headlamp-halogen
Heater & Defroster
Lights-dome & glove box
Mirrors-inside rear view, 10in day/night-black
Power Steering
Radio-AM/FM ET stereo and clock w/2 speakers
Restraint System front & rear 3-point lap & shoulder belts-outboard
Steering Damper
Steering Wheel-3 spoke
Warning System-key in ignition, seat belt
Ignition & Lock Set-single key
Windshield Wiper/Washers-electric 2-speed, intermittent

Optional Equipment

Air Conditioning
Defroster, rear window
Engine Block Heater
Light Group
Modlings, Bodyside
Power Windows & Door Locks
Radio-delete AM/FM stereo radio w/2 speakers (credit option)
Radio Prep Group (incl. antenna, speakers & wiring)
Roof Rack
Skid Plates Group
Off-Road Suspension
Speed Control
Two Hooks
Trailer two Groups
Trac-Lok Differential, Rear
Deep Tinted Quarter Glass
2 Door
4 Door
Rear Window Wiper/Washer

The University of Central Florida Police makes good use of their Jeep Cherokee. *John Bellah*

This 4.0L Cherokee police package guards the Chrysler Chelsea Proving Grounds. *Greg Reynolds*

References

"4 x 4 x 4," Daniel Charles Ross, Motor Trend, September 1991
Jeep Cherokee for Fleet, Chrysler Corporation, 1992, 1993, 1994, 1995, 1996
Patrol Vehicle Specification, Evaluation and Purchasing Program, Michigan State Police, 1992, 1993, 1994, 1995, 1996

The Perry County, Illinois Sheriff patrols in this police package Cherokee. *Greg Reynolds*

Chapter 21

1993: Dodge Intrepid: Academy Class of 1997

The 1993 Dodge Intrepid was the latest passenger car from Dodge to be considered for police work. The Intrepid was one of the long-awaited LH platform cars slated to replace the Dodge Dynasty. Like the Dynasty, the Intrepid was V-6 powered and front-wheel drive with 4-wheel discs and optional ABS. Unlike the Dynasty, the Intrepid was available with a 24-valve SOHC engine that could soundly thrash the Taurus, the king of the mid-size cop cars.

The Chrysler LH platform cars were the Dodge Intrepid, Chrysler Concorde and Eagle Vision. The first hint of this wedge-shaped, mid-size model was the Portofina concept car introduced at the 1988 Paris Auto Show. By the 1990 Detroit Auto Show, the LH concept car, now called Optima, looked to all the world like an Intrepid.

The Dodge Intrepid essentially made the Dodge Dynasty and Dodge Monaco obsolete. The Intrepid had a 72 percent USA content and was assembled by Chrysler Canada in Bramalea, Ontario.

The Intrepid used the much-heralded "Cab Forward" design. It was a marketing mystery how Chrysler Corp. managed to convince the public that "cab forward" was new, and that "cab forward" was a Chrysler concept.

Ignoring the dozens of concept cars over the past 3 decades that used this design, the first high-volume "cab forward" car was the 1986 Ford Taurus. Can there be any doubt that the second "cab forward" car was the 1991 Chevy Caprice? It was so "cab forward" that the Caprice suffered premature brake pad wear.

At any rate, "cab forward," as half the planet now knows, means:

1. move the wheels more toward the corners of the vehicle
2. move the windshield forward and give it a greater slant.

Moving the wheels outward from the center of gravity gave the Intrepid a wider track and a longer wheelbase. The wider track (distance between wheels on same end of car) gave the car better stability and better handling. The longer wheelbase generally results in a smoother ride and more interior room. The Intrepid wheelbase was 112.0in compared to 112.7in for the Diplomat.

The forward and more slanted windshield also increased interior room. The Intrepid had a 63 degree windshield rake angle. As a comparison, the radical 1993 1/2 Camaro had a 68 degree windshield angle.

The biggest risk when going to a longer wheelbase was the loss of structural rigidity. This was no problem from the folks that have made Uni-Body cars since 1960. Chrysler Corp. used

The 1993 Dodge Intrepid ES that ran at the MSP tests was powered by a 214 hp SOHC V-6.

Cops may get their choice of two power plants, a 3.3L OHV V-6 or a 3.5L SOHC V-6 (shown).

structural analysis computer modeling to increase crash surviv-ability by controlled crushing in the front and rear quarters.

The Intrepid was generally considered a mid-size vehicle. However, this is technically not correct. The EPA interior vol-ume index qualifies the Intrepid for a "large-car" classification. (Remember the EPA index from the K-car era?)

A great deal of wind tunnel testing has resulted in the rounded, wedge-shaped, profile of the Intrepid. The low hood line, low belt line and high tail result in a drag coefficient of just .31—very good for a car this large.

Some of the slippery aerodynamics were made possible by the use of reaction injection molded (RIM) composite plastic body panels. The Intrepid used a MacPherson strut front suspen-sion and gas shocks and sway bars on both ends of the car.

A 'first' time for a Dodge, the Intrepid used a fully-indepen-dent, multi-link, Chapman strut rear suspension. The stiffest sus-pension, since a police package was not officially available, was the "road handling" package. In addition to 4-wheel disc with ABS, the Intrepid had dual air bags.

The Intrepid was also available with Traction-Control. This was very different from a limited-slip (Sure-Grip) rear-wheel dri-ve differential, but it accomplishes the same task. Traction Con-trol prevented the front drive wheels from spinning during accel-eration on wet or snowy pavement, on gravel or mud, or on dry pavement during heavy acceleration.

Traction Control was the logical reverse of an antilock brak-ing system (ABS). The same ABS sensors that detect wheel lock-up while braking, also sense front wheel spin while accelerating. While braking, the ABS pulses the brakes on and off to prevent

lockup. While accelerating, Traction Control pulses the brakes, even though the brakes are not being manually applied, to pre-vent wheel spin.

This was an excellent system. Powerful front-drive cars needed some kind of limited-slip just like powerful rear-drive cars needed the Sure-Grip. On a front drive layout, however, it was too mechanically complex and too crowded for a limited-slip differential.

Traction Control was an extremely good use of the ABS logic even though it sounded exactly backwards to activate brakes while accelerating. The facts are, road racers have for years used both the brakes and the gas on front wheel drive cars to shift weight while cornering to reduce understeer. Traction control is just as clever, and it happens automatically. Traction Control deactivates at speeds over 25mph.

The Intrepid was powered by one of two very different transverse mounted V-6 engines. Which one will join the police force remains unknown. Both used sequential, multi-point elec-tronic fuel injection. Both were bolted to a Chrysler engineered and built A606 electronic, four speed overdrive automatic transaxle. The A606 was a beefed up version of the A604 Ultra-drive used on the Dynasty.

The 3.3L standard engine used conventional pushrods and overhead valves. The V-6 produced 153 net hp. This was also the engine deemed not powerful enough for the Dynasty test mule. As a comparison, the 1993 Lumina B4C was powered by a 3.1L V-6 producing 140 hp. By 1995, Chevy got tired of getting sand kicked in its face by the 160 net hp Taurus 55A 3.8L. The 1995 Lumina used a 160hp 3.1L V-6.

With this competitiveness in mind, it is unlikely Dodge would opt for the 3.3L 153 hp engine for police work, although it's possible. Wanting to avoid a complex valve geartrain for police duty, it is also possible Dodge could shoe-horn a version of the 3.8L V-6 engine into the Intrepid. This too is unlikely due to the very low hood line.

This leaves the optional 3.5L V-6 as the only, most reasonable and certainly most potent option for a police car.

The 3.5L is based on the 3.3L engine. They share a similar block design and stroke. The 3.5L has a slightly larger bore which explains the larger displacement. However, displacement alone does not describe the 3.5L any better than 426ci explains the difference between the 413ci wedge and the 426 cid Hemi. The secret to the 3.5L engine is in the heads.

The 3.5L engine uses a single overhead cam (SOHC) valvetrain, 4 valves per cylinder and a whopping 10.5:1 compression ratio. The last time any Dodge had over a 9.7:1 squish was 1969 with the 10.1:1 440ci. Yes, 27 years ago.

As a reference, the Lumina 3.4L V-6 and Taurus 3.2L V-6 are 24-valve engines, but use a dual over head cam (DOHC) valvetrain. Dodge selected the SOHC heads because they are simpler and more compact to fit under the low hood.

Neither the Lumina DOHC engine nor the Taurus DOHC engine are used in their police packages. The engines are complex and costly and the baseline OHV engine is doing a good enough job for urban-patrol. However, the Crown Vic battle cruiser is powered by a SOHC V-8 engine, the first time ever for a police car. If and when the Intrepid joins the fight against crime, the toughest decision of all will be which engine to include in the police package.

More than the valvetrain, the 3.5L V-6 has a ram tuned induction. Each bank of cylinders has its own throttle body, its own plenum and three individual intake runners. Best of all, the 3.5L engine allowed Chrysler engineers the chance to dust off ram-tuning skills they pioneered on cop cars in the 1950s.

The intake-pulse timing from the bank of three cylinders produces a "ram" effect which increases torque at both low rpm and high rpm but not in the mid-range. The intake-pulse from all six-cylinders produces "ram" effect which increases mid-range torque.

Once Chrysler engineers discovered these traits, the solution was simple. They engineered a valve that opened a cross-over tube which connected the two independent plenum chambers. The valve closed at low and high rpms and opened at midrange rpm. The result was a flat but peaked torque curve. The 3.5L engine produced 90 percent of its torque between 2100 and 5800rpm.

With 214 net hp, the Intrepid 3.5L easily outpowered both the Taurus 55A and Lumina B4C. In fact, the Intrepid 3.5L was tied with the Caprice 9C1 5.7L as the fastest 4-door police sedan. This was a fact no one at the 1993 Michigan State Police runoffs missed. If they did miss it, Chrysler Fleet stopped bragging about the incredible Cherokee just long enough to point it out.

The Michigan State Police have a policy to test only police package cars. However, they also have a commitment to work with all car makers to improve overall police car performance. As such, and completely off-the-record, they occasionally test prototypes or proposals for future squads. This gives the car makers a true vehicle analysis with the same MSP drivers, test equipment and track conditions of how the prototype squad stacks up to the current cop cars.

Half the annual MSP testing takes place at Chrysler's Chelsea Proving Grounds. This was true even for the years when Chrysler Corp. made no police cars. It is easy to see why the MSP agreed to run the non-police 1993 Intrepid through their famous battery of vehicle tests. The MSP also performs this kind of testing for Ford and Chevrolet on non-police or police-prototype vehicles. However, in all cases, agreement to test is handled on a car by car basis and the testing takes place only as time, or some years, weather permits.

The performance figures for these non-police package cars are considered strictly unofficial, since the cars are not tech inspected by the MSP. As a result, these unofficial figures are not published in the MSP annual evaluation. The MSP does not warrant the figures, good or bad, to be representative of how the prototype might perform when it does get upgraded to "police package."

With those remarks as a caution, the Intrepid blew the doors off the Lumina, Taurus, Crown Vic and 305ci powered Caprices. The 350ci Caprice could not outrun the Intrepid and the Mustang 5.0L pursuit car just barely did.

The Intrepid may just be the ideal cop car for the 1990s. This 4-door sedan has all the right stuff for the 1990s, including a size midway between mid-size and full size. With the OHV en-

The prototype Dodge Intrepid was the fastest front-drive police car at the 1993 MSP vehicle tests.

gine, it is the economical taxi that detective and urban patrol officers need.

With the SOHC engine, the Intrepid appears to fill the patrol boots of both a highway-squad and a pursuit-squad. This pursuit-squad however, has 4-doors. Dodge has not had a car like this since the 360ci, 4-bbl St. Regis in 1980.

In mid-1993, Chrysler Fleet continued to deny any knowledge of a Dodge Intrepid police package vehicle. At this time, no test mules had been sent to the field for in-service police testing. It appears 1997 will be the soonest model year possible for a police Intrepid, if one ever becomes available.

The demand for all three LH passenger cars is so strong, Chrysler started building the Intrepid at its Newark, Delaware assembly plant. This is in addition to the Intrepid and Concorde coming in from Ontario. As long as the retail market continues with demands that far exceed supplies, the Intrepid will remain a passenger car.

As of the 1996 model year Dodge still has not released a police package Intrepid, even though a fully-developed package of police components has been on the shelf since 1993. In 1993 and 1994, Dodge Chrysler and Eagle were at full capacity producing the LH-body cars for the retail market and still not able to keep up. Statements from Chrysler Fleet officials indicated that Dodge would not offer the Intrepid for low-margin fleet police sales as long as retail demand exceeded production capability.

In 1995, Dodge finally caught up with the demand for the Intrepid. In fact, one of the production plants was idled for a few weeks due to excess supplies of LH cars. This should have been the trigger for the release of the police Intrepid, especially since the 1996 Ford Taurus would not be available with a police package. This left the Chevy Lumina all alone in the urban-patrol, front wheel drive market for 1996.

Even still, as of mid-1996, Dodge has not entered the police market with their Intrepid. This is in spite of the fact that numerous police agencies are using the retail Intrepid as a police car, especially the northern states and Canada. In a wet and snowy patrol environment, the powerful, yet front wheel drive Intrepid would make an excellent cruiser.

1993 Dodge Intrepid ES
(non-police)
General
Body style	4-door sedan, 5-passenger
Drivetrain	front engine, front drive

Dimensions
Wheelbase	112.0in
Track, f/r	62.0/62.0in
Length	202.8in
Wind Drag	.31Cd

Engines
	Standard	Optional
Type	Transverse	Transverse V-6, SOHC
Displacement	3.3L 201ci	3.5L 215ci
Bore & Stroke	3.66x3.19	3.78x3.19
Compression	8.9:1	10.5:1
Induction	Seq. Multi-point EFI	Seq. Multi-point EFI
Throttle Body	Single	Dual
Horsepower	155 @ 5300rpm	214 @ 5800rpm
Torque	177 @ 2800rpm	221 @ 2800rpm

Drivetrain
Transaxle	A606 Ultradrive 4-speed auto. overdrive, electronic. Lockup converter
Final Drive	3.42:1

Suspension
Front	MacPherson strut, heavy duty coil springs, gas-charged, front sway bar (road-touring)
Rear	Fully independent, multi-link, Chapman struts, rear sway bar, (road-touring)

Steering
Tilt, rack & pinion, power-assist, 17.0:1 ratio
Brakes
4-wheel disc, anti-lock braking system, power-assist, dual side air bags
Wheel/Tires
P205/70R15, P225/60R16

1993 Police Car Comparison*

Vehicle	0-60 mph	0-100 mph	Top Speed	Brake Power
Dodge Intrepid 3.5L	9.02sec	24.64sec	126.2mph	26.17fps2
Ford Taurus 55A 3.5L	9.55sec	29.89sec	123.0mph	29.08fps2
Chevy Lumina B4C 3.1L	11.18sec	38.23sec	114.1mph	24.16fps2
Ford Crown Vic 55H 4.6L	9.57sec	27.91sec	123.0mph	27.21fps2
Chevy Caprice 9C1 5.7L	8.77sec	25.86sec	132.0mph	27.69fps2
Ford Mustang SSP 5.0L	7.98sec	22.34sec	135.1mph	23.76fps2
Chevy Camaro B4C 5.7L	6.18sec	15.82sec	154.0mph	30.34fps2

(fps2=feet per second squared)

*Michigan State Police testing. The Dodge Intrepid was not a police package. Intrepid results are unofficial, hand-timed results supplied by Chrysler Fleet and were not published by the MSP.

References
Patrol Vehicle Specification, Evaluation and Purchasing Program, Michigan State Police, 1993
"Chrysler's Top Secret LH," Paul Lienert, Automobile, April 1991
Chrysler Concorede, Chrysler Corporation, 1993
Personal communication with officials from Chrysler Corp. Fleet Operations

Chapter 22

Police Cars of the Future

In the immediate future, the cop car of tomorrow will remain the full-size, long wheel base, rear wheel drive squad like the Caprice and Crown Vic. However, as front-drive "passenger cars" and front-drive police cars become more accepted, the large car market will disappear.

The squad cars of today are a mix of:

URBAN-PATROL: Mid-size, front-drive, medium-power V-6
Taurus 3.8L V-6
Lumina 3.1L V-6
URBAN-PATROL: Full-size, rear-drive, medium-power V-8
Caprice 4.3L V-8
Crown Vic 4.6L V-8 SOHC
HIGHWAY-CLASS: Full-size, rear-drive, high-power V-8
Caprice 5.7L V-8 LT1
Crown Vic 4.6L V-8 SOHC
UTILITY-CLASS: Four-wheel drive, medium-power, V-6
Cherokee 4.0L
Explorer 4.0L

UTILITY-CLASS: Full-size, rear-drive, V-8, station wagon
Caprice Wagon 5.7L
PURSUIT-CLASS: Mid-size, rear-drive, high-power pony car
Camaro 5.7LT1
Mustang 5.0L HO

Listen to the predictions from the most influential cops in the country when it comes to police cars of the immediate future:

"With faster sedans, we may not have a need for the high-speed Mustang or Camaro in the future. We are headed for a time when we will no longer need a sporty car for speed!" West Barker, Commander of the California Highway Patrol's Motor Transport Section, March 1983.

"The optimum police vehicle would be a full-size police package vehicle that performs like the special service package Ford Mustang. Most officers prefer the safety and utility of a larger vehicle, but like the high performance speed and handling of a vehicle like the Mustang." F/Lt. Curtis VanDenBerg, Michigan State Police, Officer-In-Charge, Vehicle Evaluation, December 1989.

The Ford Taurus 55A has been the front-drive, car-to-beat since 1990. The Dodge Intrepid can beat it. *Ford Div.*

4-Door Sedan vs. Pony Car

Vehicle	0-60 mph	0-100 mph	Qrt. mi ET	Top Speed	1.63 mi MIS Road Course
1993 Mustang 5.0L HO	7.98sec	22.34sec	16.24sec	135.1mph	1:23.4min
1994 Caprice 5.7L 350ci LT1	8.30sec	21.64sec	16.18sec	141.2mph	1:23.8min

The prediction of both men has come true. In 1994, Chevy released a 260 net hp version of the 350ci small-block in the Caprice. This is the "LT1" Corvette engine which became available in the 1993 Camaro and the 1994 Caprice.

The LT1-powered Chevy Caprice ran 141mph almost like the 1969 Dodge Polara 440ci. The LT1 Caprice hit 100mph in 21-1/2 seconds (versus 26 seconds for the non-LT1). On the 1.6 mile MIS road course, the LT1 Caprice was equal in overall lap time to the 5.0L Mustangs.

With that kind of performance, the LT1 Caprice is what the CHP and the MSP considers the ideal squad car. Ford is ready to meet the competition with its 24-valve (modular) V-8 which puts out 285 net hp. This kind of performance will, in fact, obsolete the Camaro-pursuit and Mustang-pursuit.

However, the problem with these powerful "full-size" rear wheel drive cars is not restoring 1960s big block power to full-size cruisers. Engine technology has done that. The problem is the longevity of the full-size, rear wheel drive, 4-door sedan itself.

Here is the key. When fleet sales of any car becomes half of retail sales, the car is in trouble. Fleet sales include taxi, police and rentals. The fleet sales measure is a cut-throat, competitive, low bid process that leaves almost no margin of profit for anyone. As an example, the Chevy Caprice 5.0L retail car on the showroom in 1993 listed for $22,000. The Caprice 9C1 police car with a special 5.7L engine and heavier duty suspension, cooling and brake components was bid out at $12,400.

In the mid to late 1980s, sales of the Diplomat and Gran Fury were equally split between retail and fleet. Because fleet sales could not carry that load, both cars were discontinued. With total police vehicle annual sales of 60,000 vehicles, split between all car makers, Ford and Chevy have to find sufficient retail buyers for their high-powered, rear-wheel drive, full-size sedans. One example is the police package-based Impala SS. Without the help of retail sales, the CHP/MSP optimal squad car would have a very short police career.

The squad car of the late 1990s is easy to predict. As in the past four decades, police cars are simply beefed up versions of whatever was available in a passenger car. When passenger cars shrank, so did cop cars, against police protest. An example of this was the Diplomat. When passenger cars stopped using big block V-8s, engines like the 360ci St. Regis and then the 318ci St. Regis were soon unavailable to cops. When passenger cars went to fuel injection, anti-lock brakes and rear discs, so did cop cars, after a respectable delay.

Here is how retail cars were divided up in 1993 according to the Automotive News Data Center.

Car Class	Best Selling Car	Drivetrain	Percentage
Mid-Size	Taurus & Accord	fwd	37.3
Sub-Compact	Escort & Civic	fwd	25.6
Compact	Cavalier	fwd	14.7
Large	LeSabre	fwd	10.5
Near-Luxury	Park Avenue	fwd	3.5
Specialty	Mazda Miata	fwd	1.3
Luxury	Cadillac DeVille	fwd	7.0

What will the cop car of the future be? The same as the passenger car of the future. With near certainty, it will be a front-wheel drive, 4-door sedan. The future cop car will be the largest

Dodge has indeed developed a police package for the front-drive Intrepid. So far the retail demand has been too strong to release a fleet car.

of these sedans, such as a 5-passenger or perhaps (strictly by EPA definition) a 6-passenger such as Lumina, Taurus or Intrepid.

The squad will be powered by an extremely sophisticated engine. It will obviously be multi-point fuel injected. Most squads today already are. Today's cars have OHV engines. Tomorrow's may have single overhead cams like the Ford 4.6L engine already on the police force. The future squad will have 4-wheel discs, antilock brakes, traction control, dual airbags and heads-up instrument display. It may have dual overhead cams.

The future squad car will have top speeds around 140mph, but most importantly, it will get to 100mph in under 25 seconds. As a reference, the fastest front-drive squad car, the Ford Taurus 3.8L now takes 29 seconds. Absolute top speed will never be as important to cops as rapid acceleration. Cops are most concerned about rapidly closing in on a violator, the "catch time."

The police car of the future will be front wheel drive, for better or for worse. Chrysler Corp. was the first domestic automaker to release a front drive police package car. This was the 1982 Aries K and Reliant K powered by the 135ci/2.2L Inline 4-cylinder. The K-car was not well accepted by cops, even for the light-duty jobs the K-car was able to do. It was dropped after 1987.

Chevrolet was next with their 1984 Celebrity police car. Powered by the 2.8L V-6, the Celebrity was a far better squad than the K-car. However, it did not sell well. It had almost enough room, acceptable acceleration up to 75mph and excellent handling characteristics. The car needed far more top end power and drivetrain durability even for routine traffic enforcement.

Chevrolet also noted:

Front end problems, plus engine, transaxle and drivetrain damage due to the severe service of police work. Improved designs and technology have answered some of those problems. However, the sales were not enough to pay for additional research and development. Reliability is so important in police work.

Giving credit where it is due, Ford released the first acceptable front drive cop car—the Taurus 55A. Powered by a 3.8L OHV V-6, the Taurus was loaded with engine, transaxle and power steering coolers. It had heavy-duty wiring, battery, alternator, suspension and transaxle. The Taurus also had heavy-duty 4-wheel disc brakes.

Released for police mule tests in late 1988, the Taurus achieved "police package" status by 1990. This was a heavy-duty, full-bore police package car, not a limited use "special service vehicle." Led by the Wayne County, Michigan Sheriff, Baltimore, Maryland Police and the Utah Highway Patrol, the Taurus shattered old myths and realities about front-drive squads. The Taurus 55A has been extremely well accepted by law enforcement. It must be considered the first of the true police front wheel drive squad cars.

Today front wheel drive cars hold up marginally well under the strain of police work. They do not have constant front end alignment problems, or excessive tire wear. Once equipped with engines too small for serious police work, this is no longer the case. However, they are certainly not too powerful! The interior on the large front drive cars, such as Taurus and Lumina is marginally large enough for solo cops, their gear and occasional prisoners. However, this is still not true for 2-officer patrol cars.

The problem for mid-size squad cars is legislation requiring dual air bags. This has forced gear off of the dash, and into console and passenger space. This is even crowding solo officers. Clearly, not enough room exists for 2-man units. The space problem is the last issue to solve for front-drive squads.

At one time, long wheelbases were considered critical for good high speed handling. Cops later discovered that suspension design, not wheelbase length was the key to handling and stability. They also discovered large displacement engines are only required for patrol-class speeds, if the car is large. Cops everywhere learned a valuable lesson during the 1991 MSP runoffs.

In its first year as a police package, the 1990 Taurus performed better than even the 351ci Ford. It did not, however, equal the 350ci Caprice. The 1991 model year Taurus with 15 more horsepower, was a historic turning point for the police Taurus in particular and front wheel drive police cars in general.

Front Wheel Drive vs. Rear Wheel Drive

	1991 Caprice 9C1 (non-LT1)	1991 Taurus 55A
Layout	rear wheel	front wheel
Engine	5.7L V-8	3.8L V-6
Horsepower	195hp	155hp
0-60mph	9.88sec	9.88sec
0-100mph	29.24sec	29.62sec
Top Speed	130.0mph	129.4mph
Brake Power	24.9fps2	23.5fps2
MIS Road Course	1:28.07min	1:27.05min

Since 1990, nearly every major police department in the U.S. has experimented with the Taurus, or the Lumina cop car (introduced in 1992). In cases such as the St. Louis, Missouri Police, the agency actually wanted a squad like the front drive V-6 mid-size. In most cases, however, cops were just getting prepared for the inevitable, just like they tested mid-size cars in the mid-1970s.

"In actual street experiences, Taurus-driving officers have been able to catch fleeing 5.0L Mustangs in city and urban pursuits. While the Mustangs could run away on long straight areas, the Tauruses caught up going through corners."—Ed Nowicki

If we could pick one point in time when front wheel drive squads gained real credibility, it would be during those 1991 tests. Sheer vehicle performance was no longer a major issue.

The next issue is safety. Larger, heavier vehicles do have a better high speed survivability than smaller, lighter vehicles. However, technology has cheated the law of physics in the late 1980s and early 1990s. Antilock brakes make cars stop quicker than ever before. Better yet, they allow the officer to steer around an obstacle even with the brake pedal smashed to the floor, or panic brake in the middle of a turn. That was never before possible.

Air bags (supplemental restraint system) have even further protected the front occupants of a vehicle if a collision cannot be avoided by braking. This is a new level of safety and it has nothing to do with vehicle weight or size. Computer simulated impacts allow vehicle designers to design the safest way for a vehicle to crush during an impact.

All this confirms that front wheel drive cars are the squads of the future. Chrysler Corp. got out of the police business in 1989 because they were a "front wheel drive company." Can a Mopar squad now be far away? See Chapter 22 on the Dodge Intrepid.

The Intrepid has everything the squad car of the future will have. It even has the ability to step up from patrol-class to pursuit-class. The Taurus is the standard by which all front-drive squad cars must be compared, according to MSP test results and actual street experience. But the Intrepid is better than the Taurus in every single area of performance and ergonomics.

At 214 net hp, the 3.5L powered Intrepid is much faster and a little roomier than the Taurus 55A and Lumina B4C. These factors will become important as the pressures increase from fleet managers to replace the Camaro B4C and Mustang SSP with

The Michigan Sheriffs Association has the right idea for a Mopar pursuit car: the Dodge Viper. *Mopar Muscle*

faster 4-door sedans. They will also have an impact as the car companies force cops away from full-size, rear-drive sedans. The Intrepid could emerge as the ultimate cop car.

Sure, Chevy and Ford have DOHC V-6 engines to stuff in the Lumina and Taurus to keep up with the Dodge. No problem. Without those engines, the Blue Oval and Bowtie would not stand a chance. However, even with roughly the same engines, Chrysler products have always had an edge. Changing the drive wheels from the rear to the front does nothing to affect that. In fact, Chrysler has produced high performance front-drive cars longer than any automaker.

The cop cars of the future could be:

PATROL-CLASS: Mid-size, front-drive, Medium-power V-6
Lumina	3.1L OHV
Taurus	3.8L OHV
Intrepid	3.0L OHV

HIGHWAY-CLASS: Mid-size, front drive, high-output V-6
Lumina	3.4L DOHC
Taurus	3.2L SHO (3.4L V-8)
Intrepid	3.5L SOHC

UTILITY-CLASS: (K9, supervisors, rugged terrain):
Four-wheel drive, medium power V-6
Jeep Cherokee	4.0L
Ford Explorer	4.0L/5.0L
Chevy Blazer/Tahoe	4.3L/5.7L

*Notice that this time around, Chrysler Corp. already makes everyone of these as passenger vehicles.

In the past, we have had the same squad with different engines for different uses: The Inline 6 and small V-8 were used for patrol and the big V-8 used for highway use. We may get to a time where once again the "patrol" class car has an economy OHV V-6 and the "highway" class car is the same car with the multi-cam V-6.

Think back over all the years of Mopar police cars since 1956. In heads-up performance and bidding competition, Dodges, Plymouths and Chryslers have always been the best overall police cars. We both look forward to the return of Pentastar cop cars.

(This chapter was presented by Ed Sanow during the Awards Banquet at the 1994 PCOOA National Convention held in Eureka Springs, Arkansas.)

As this book goes to print in 1996, Chevrolet Motor Division announced the rear-wheel drive Caprice, will be discontinued after the 1996 model year to free up capacity at the Arlington, Texas assembly plant to make their more profitable trucks. Ford Motor Company has announced the new-for-1996 Taurus will not be available with a police package.

References

"The Great American Police Car," Ed Nowicki, *Police,* December 1989

"Police Cars for 1977," staff report, *The American City and County*, October 1976

"Readying Our Cars for Patrol Duties," Hal Rubin, *The CHP,* March 1993

"Front Runners," Tom Yates, *Law & Order,* January 1991

"Experimental Squad Car," Massad Ayoob, *Law & Order,* November 1977

"Garden Grove Police reserves and Unit 32-900," Sgt. Paul McInerny, *The Backup,* Winter 1991

"Ford's High Technology Approach-A Major Advance in Police Car Design," Ken Garrett, *International Law Enforcement,* September 1986

Chapter 23

Police Car Owners of America

The Police Car Owners of America (PCOOA) is a cop car enthusiast club organized in early 1991 by retired Kansas City, Missouri police sergeant Jim Post. In just a few years, this club has grown to over 650 members, mostly by word of mouth. Members now hail from 46 states and nine foreign countries.

After a formal gathering at the California Highway Patrol Academy and their first National Convention in Sparta, Illinois, the PCOOA has started to receive national and international attention.

By the way, Sparta, Illinois was selected as the Nationals site because Sparta was celebrating the 25th anniversary of the on-location filming of the movie, "In the Heat of the Night." This 1967 Academy Award winner was filmed in and around this southern Illinois town. The epic cop flick that spawned a sequel and a current television series, used a 1964 Plymouth Fury as patrolman Sam Woods' (Warren Oates) squad car. Chief Bill Gillespie (Rod Steiger) used a 1966 Plymouth Belvedere.

The PCOOA has been featured in: Mopar Muscle, Super Chevy, High Performance Mopar, Muscle Mustangs, The Plymouth Bulletin, Classic American (British), and Chrysler Power.

The PCOOA is open to owners of all makes of restored police cars, owners of ex-squads used as daily-drivers, and all other car enthusiasts. Some members are federal agent pursuit instructors, while other members are too young to drive. Many members are current and former police officers and reserve officers. Since most fire departments use police package cars, members also include full-time and volunteer firemen. The car shows frequently include both police cars and fire trucks.

The purpose of the club is to promote the joy in ownership of all makes of squad cars. About half the PCOOA favors the Mopar squads while the balance is split between the Ford Blue Ovals and the Chevrolet Bowties. While founded in Kansas City, the PCOOA membership is evenly spread across the fruited plain. California and New York have the most members, followed by Missouri, Illinois, New Jersey, Virginia and Wisconsin.

The PCOOA encourages a wide range of uses for retired squads. This means everything from the display of a fully restored, completely authentic squad at a car show to driving the car back and forth to work. Some members drag race their car. Some road race or autocross with the squad. Others put their squad right back into emergency service as a part of a fire or police reserve organization.

In fact, the only use of ex-squads that is not tolerated is taxi duty. That is considered a dishonorable discharge from the police force.

Apart from national or regional PCOOA car shows, members are encouraged to show their squads at local car shows or events. Post believes the restored cruisers are great "public relations" vehicles for an occupation that receives far too much bad press. They are a great attraction at county fairs. Some have been converted to D.A.R.E. squads to help educate kids about the dangers of drugs and drunk driving. PCOOA squads show up in shopping mall attractions, civic parades and even as extras in movie filming.

Ownership of a police car is not required. In fact, some members join just to find the right connections and information

The PCOOA is the source for sirens, lightbars, badges, memorabilia and even used squad cars.

PCOOA badges are available to members to display with their vehicles.

Here's a pair of restored Kansas Highway Patrol cars from a PCOOA regional event. That's an 1988 Diplomat and 1967 Belvedere. *Dave Dotson*

The first PCOOA National Convention was held in Sparta, Illinois. This was the actual setting for the movie, "In the Heat of the Night". *Mark Redelberger*

to get the "perfect" squad. Some PCOOA members own up to six genuine ex-squads, while most own just one.

Significantly, a fair number own a vehicle of the same make and model as was once a police car, but their car was not. These members set about to find and install the beefed up and reinforced police parts, one at a time, on their passenger cars. These cars are either turned into what appear to be police cars—aka: replica police cars. Or they in fact build them all the way up to where everything but the VIN is genuine police package spec.

The key to finding parts, and finding shows, is the PCOOA quarterly newsletter, *Rapsheet*. This publication has "wanted" and "for sale" ads which are critical for the club to continue to gain new members, maintain the current cop cars and restore additional squads. The newsletter also features black and white photos of the members' Black and Whites.

The newsletter contains a calendar of events which includes regional and national shows. It also includes police badge and

patch shows, fire truck shows and police and fire memorabilia shows. Finally the newsletter contains brief articles ranging from the history of Georgia State Patrol squads to the latest vehicle test results from MSP and LAPD/LASO.

The focus of any car club is, or should be, the cars themselves. PCOOA members have the very best squads from all the eras. Post himself, sets a pretty high standard. His 1984 CHP Diplomat is the best of the best, and every bit of it was done the hard way with many hours of tedious labor. This 1984 squad is a replica of the highest order.

The AHB police package car was originally ordered by the Atlanta, Georgia Police (APD). When budget problems set in, APD had to pass on some of the cars. Post's car was sold to the

The second PCOOA Nationals were held in conjunction with the Indiana State Police museum.

For the PCOOA Nats, Chrysler, Chevrolet and Ford sent the Cherokee AHB, Camaro B4C and Mustang SSP fleet cars.

Kansas City, Missouri Police where it served as an unmarked unit. Post got the squad from his former Department and began a painstaking task to build a CHP cruiser from scratch.

The finished product boasts an issue Jetsonic light bar with the correct color and properly placed grille and deck lights. The siren, pusher bars, shotgun and mount and door shields are all CHP-spec. Post even welded a CHP optional support plate for the side-mounted trunk whip antenna. The vehicle has the original Motorola radio gear.

Under the hood remains an original ELE 318 ci, 4-bbl, to which Post even installed the N95 California Emissions Pack-

age. The right A-pillar sports a white spotlight while the left A-pillar has the California-required "continuously glowing" red spotlight.

The exhaust system has been upgraded to the CHP St. Regis system of dual cats and no mufflers. Even the Goodyear GT+4 pursuit tires are correct. And a complete duty uniform of a CHP sergeant hangs in the left rear window. Perfect.

The CHP is by far the most frequent police trim for squad car restorations. After the CHP, the most frequent choices are the squad's original agency or the colors of a department with whom the owner is affiliated. The latest trend is to pick a police depart-

The third and fourth PCOOA Nationals were held at the club headquarters in scenic Eureka Springs, Arkansas.

The competition at the PCOOA Nationals is tough. Judges want to see engines, trunks and interiors.

The PCOOA Nats have a dozen different show classes. This 1987 Diplomat won an in-service police car class.

ment with more graphic, colorful and distinctive colors like New York State Police and the Nevada Highway Patrol.

The decision on police colors and trim are frequently based on the availability of authentic or period parts, and on the ease of finding accurate information about the as-issued specifications for these cruisers. Here is where the PCOOA membership comes to play.

The *Rapsheet* plays a major role in parts sourcing, agency information, and police car literature. Information can be found on sirens, lightbars, radios, radar units, badges, uniforms, spotlights, rust-free fenders and all manner of A38/AHB components.

Many times the original police agency will even have some of this gear laying around, since police equipment is constantly being updated. Most departments are extremely cooperative and supportive of the restoration effort.

One word of caution is in order. Check the local laws before you hook up all the cop stuff. It is a crime in all 50 states to impersonate a police officer, to use police emergency equipment, or in some states to even possess a police-band two-way radio. Do not be discouraged. Just follow the law. The California vehicle code is quite clear what can and cannot be displayed or be functional. Each state is different, so be sure to check out the local law.

California law requires that the vehicle be painted or partially painted by the seller so that it no longer resembles a vehicle used by a peace officer or traffic officer while on duty. This means the white front doors on X-CHP cars get painted black.

The Michigan State Police uses a unique shade of deep blue on their cars. Part of the sale to civilians is a contracted agreement to have the buyer repaint the car some other color within a specified period of time. On the other hand, no such statutes apply to the special two-tone, brown and tan colors used by Sheriff's Department vehicles in Indiana. Seller paints it; buyer paints it; no repaint is necessary. The laws vary.

The laws also deal with the police or sheriff door shield or other insignias that identify the car as a traffic enforcement or police vehicle. Simply put, door shields are a no-no almost everywhere. Three California options exist. First, California allows

The M-body Diplomat and Gran Fury are the most popular PCOOA vehicles. Most are daily-drivers.

cars to be fully marked as long as the term "movie car" is displayed prominently on the doors. The law reads these must be used exclusively for movie or television production, which appears to exclude enthusiasts from using this option.

The second option, and one widely used, is that of removable magnetic signs. These can be made up by local sign shops to exactly reproduce the official door shields. Put them on for the event. Take them off when the event is over. Don't forget to take them off! And again, check with the laws of your state.

The third option, at least addressed by California, is that of vehicle age. Vehicles can be painted exactly like a genuine police car as long as the vehicle was originally registered on or before January 1, 1979. You still cannot use door shields.

The same sort of restrictions apply to light bars, grille and deck lights and sirens. In some states, the switch for the siren must be under the hood instead of inside the car. Some states require the gumball light or light bar to be covered while on public roads. The fact that these are wired or not wired to produce any light output at all, may not make any difference.

The same is true for the color of front-facing or rear-facing auxiliary (grille or deck) lamps. State by state these colors mean something. Red and blue almost always means police. Blue means police in many states but fire in others. Red means fire in many states but police in others. Wig-wag or impulse-flash headlights mean police almost everywhere but may mean fire. Again, do the restoration, but just find out what the laws are.

There is a sufficient amount of attention placed on the exact, authentic and complete restoration of vehicles back to police trim. But PCOOA's Jim Post is quick to point out that these aren't the only types of police car enthusiasts in the PCOOA. Ex-squads used as daily drivers are the backbone of the club. Post drives his cars to all the events, and expects everyone else to do the same. And they do! Fully-restored, fully-marked cruisers

PCOOA members actually drive their cars across country to events. Sometimes they meet people they were not planning to meet. *Rocky Finlayson*

came from both coasts to the first National Convention. And so did daily drivers, unmarked but still very obviously heavy-duty battle cruisers.

The PCOOA is about enjoying all former squads. It really does not matter how detailed or how original the squad is. What matters is enjoying the squads for the heavy duty examples of Detroit iron that they really are.

PCOOA events are held both indoors and outdoors and frequently along with fire truck and patch collecting events.

Here are two clean, ex-Illinois State Police 1987 Diplomats used as daily drivers. The PCOOA is open to all car enthusiasts.

Here's an 1987 Calgary Police Service Plymouth Caravelle protecting a donut shop. PCOOA members come from 9 foreign countries. *Rob Elliott*

The spirit and enthusiasm of the PCOOA is personified in Mike Hallenbeck of New York. He is the current owner of an X-CHP 1969 Dodge Polara 440 Magnum. It is not restored. In fact, it was handed-down from the CHP to a local California police department in 1971 when it had 85,000 miles on it. It picked up three times that number of miles in various police jobs in Southern California.

Hallenbeck read an ad for the squad in Hemming's Motor News and bought the car sight unseen. He flew to California and drove it back to New York! At the time, the certified speedometer read 339,000 miles.

Before he had a chance to freshen up the ultimate big block, he ran the Polara at the wide open Lime Road road racing course during a SCCA Solo I event. He left the road course, after embarrassing some Porsches as CHP Polaras always did, and drove half way back across the country to attend the first PCOOA Nationals. The club is loaded with that kind of member.

Both this 1972 ex-Washington State Police Polara and 1965 ex-CHP Polara have been restored to show quality. *Darryl Lindsay*

172

Here's an 1980 Dodge St. Regis headed to a PCOOA show. PCOOA members hail from 46 states. *John Bellah*

For membership information contact:
Sgt. James Post (ret.)
Police Car Owners of America
Route 6, Box 345-B
Eureka Springs, AR 72632

Car enthusiasts have always had a special respect for police cars. This has made police car collecting and restoration the latest trend. It combines the mystique of the cop car with the power, in most cases, of a muscle car, and reliability unmatched by any car. It is a totally new kind of excitement to go cruisin' in a real cruiser.

The PCOOA has patches, T-shirts, ball caps, satin jackets, window decals and key fobs. The club even has 7-point, CHP-style, gold badges with the PCOOA center crest and the embossed club member's number. It will not, however, help you get out of a speeding citation. Don't even try.

Used Police Cars The enthusiast can find a used police car the same way as a normal used car. Classified ads in national

Here's a restored 1963 ex-CHP Dodge 880 and along with an in-service 1988 California State Police Diplomat. Some PCOOA members are police officers, jail officers, firemen and dispatchers. *Teresa Troutman*

Some PCOOA members drag race, oval race and solo race their ex-squad cars. Here's a 1975 Plymouth Fury stocker. *Omar Caraballo*

magazines like Autoweek, Hemmings, Old Cars, Cars & Parts and others provide information. Used police cars are advertised in the PCOOA newsletter. Ads also run in the local "Trader" newspapers. Seeing an ad for a 1959 X-CHP Dodge Coronet D-500 stirs the soul, and quickens the heart rate.

Two other approaches are much more to the point. The first is to buy the squad at auction right from the police department. The second is to buy a squad from a fleet wholesaler.

As a rule, all police cars are sold at public auction after their retirement age or mileage is up. A few exceptions exist. The Missouri State Highway Patrol will only sell to another government agency, not to the public at large. Other state police or highway patrols may have similar policies, but again they are the exception.

Most fleets are replaced on very rigid schedules. The CHP rotates their squad cars out at 85,000 miles. The Michigan State Police sell theirs at 60,000 miles.

As a rule, most state police and highway patrol cars are sold off with 50,000 to 80,000 miles and a maximum age of 3 model years old. These are the most desired squads. They have the most powerful engines, the most options and, as a rule, the best care and the easiest life.

Many of these agencies have only a small detective unit, or detectives often drive urban patrol-class cars, even front wheel drive cars. Once the trooper's battle cruiser reaches the maximum miles, there is no non-emergency place within the department for the car. They become for sale.

City and counties generally hold on to their squads much longer. Once they reach maximum miles or years, they are passed on to one of the numerous detective or non-emergency roles. Many departments pass on the oldest cars to reserve organizations. Happy is the reservist who gets assigned a squad with only 100,000 miles on it. (Really!)

Some states have very restrictive laws about police car markings. Note the "not in service" and "movie car" decals. *Rhonda Madden*

Check local and state laws before restoring or operating a replica police car. Some states limit the paint scheme and even the shade of paint. *Rhonda Madden*

The PCOOA encourages restoring old Mopars but insists its members follow the law. The lettering and shield of this CHP 1969 Polara have been properly deleted for travel. *Rhonda Madden*

When these city and county cars finally come up for sale, they are beat. Our Sheriff's Dept. routinely puts 175,000 to 200,000 miles on a squad. This makes the auctioned state cars look showroom new.

Perhaps the best place to find an auctioned off squad is from one of the thousands of small town marshals across the nation. They must advertise the auction just like any government entity. The chances of getting a good one here are the best if you pay attention.

Some cars, depending on local politics, get sold off with relatively low miles, as low as 50,000. Further, the reputation of the law enforcer is well known in the small community. Is he or she easy on the car? Is he or she picky about keeping it clean and well-maintained? You cannot buy a better vehicle than from such a small town law officer.

Regardless of which police department the squad comes from, you should expect the interior and dash to have mystery holes and the carpet may be slit to allow for running wires. The police department may even remove the heavy duty alternator and regulator and replace it with a standard duty unit. This happened in the 1960s and 1970s, but much less so in the 1980s.

The Goodyear Eagle GT+4 is the correct tire for restoration of late-model Dodge Diplomats and Plymouth Gran Furys. *Goodyear*

This yellow and blue ex-New York State Police Gran Fury is the basis for a great restoration. *Ned Schwartz*

This restored 1988 Kansas Highway Patrol Diplomat hits all the Midwest car shows. *Dave Dotson*

The other approach is to go directly to a company that reconditions police cars. Some examples of such organizations are:

Blue Streak Motors
1703 Cannonsburg Rd.
Ashland, KY 41102

Diversifleet, Inc.
7150 KAW Drive
Kansas City, KS 66111

Veto Enterprises
212 W. Exchange Street
Sycamore, IL 60178

Recondition is the key word for the service these companies do, not rebuild. If they need rebuilding, these folks avoid them. They also avoid vehicles from northern climates where road salts and sand can cause damage. Finally, for obvious reasons, they avoid cars from "large metropolitan agencies." All three companies try to get cars from the Midwest, southeast and southwest, and from agencies with budgets that allow annual car purchases and well established maintenance programs, according to Bob Veto, PCOOA member and enthusiast.

Tricks of the trade allow these enthusiasts to find the best possible used police package squads. These fleet experts find that agencies who use premium fuel have fewer injector and carburetor problems.

In general, these outfits:
1. Replace brake pads
2. Scrutinize front brake rotors
3. Replace shocks
4. Replace wiper blades
5. Replace fan belts, radiator hoses
6. Replace worn tires with pursuit radials
7. Compression tests and tune engines
8. Interior inspected and replaced if needed
9. Paint touched up or repainted if needed
10. Front end inspection, repair, alignment

This 1980 New York City Police Gran Fury "Highway" car had the lightbar removed before it was sold at auction. *Ned Schwartz*

As for the cop stuff, most any police equipment shop can supply emergency lights, sirens, wig-wags, pusher bars, plexiglass cages with a rollbar, spotlights and shotgun racks. One of

A Kansas Highway Patrol 1967 Belvedere and 1988 Diplomat join a Missouri State Highway Patrol 1964 Enforcer at a PCOOA show. *Dave Dotson*

the best mail order houses in the country for all this gear is in the Appendix.

As this book goes to press, the fourth PCOOA National Convention is history. It was a return to historic Eureka Springs, Arkansas: Elvis-impersonators, southern-style BBQ sandwiches, mountain music, Ozark scenery and squad cars at literally every traffic intersection.

The first PCOOA Nationals in 1992 were held in Sparta, Illinois. One of the judges for the car show was Bruce Cameron, editor of *Law and Order* magazine and PCOOA member.

The second Nationals in 1993 were in Indianapolis. The PCOOA helped the Indiana State Police celebrate 60 years of service to Hoosiers. The Nats were held in conjunction with the Grand Opening of the ISP Museum.

As evidence of the popularity and influence of the PCOOA, Chrysler, Chevrolet and Ford each sent a fully-marked, fully-equipped police car for members to view. The Cherokee AHB, Camaro B4C and Mustang SSP added prestige and credibility to the young club. Frank Goderre's 1973 New York State Police Plymouth Fury I and 1974 New York State Police Dodge Monaco were awarded Best-Of-Show.

The third PCOOA National Convention was held in Eureka Springs, home of the PCOOA. The Arkansas State Police and Oklahoma Highway Patrol sent both officers and show cars. A lights and siren parade through the downtown district was led by the Eureka Springs police chief, the county sheriff and a sergeant with the state police.

The Nationals included a formal awards banquet with talks by Lt. Monty McCord, author of Police Cars, A Photographic History, and Cpl. Ed Sanow, co-author of Dodge, Plymouth &

Chrysler Police Cars, 1956-1978. As always Mopar owners took their fair share of trophies including Best-Of-Show and In-Service Police Car.

An evening cruise-in at McDonalds and a 27-mile daybreak scenic tour through the Ozarks rounded out the 1994 Nationals. With these vintage black-and-whites in the 'hills,' the local moonshiners must have suffered "revenuer" flashbacks.

As many older model police cars are restored by PCOOA members as late models. Here's a 1964 Dodge 880 from the Missouri State Highway Patrol.

This 1969 Kansas Highway Patrol Plymouth Fury I with a 440ci V-8 is one of the era's most classic squad cars.

Fire departments frequently use police package cars and are a good source for restoration. *Greg Reynolds*

Some PCOOA cars are used in movies. This 1980 Gran Fury was featured in "Code of Silence". *Greg Reynolds*

References

Rapsheet, Jim Post, President PCOOA, Vol. 1, Issue 1, through Vol. 3 Issue 3.

"Smokey, But No Bandits," Colin Peck, Classic American, 1992

"Return to Mayberry," Jerry Heasley, Car Exchange, August 1986

"Auto Auctions," Staff Report, Motor Trend, 1966

"What is Black and White and Can Save You Money," Staff Report, Motor Trend, June 1971

"Getting a New Fleet for a Steal," Tom Ellis, Law Enforcement Technology, September 1990

Chapter 24

Chrysler Cop Car Quiz

It is now time to check how much you really know about Mopar squads. Keep track of the number of right answers.

Q: What was the lowest numeric rear gear ratio for any Mopar squad?

A: 2.24:1 with the mid-1980s 318ci, 2-bbl.

Q: What change was made to the exhaust of all Mopar squads in 1987?

A: stainless steel.

Q: With the exception of stainless exhaust (1987) and a driver's side air bag (1988), the 1986 through 1989 Diplomat and Gran Fury were absolutely identical. True or false.

A: True.

Q: From the late 1970s to the mid-1980s, the Michigan State Police proved by testing and bidding that the Mopar squads had the most performance for the dollar. True or false.

A: True.

Q: A major carburetion change took place in 1985. What was it?

A: Rochester QuadraJet replaced Carter ThermoQuad.

Q: In the history of Chrysler Corp. police cars, what were the only fuel injected squads?

A: 1986 and 1987 Reliant K and Aries K.

Q: What prior experience did Plymouth use in building police cars?

A: Building taxis.

Q: What happened to most police engines in 1970?

A: Lower Compression Ratios.

Q: Starting in 1972, most police engines used what Carter 4-bbl carb?

A: ThermoQuad.

Q: What Three years were the R-body Newport, St. Regis and Gran Fury available to police?

A: 1979, 1980, 1981.

Q: The St. Regis came with aluminum bumpers front and rear. True or false.

A: True in 1979 only.

Q: At what speed should the pursuit-class car start to generate the most performance?

A: Max. Legal speed limit.

Q: What size engine is required for a police car or police package car?

A: Engine size has nothing to do with the police package.

Q: Police cars have always been available with the most powerful engines made by the company. True or false.

A: False. Until the mid-1970s, passenger cars could have more powerful engines than police cars.

Q: What are the top five "favorite" Mopar squads?

A: 1st-1980 Dodge St. Regis, 360ci, 4-bbl
2nd-1978 Plymouth Fury, 440ci, 4-bbl
3rd (tie)-1969 Dodge Polara, 440ci, 4-bbl
3rd (tie)-1969 Plymouth Belvedere, 383ci, 4-bbl
5th 1984 Dodge Diplomat, 318ci, 4-bbl

Q: What is the reason the 383 powered Road Runner had a better quarter mile time while the 383 powered police Belvedere had a higher top speed?

A: Cop cars had 3.23 rear gears versus civilian 3.55, 3.91 or 4.10 rear gears.

Q: What police car had a true top speed of 147mph as measured at the Chelsea Proving Grounds?

A: 1969 Polara 440ci Magnum.

Q: What police dept. began measuring the temperature of oils and fluids to predict failures and promote use of fluid coolers?

A: Los Angeles County Sheriff's Dept.

Q: In patrol use, the 2-bbl V-8s get better fuel economy than 4-bbl V-8s according to LASD testing. True or false.

A: False.

Q: Cars with 122-inch wheelbases and 3800 pound curb weights have better high speed handling and hold the road better than shorter or lighter cars. True or false.

A: False.

Q: Canadian police engines often had more compression and a less restrictive exhaust than the American federal engine. True or false.

A: True, especially 1980 360ci, 4-bbl.

Q: In the early 1950s, what was considered a requirement for police engines?

A: Overhead valves.

Q: The first Chrysler Corp. police package car was the 1956 Dodge "230" Pursuit. What did "230" mean?

A: 230hp from the 315ci, 4-bbl V-8.

Q: What was the first Chrysler Corp. cop car to come with a Hemi engine?

A: The 1956 Dodge with the D-500 315ci, 4-bbl and 260bhp.

Q: What car was the Bluesmobile?

A: Ex-Mount Prospect, Il Police 1974 Dodge Monaco 440ci.

Q: What two things make up firm-feel steering?

A: 1. Sorted and paired gears; 2. High rate internal spring.

Q: In 1980, the New York City Police Dept. used the Plymouth Horizon as a squad car. True or false.

A: True, but they were removed from service after just 2 months.

Q: When did air pumps and catalytic converters first appear on most police cars?

A: 1975.

Q: Which Mopar squad used an overhead cam engine?
A: The 4-cylinder K-car engines.
Q: What period of time did Dodge and Plymouth squads have access to the exact same police engines?
A: 1967 to 1989.
Q: What police dept. insisted on rear sway bars and 11x3-inch rear drum brakes on their 1968 Belvedere?
A: Los Angeles Police Dept.
Q: What engine was Chrysler Corp.'s most produced police V-8?
A: 318ci LA small block.
Q: What engine has the longest police career of any Chrysler Corp. engine?
A: 225ci Slant Six.
Q: What was the longest wheelbase police car from Chrysler Corp.
A: 1976 Chrysler Newport A38 at 124 inches.
Q: What famous engine control was added in 1976 on most big blocks?
A: Electronic Lean-Burn System.
Q: In 1975, Chrysler Corp. produced how many different police cars? (This was a record.)
A: 7-Monaco, Coronet, Dart, Gran Fury, Fury, Valiant, Newport
Q: The first Chrysler Corp. police car was available with a Hemi-engine, Airtemp air conditioning, power steering, electric clock, 4-way power seat and pushbutton automatic transmission. True or false.
A: True.
Q: What was the first year for a Plymouth police car?
A: 1957.
Q: What was the first year for a Chrysler-marque police car?
A: 1961.
Q: What year were torsion-bars first used on Chrysler Corp. cars?
A: 1957.
Q: What was the first year for the 3-speed TorqueFlite?
A: 1957.
Q: The K-car was a "scout" or police car during what period?
A: 1982 through 1987.
Q: The Aries K and Diplomat have the same front leg room, hip room, shoulder room and headroom. True or false.
A: True, within a 1/2 inch.
Q: What problems could the transverse torsion bar front suspension cause?
A: 1. Uneven tire wear (negative camber); 2. Poor high speed handling (toe-out); 3. Severe brake pull (toe-out).
Q: What small block was new for 1967?
A: The 318ci LA wedge.
Q: The big block 318 V-8 produced more power and torque than the small block 318 V-8. True or false.
A: False.
Q: What were the first police cars to use the "isolated transverse torsion bar" front suspension?
A: 1977 Aspen and Volare.
Q: At one time, the 440ci, 4-bbl cars were equipped with an air pump and three catalytic converters. True or false.
A: True, 1977 in California trim.
Q: In 1977, Chrysler Corp. made 17 different police engines. True or false.
A: True, Federal (7), California (5) and High Altitude (5).
Q: After 1977, all police "models" were dropped. Starting in 1978 police cars were made from police "packages". True or false.
A: True.

Q: During the 1960s and 1970s, what axle ratio was used on most Mopar V-8 squads?
A: 3.23:1.
Q: During the 1980s, what axle ratio was used on most Mopar V-8 squads?
A: 2.94:1.
Q: Dodge did something to the 1965 Polara just to meet police demands. What?
A: Altered the wheelbase from 121 to 122in.
Q: The Chrysler sales coding system changed from alpha-numeric (like A38) to alphabetic (like AHB) in what year?
A: 1984.
Q: The M-body 318ci, 4-bbl cars had what transmission change in 1984?
A: The big block A727 was replaced by the small block A999. Also, the 4-bbl cars got wide ratio planetary gears.
Q: The 360ci, 4-bbl Aspen was almost as fast in the quarter and top speed as the 440ci, 4-bbl Monaco. True or false.
A: True.
Q: In 1977, the 360ci, 4-bbl Dodge Aspen Pursuit had better overall performance than the 400ci Pontiac Trans Am. True or false.
A: True.
Q: The M-body Diplomat, LeBaron and Gran Fury were produced at three locations in the 1980s. Name them.
A: 1981-83 Windsor, Ontario; 1983-87 Fenton, Missouri; 1987-89 Kenosha, Wisconsin.
Q: What was the last year for the 400 and 440ci police car engines?
A: 1978.
Q: In 1978, the fastest car of any kind made in North America was what vehicle?
A: Plymouth Fury A38 with 440ci, 4-bbl at 132.7mph.
Q: From 1956 to 1988, the California Highway Patrol selected Dodge or Chrysler how many times as their main patrol car?
A: 28 of the 33 years.
Q: What big block V-8 police engine appeared in 1966?
A: 440ci Wedge @ 350bhp.
Q: What was the change to the brakes in 1965?
A: Front discs optional on Polara and Fury.
Q: What was the Chrysler-marque squad car in 1981? The last Chrysler-marque squad?
A: LeBaron.
Q: What was the last year for a high compression and premium fuel police engine?
A: 1971, E86 440ci, 4-bbl @ 9.5:1.
Q: Mopar police cars got lockup torque converters in what year?
A: 1981.
Q: The 318ci, LA was first available with a 4-bbl in what year and with what restriction?
A: 1979, California only.
Q: The 318ci, 4-bbl used heads from what engine?
A: 360ci H.P.
Q: Which 318ci engine was fuel injected?
A: Option on 1981 to 1983 Chrysler Imperial only.
Q: The first Plymouth to come with over 300bhp used what engine?
A: 1958 dual quad 350ci, Golden Commando producing 305bhp.
Q: What year was the Sure-Grip Differential with Automatic Traction Pilot introduced?
A: 1958.

Q: In what year did "constant control" power steering become the first attempt at gaining more road feel from power steering?

A: 1958.

Q: After 1983, the Diplomat and Gran Fury were the only rear wheel drive, V-8 powered cars produced by Dodge Div. and Plymouth Div. True or false.

A: True.

Q: What was the name of the Chrysler-marque police car made from 1961 to 1964?

A: Newport-based Enforcer.

Q: During the 1971 changeover from the Carter AVS 4-bbl to the Carter ThermoQuad 4-bbl, what carb came on some big block engines?

A: Holley 4160 4-bbl.

Q: What year did horsepower ratings change from brake (SAE gross) to SAE net?

A: 1971.

Q: What did Dodge do special for the California Highway Patrol in 1961?

A: Released a police package version of the Dodge Polara, 122-inch wheelbase.

Q: The mid year release of the 62-1/2 Dodge 880 was a combination of which two vehicles?

A: 1962 Chrysler body and 1961 Dodge frontend.

Q: Chrysler Corp. purchased American Motors including their Kenosha, Wisconsin facility in what year?

A: 1987.

Q: What one engine improvement did police fleet managers insist Chrysler make in 1987?

A: Fuel injection on the 318ci V-8.

Q: What famous big block engine became available on Mopar police cars in 1963?

A: 413ci, raised block, B-engine.

Q: Which police engines are considered the four best ever made by Chrysler Corp.?

A: 1. 318ci (LA), 4-bbl; 2. 383ci, (B), 4-bbl; 3. 413ci (RB), 4-bbl; 4. 440ci (RB), 4-bbl.

Q: In 1971, Plymouth made a major policy decision on the A38 police package. What?

A: A38 available on wide variety of non-traditional 2-door and 4-door vehicles.

Q: Which car with exactly what engine was called a "dog" by the largest newspaper on the west coast?

A: 1980 CHP Dodge St. Regis 318ci, 4-bbl.

Q: What new police big block engine was introduced in 1972?

A: 400ci.

Q: The CHP modified the 318ci St. Regis by straight piping the muffler, installing a shift kit, advancing the timing and plugging the EGR. True or false.

A: False, only the shift kit and muffler were officially changed.

Q: The 1981 CHP Diplomat 318ci, 4-bbl was much faster than the 1980 CHP St. Regis 318ci, 4-bbl. True or false.

A: False, Acceleration to 60mph was just .3 sec. faster; top speed was just 1.6mph higher.

Q: In 1964, the CHP tested two kinds of brakes. What were they?

A: 1. Four piston Budd front disc brakes; 2. 4-wheel Airheart disc brakes.

Q: What is the only official Chrysler Corp. police vehicle made after 1989?

A: Jeep Cherokee starting in 1992.

Grading Scale:

82-89 correct	excellent, genuine Mopar historian status
79-81 correct	very good, consider writing for the PCOOA newsletter
71-79 correct	good, but you probably like Chevys, too
66-70 correct	fair, is that a Ford in your garage?
65 or less correct	poor, an obvious Volvo-lover!

Chapter 25

Cop Quotes: Observations on Mopar Squads

"The Diplomat is the only car that looks like a police car; the only car that acts like a police car. The Diplomat is what a police car should look like," said Marshal Ernie Winchester, Oxford, Indiana Police the day he turned in his 1987 Dodge Diplomat A38, and very reluctantly picked up a 1991 Chevy Caprice.

"The police car itself is as much a symbol of the police officer as his gun or badge. The car itself becomes something special, much different than a mere car. It becomes part of the officer." Frank Goderre, Revolutionary Auto Body, owner of two New York State Police Plymouths.

"I am a retired LAPD officer and I get a big bang reading what people say about certain makes of domestic cars; which one is best, faster, quickest, etc., etc. I have been in hundreds of chases, and during these chases, it becomes abundantly clear what domestic cars lack, especially in high-speed acceleration, braking, and cornering. All GMC products rate very, very poor in braking power, cornering ability and stability. FoMoCo is not much better. Surprisingly, Mopar rates way ahead. Anyone that has been in a 100mph-plus chase finds out real quick how utterly lacking GMC and FoMoCo products are." Chester Seaton, *Motor Trend*, June 1971.

"The only thing this officer can say is that this vehicle is the most inferior vehicle ever driven. It may make a good family car." Anonymous trooper with the Maine State Police referring to the 1978 Plymouth Fury E68.

"The Central City, Nebraska Police Dept. purchased this car from the Nebraska State Patrol on August 21, 1970. This is the exact car that used to chase us kids when we were in high school. When I said I was chased by it, I wasn't kidding. Before a bunch of us had cars of our own and were old enough to understand how stupid we were, we used to throw green pears at anything going down the highway. I recall drilling this big white behemoth with a pear and hearing the AVS kick open. We were running in all directions with the Ply-mobile hot on the trail of a few who hadn't hid in the bushes. Anyway, I got away, but I sort-of fell in love with that sound. Didn't know I'd have it to myself 15 years later. The local patrollers said that was probably the fastest car they had available to chase speeders with because it would go in excess of 125. I had to have it." Rocky Finlayson, about his totally restored X-NSP, X-CCPD Plymouth Fury I.

"The 1978 Plymouth Cruiser is the worst state police cruiser that this officer has driven since 1961. No Power, No Speed, No weight, No room, and poor handling qualities in the rain and wind make this vehicle dangerous as a State Police Cruiser." Anonymous, Maine State Police.

"Don't kid yourself, partner. She'll run the tires off anything on patrol today. This baby tops out at around 135mph and will cruise forever at 100mph plus." LAPD detective Paul Bishop, describing a 1965 Plymouth Fury freeway interceptor in his book, *Citadel Run*.

"I think most people don't realize how different the police cars were from the regular "civilian" models. Chrysler Corporation made a big mistake, dropping the V-8, rear drive Gran Fury and Diplomat in 1989. I think if Chrysler started the Fury and Diplomat again they would sell like hotcakes." John Crawford, Mopar police car historian.

"I was surprised such a big car could handle so well. One high point was the alignment. It was always straight. The front tires never showed any irregular wear. Overall, the car ran strong. Never any problems with the engine. It never overheated. It was holding up good when I saw it last, but it wasn't cared for well. If it wasn't a Chrysler Police Car, it would have died by now. My personal opinion is the 1979 to 1981 R-bodies were the best police cars ever made." Sgt. Joe Gavula, Philadelphia, Pennsylvania Police, concerning the 1979 Dodge St. Regis A38, sold at 105,015 miles.

"In the early 1970s, they were excellent. From 1975 on they were just low bid junk." Lt. J.G. Hippert, Winston-Salem, North Carolina Police.

"Plymouth was known as a police car maker. You could not kill a Chrysler product, even though it was worn out. You were not a police officer unless you had a Chrysler. There were police cars and reborn police cars. You had to have a Chrysler product or you were not a cop and the vehicle you were driving was not a police car. CHRYSLER spells police car. That is what they built: real police cars." P.O. Howard Kotarski, New York City Police, Hobbs, New Mexico Police; Mansfield, Texas Police.

"The 1980 Dodge is probably the finest cruiser that the Maine State Police has had in a long time. The Dodge has both performance, power and better gas mileage than the 1979 Chevrolet Impala that this officer had for one year." Anonymous, Maine State Police.

"I remember an interceptor from 1965. It was cruising in the fast lane at about 110mph. Unknown to the two cops, a car had stalled in the fast lane ahead. The interceptor hit the car, rolled over end for end and then side over side like a NASCAR stocker. The trunk and hood both flew off. The two officers were shaken, but saved by the roll cage." Anonymous, Detroit, Michigan Police.

"The vehicle is preferred by this officer over the 1979 Chevrolet with which much more trouble and maintenance problems were experienced." Anonymous, Maine State Police trooper reporting on the 1980 Dodge St. Regis.

"Chrysler was the acknowledged leader in police package production. Chrysler police package cars were built with a very complete combination of high-performance and long-wearing, heavy-duty parts. When you passed a Chrysler-built highway patrol car laying low in the interstate median, you got slightly antsy even if you weren't speeding. You knew it was an all-out, no-compromise machine, a true muscle car." Greg Rager, 17-year veteran of the Johnstown, Pennsylvania Police, editor of *Mopar Muscle* magazine.

"I strongly feel Chrysler Motors did a great disservice to all the Police Departments when they discontinued making the police package Diplomat." P.O. Scott Zane, Galena, Illinois Police.

"Chrysler products projected a square, tough, no-nonsense image." Sgt. Rodger Jincks, Oregon State Police.

"Glad to see they are gone. Never was a good squad car." Anonymous, Illinois State Police.

"In 1968, the Greenwich cars were actually Plymouth Road Runners in police paint. They were not outrun very often. Many complaints from residents near headquarters came in at shift change as each car headed out to post. Burning rubber up the street was the norm." Patrolman Mark Wilson, Greenwich, Connecticut Police, owner of a 1964 Plymouth Savoy squad.

"Never flunk the "attitude test" when given by an officer of the law. Quite a few officers own Mopar muscle cars. So don't be surprised if they pull you over just to check-out your ride." Mopar Rule of Thumb #5, Roland Osborne, editor of *Chrysler Power* magazine.

"On the Fourth of July, 1969, I was driving a new 1969 CHP Polara northbound on U.S. 101 near San Luis Obispo, California. I observed a new bright red Porsche going southbound at about 100mph. I made a U-turn through the center divider to pursue.

"Approximately 10 miles down the road, I caught up to the Porsche. Then the race was on, with red light and siren, we were flying. I looked at my speedometer to see how fast we were going and there was nothing there. I think it was over in the glove compartment. Anyway, the Porsche finally stopped, the driver stating, 'I thought my Porsche would outrun your Dodge, but we can see it didn't.'

With this, I asked the driver exactly how fast were we going as my speedometer had disappeared. He stated, 'Well, I shouldn't say, but mine was reading about 158.' I was one hopped up CHP officer and escorted the driver to jail for reckless driving (five days and $250)." Ira F. Bogard, *Old Cars*, February 25, 1993.

"I finally got the Diplomat and after comparing the two, I have to say that I like the ride and engine feel better in the St. Regis. The St. Regis being a bigger car, had a smoother ride to it

and the engine, a 318 2-barrel seemed to be smoother also. It wasn't the fastest but it could get up there. The Diplomat has a rather harsh ride and the engine (a 318 4-barrel) is not as smooth, it is quicker though." Sgt. Joe Gavula, Philadelphia, Pennsylvania Police, comparing the St. Regis to the Diplomat.

"Cops and emergency-room orderlies have a lot in common: Every day they get an up-close look at how stupid and helpless most of us are." Brock Yates, *Car & Driver*, September 1975.

"A race car driving instructor drove the course in a Plymouth freeway interceptor. He did a good job. Then I told him to run the course with lights and siren. His driving became sloppy due to loss of speed sensation caused by the siren, and by changes in visual depth perception caused by the adrenalin rush. I told him he was a police officer, working alone, in pursuit and he must use the radio to broadcast his location. The race instructor ended up wrapping the microphone cord around the steering wheel twice and ran off the road in a locked-up, 4-wheel slide." Lt. Jerry Trent, (ret.) LAPD, the officer who started the LAPD pursuit driving school, explaining why pursuit instruction is needed.

"The best police vehicle I have ever driven was the 1968-69 Plymouth Belvedere. It was, for all practical purposes, a four-door Plymouth Road Runner. With 383 cubic inch V-8 and the 440 V-8 heads and a 4-bbl carburetor, the car would fry the tires all the way through first gear. Other manufacturers would build cars with bigger engines, such as the 429 Fords in 1971, but none had the straight line acceleration and cornering of those Plymouths." Sgt. Tim Bauer, Santa Monica, California Police.

"Cops have all the fun. Not only do they get to write tickets, they ride around all day in trick cars." Patrick Bedard, *Car & Driver* describing the 1977 Dodge Monaco Police Pursuit.

"The Dodge Diplomat is one of the most bullet-proof cars ever built." Chuck Swift, the Dodge dealer who supplied the CHP with pursuit-class squad cars for decades.

"Rear wheel drive involves a totally different set of technologies, like drive shafts and differentials. Our engineers were concentrating on other things. Chrysler is a front wheel drive company." Tom Houston, spokesman for Chrysler Corp. explaining why Chrysler dropped the Diplomat and Gran Fury and pulled out of the police car business.

CHP Polara: Free to a Good Home
"I bought the X-CHP Dodge Polara from a young lady who purchased it from CHP in early 1967.

"This particular vehicle was unmarked throughout its use with CHP. Research has been very difficult. However, in talking with officers that were there during this time frame, they believe that my vehicle was probably a captain's unmarked car, or something similar. They also think this is true due to the outstanding original condition that it is in.

"Sue Coe, of Long Beach, California is the person I purchased the car from. She had done regular oil changes every 3,000 miles since the day she got the car! No wonder the engine was in such excellent condition.

"Buying the car from her was real interesting. The reason is that I first saw the car for sale in an "old Car Trader" book about three years ago. Sue was selling the car then, and if I remember correctly, she was asking about $3,000 for it.

"Long Beach is about 600 miles away from where I live. But I called her anyway, and she had said that she had received numerous calls on the car and had lot of people interested in it. I went and looked at the car anyway and decided to pass, mainly because I didn't have that kind of money at the time or the space to take on such a project. It also sounded as though she wouldn't have any trouble selling the car, with all of these people interested in it. So, I let it go and we kept in touch off and on.

"At least a year went by and I hadn't talked to Sue. One Sunday afternoon I came home and had a message on my machine from her asking me to call her back. So I did and eventually got around to asking her if she still had that old Dodge CHP car. She said that she still did and I about fell outta my seat. She then told me that she was kind of disappointed because all of these interested people for one reason or another fell through. She had talked to several people that did in fact want to buy the car, but all of these people consisted of young kids or adults who wanted to strip the car and pull out the high performance 413 V-8 and put it in some other Mopar. She said that she couldn't stand to do this to a car that she had grown so attached to and taken care of for so long.

"Then she asked me if I was still interested in the car, because I was the only one out of all these people that ever expressed an interest in restoring the car. I said I was still interested, but the month was November and Christmas was coming and I didn't have a whole lot of cash available for a new hobby. She basically said that she wanted me to have the car because the money was not as important as finding somebody who would appreciate the car for what it was. She then was extremely helpful in reaching a very fair price and the next weekend my girlfriend and I flew down to Long Beach to pick up the car.

"I hadn't seen the car in about 18 months and couldn't really remember what kind of shape it was in. When we got there, I remembered looking at the car before. The body was in pretty good shape for its age but it had a dent about the size of a shoe in the left rear door and the chrome on both bumpers was bad. The interior was in good shape with the exception of the front seat where the material was worn and torn. I got in the car and started, and it sounded great except for very loud exhaust.

"We took care of the paperwork and I headed for the nearest muffler shop. Upon arrival, we determined that the mufflers were fine, just one very holy pipe. We repaired that and restarted the car and it was the most pleasant sound I had heard in a long time. It was then that I realized what excellent mechanical condition the car was in. We then drove the car home and even got 19mpg with that 413. The rest as they say, is history.

"I put about $500 into rebuilding the front end and then proceeded with the body work and the interior. This past summer I drove the car to a PCOOA Police Collectors meet which was held in Kansas City, Missouri. This particular year, they also had a car show for restored police vehicles. I competed with about 25 other police vehicles and was very happy to take first place! The car ran excellent driving both to and from this show. I got some strange looks from officers along the way but most of the time stopped to show them the car and listen to their own old 440 pursuit stories."

Communications Officer Darryl Lindsay, Sunnyvale Public Safety Dept., describing his phenomenal 1965 Dodge Polara 413ci now fully marked in CHP trim. Lindsay is the Western States Region Director of the PCOOA.

Wheelbases and Engines Over Time

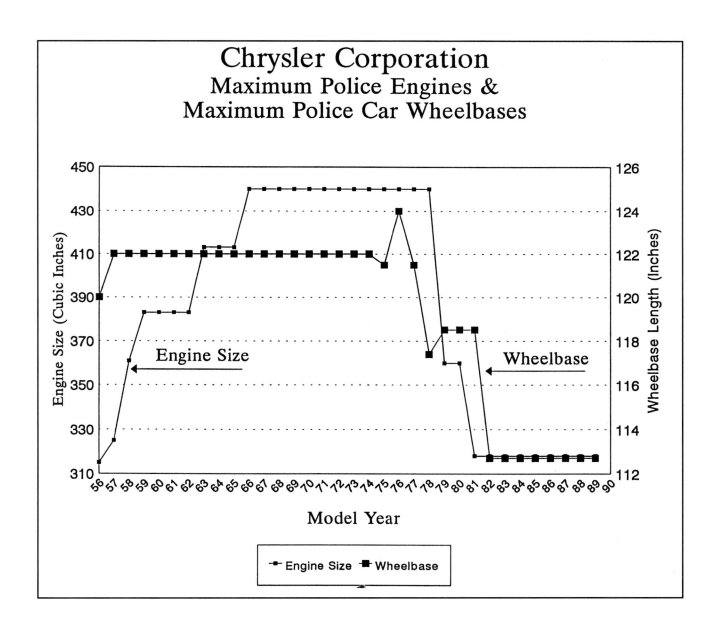

Appendix B

Sources for Cars and Parts

Resources Available to the Police Car Builder

A. Historical Data/Photographs:
Police Cars: A Photographic History by
 Lt. Monty McCord
Cars of the State Police and Highway Patrol by Lt. Monty McCord
Dodge, Plymouth & Chrysler Police Cars,
 1956-1978 by Cpl. Ed Sanow &
 Ofcr. John Bellah

All are available from Classic Motorbooks, P.O. Box 1, Osceola, WI 54020;
(800-826-6600)

B. Obsolete Police Car Literature:
Walter Miller
6710 Brooklawn
Syracuse, NY 13211

Ed Faxon's Auto Literature
1655 East 6th Street
Corona, CA 91719

C. Used/Rebuilt Emergency Equipment:
The Engine House/John Dorgan
7381 E. Stella Road
Tucson, AZ 85730

David Dotson
501 North Vine Street
Sparta, IL 62286

D. New Emergency Equipment
Police Collectibles
Route 6, Box 345B
Eureka, Springs, AR 72632

Camp Safety Equipment
8216 Blue Ash Road
Cincinnati, OH 45236

Gall's Inc.
2470 Palumbo Drive
P.O. Box 54658
Lexington, KY 40555

E. Used Police Car Dealers Including New and Used Police Equipment:
Cruisers Unlimited
1108 Malvern St.
Middletown, OH 45042

Day Ford
3696 William Penn Hwy
Monroeville, PA 15146

Diversifleet
7150 Kaw Drive
Kansas City, KS 66111

Blue Streak Motors
1703 Cannonsburg Rd
Ashland,KY 41102

Donna Motors
15 Roosevelt Ave
Bellville, NJ 07109

Excellent Auto Sales
269 Page Boulevard
Springfield, MA 01104

Live Oak Auto Center
34906 Louisiana Hwy 1019
Denham Springs, LA 70726

Mossberg Spec. Cars
Route 48
Wall, PA 15148

Pursuit Unlimited
1329 N Harrison
Shawnee, OK 74801

Rinto Enterprises
2077 W. Roosevelt Road
Wheaton, IL 60187

Sun Chevrolet
104-108 W. Genesee
Chittenango, NY 13037

Veto Enterprises
212 W. Exchange Street
Sycamore, IL 60178

Woodside Motors
43-29 Crescent Street
Long Island City, NY 11101

F. Police Memorabilia and Police Show Listings:
Police Collectors News
RR1 - Box 14
Baldwin, WI 54002

G. Car Club
Police Car Owners of America
Route 6, Box 345-B
Eureka Springs, AR 71632

Emergency Vehicle Owner's Club
501 N. Vine St.
Sparta, IL 62286